Smart
Moves

for Liberal Arts
Grads

Finding a Path to Your Perfect Career

SHEILA J. CURRAN, BA, PGCE, SPHR

AND SUZANNE GREENWALD, PhD

TEN SPEED PRESS
Berkeley | Toronto

Ten Speed Press
Box 7123
Berkeley, California 94707
www.tenspeed.com

Distributed in Australia by Simon and Schuster Australia, in Canada by Ten Speed Press Canada, in New Zealand by Southern Publishers Group, in South Africa by Real Books, and in the United Kingdom and Europe by Airlift Book Company.

Text design by Jeff Puda
Cover design by Betsy Stromberg

Library of Congress Cataloging-in-Publication Data on file with the publisher.
ISBN-13: 978-1-58008-709-4
ISBN-10: 1-58008-709-4

Printed in the United States of America on recycled paper
First printing, 2006

1 2 3 4 5 6 7 8 9 10 — 10 09 08 07 06

CONTENTS

2 Up, Down, and Sideways, in the Business World

3 A Life of Service

4 Fulfilling Creative Passions

5 Taking Your Degree Abroad

6 Offbeat Passions: Doing the Unexpected

This book is dedicated to our most patient and supportive husbands,
Joe and Jeff. We could not have asked for a better fan club.

We give special thanks to John Grossmann, writer extraordinaire,
who has shared this labor of love and without whose help this book would not
have been possible.

Credits

❖

As we have gone along our own journey of writing *Smart Moves*, we have been inspired by literally hundreds of people and nurtured by the excellent food and ambience at our "office"—the 729 Hope Street Café in Providence, Rhode Island. It would be impossible to individually thank all those who have given us insight and inspiration, but their help is warmly appreciated. We are especially grateful for the patience, time, expertise, humor, and helpful hands of the following people:

Family and special friends

Joe Curran, Peter Curran, Chris Curran, Alison McGowan, Pat McGowan and (late) Bruce McGowan, Bridget and Richard Simpson, Stuart and Siew Li McGowan, Jeff Greenwald, Don and Beverly Bavly, Eric and Miriam Bavly, Lawrence Bavly, Benjamin, Ariel, and Jessica Bavly, Barry and Marjorie Greenwald, Garry, Jessica, Alexeya, and Nathaniel O'Brien, Leslie Bash, Alexander, Isobel, and Oliver Genn-Bash

Professional inspiration

Colleagues in the Duke University Career Center and Division of Student Affairs, the Ivy+ Career Directors group, the SEACNET career group, the University Network career group, staff of the Cambridge-MIT Institute, the Brown Office of Institutional Research, and the University of Chicago Admissions Office

Friends and colleagues

Larry Moneta, Zoila Airall, Treat Harvey, Karen Bridbord, Ellen Welty, Bill Currin, Scott Brown, Liz Michaels, Lance Choy, Pat Rose, Skip Sturman, Kim Schliep, Steve Goldenberg, Jack Fracasso, Ruth Macaulay, Eric Broudy, Jennifer Floren, Janet Cooper-Nelson, Rhoda Flaxman, Bev Ehrich, Barbara Peoples, Jan Tullis, (late) Frank Newman, Geoffrey Hayward, Jennifer Kay.Goodman, Monica Brady,

Ricardo Wellisch, Cary Friedman, Susan Graham, Sarah Steen, Stuart Canning, Nicole Stark, Sarah Feldman, Lucinda Jewell, Elena Zezlina-Philips, Karim Malek, and Amani Michael

Liberal arts friends and muses

Jonathan Bigelow, Anthony Vitarelli, Philip Kurian, Mike Sacks, Elizabeth Dixon, Liz Reaves, Michael Otto, Luz Herrera, Lisa Price, Elizabeth Shammash, Katharine Woodhouse-Beyer, Mike Smith, Allison Macmillan, Leon Richter, Aliza Gutman, Leon Dunkley, Doug Kezirian, Anuja Khemka, Dave Brown, Adam Decker, Rob Howe, Tim Taylor, Clarissa Quintanilla, Paul Doscher, Jeff Shesol, Chris Engles, Leta Malloy, Milena Ivanova, Tara Fiscella, Brad Weinberg, Jeffrey Ganz, Joy Ridgeway, A. Craig Powell, David Cicillini, Will Tams-Wadman, Christian Anthony, Taylor Margis-Noguera, Lillian Zhao, and Noi and Josh Reineke

Special thanks

Carrie Rodrigues, our editor at Ten Speed Press; Christopher Ladner, Ladner Bond Literary Management, our agent; and Sabrina Spitaletta, who was instrumental in helping us in the early stages of this book

Foreword for Students and Graduates

Ever since you were in grade school, people have been asking you what you're going to do when you grow up. Generally, it's a throwaway question— a bit like routinely asking you how you're doing. Unless you're truly Machiavellian, this is not the time to proclaim to your parents or your Aunt Mildred your desire to go off and join the circus.

Little wonder so many students simply answer lawyer, doctor, engineer, or perhaps teacher. And for many, the more times they reply, the more their answer becomes a self-fulfilling, though often unfulfilling, mantra. Unfortunately, choosing a career this way is a little like saying you want to read a book because it has an attractive cover.

The fact is, beneath this kind of standard-issue campus bravura, most students are clueless about what they really want to do when they graduate. Surprisingly, the few who admit their uncertainty often hold a distinct advantage over those students who claim to know where they're bound after they graduate. Why? Because embracing uncertainty encourages you to go beyond the attractive cover of those prestigious but knee-jerk careers and, metaphorically, actually read the book. You start to examine what it really means to be a doctor. You discover that most lawyers do work that bears little resemblance to what's on *Law and Order* reruns. Or a little real-world investigation helps you realize an engineering career is not for you, never mind your prowess as an eight-year-old Lego whiz.

> **S**urprisingly, the few who admit their uncertainty often hold a distinct advantage over those students who claim to know where they're bound after they graduate.

So if you're not headed down one of those clearly marked paths for doctors, lawyers, and engineers, just what are you going to do? For one thing, you're going to work as hard at discovering a career that fits your personality, your talents, and your passion as you did at getting into the liberal arts college of your choice. Probably harder, because this discovery often takes years.

Ask any student psychological services or careers office, and they'll tell you that career decision making creates a huge amount of stress. Senior year, when the uncertainties of the future often seem overwhelming, that stress becomes epidemic.

It doesn't have to be.

Most people would love to have twenty-twenty hindsight on their careers, thus avoiding numerous mistakes of youth and inexperience and various wrong turns. We've assembled the next best thing. These are the stories of twenty-three liberal arts graduates—English majors, biology majors, psych majors, even a Far Eastern civilizations major—who have gone on, if not from the specific springboard of their major, then with a major push from their liberal arts education, to all manner of fascinating and satisfying careers. In *Smart Moves*, you'll read how Chris N. found a job as a scuba diver straight out of college and follow Thad's path from an English major to a dream job in the front office of a major league baseball team, and learn how a subway ride helped Sharon speed her intended career leap from a luxury department store to journalism.

This book presents a diverse mix of individuals from all regions of the country and all kinds of colleges and universities. Chances are, you'll see yourself, your interests, your energy, your dreams, your personality, and your indecision in several of the stories we've tracked down and brought to these pages. We're even more convinced that you'll learn from these individuals, for their stories illuminate valuable career lessons. We've annotated many of these lessons within the stories and highlighted more at the end of each narrative under the heading "Smart Moves."

Are you the first in your family to attend college? Read Adelita's story and learn how to navigate unfamiliar environments and use the skills you develop to further your career. Do you want to be your own boss? Then turn to Theresa, Warren, or Todd, who have turned their passions into a living.

This is a book you need not read front to back. The index at the back will help you identify various career issues that our liberal arts graduates have faced so you can easily hone in on the stories that will interest you most.

As much as anything, this is a book about passion. Discover your passion, what excites you most, what makes you eager to greet each new day, and you're well on the way to solving the career conundrum. Learn from our colorful mosaic of graduates. Listen to them. They've interviewed with on-campus recruiters, taken jobs they hated after six months, tried to find themselves—some successfully, some not—in graduate school, and traveled the world looking for adventure and a better sense of themselves. As you get to know them and identify with their achievements and struggles, listen carefully to the questions they ask themselves.

And do read the book's opening chapter, which talks about not only the value of a liberal arts education but also the assumptions and realities of finding careers in the twenty-first century. You'll be surprised to find that some of the "facts" you've taken for granted, like the need for further education after your bachelor's degree, may not be true for a significant proportion of graduates.

The remaining five chapters organize the stories, sometimes a bit loosely, by type of career. You'll note, after reading the stories, that some could fit as easily in another chapter. Truth is, in a year or two, some of the people profiled in this book will have changed careers (some, no doubt, by the time this book reaches bookstores).

We hope *Smart Moves* will convince you that a career is an ongoing, complex, very individual decision—but not without plenty of outside influences—and one that can often feel quite haphazard. Rarely does the path from point A to point B follow a straight line. Expect detours, switchbacks, false starts. And take heart and pleasure in the journey. Embrace the uncertainty.

The only thing that's certain in your career life is that you can't reliably predict where you'll be in five years, let alone twenty-five. There is no single career that is right for you and no dream that is too outlandish. Prepare to expand your career horizons. Prepare to learn new strategies. Prepare to act.

Foreword for Parents

---- ◆ • ▶ ----

A career is not what it used to be; it's much more interesting.

One week into a new term, the message on my voice mail was from a distraught father, claiming that his student son needed intensive career counseling. Returning the call, I inquired, "What year is he?" "Well, actually, he's a freshman," replied the father. "In fact he's still in orientation. But I need your help. You see, he's always loved computer science. He came to Brown because he knows you have a great computer science department. Trouble is, he's met some wonderful people, and now he's convinced that he should study philosophy instead." There followed a pause, and then the father said what was really on his mind, "But what can you do with a degree in philosophy?"

Actually, you can do just about anything with a liberal arts degree, as the stories in this book so vividly attest.

But if you're like most "millennial" parents, you won't be satisfied by such vague pronouncements, maybe not even by statements from Fortune 500 CEOs who say "we love liberal arts graduates." Wanting the best for your children, you're eager to know how you can help them make the most of their liberal arts education—while also preparing them to get off the family payroll!

Identifying and happily settling into a career that matches a heartfelt passion isn't easy for anyone. Think back: How quickly did you identify your own passion? How long thereafter was it until you brought your career and your passion in sync? Have you yet?

In a recent Duke University survey of its soon-to-graduate seniors, over half claimed that their primary source of career advice after graduation would be their families. But most families are ill-equipped to help with postgraduate career decisions. Your own college or work experiences no longer provide a good enough compass to guide your son or daughter from point A (graduation) to point B (career success). Why? Because in recent years the career landscape has changed dramatically. Choice has exploded, new careers have been invented, and the Internet has changed everything about the way people look for jobs. Examine the myths in chapter 1. Did you think they were true before you read them? The reality for today's liberal arts graduates may be very different from what you expect.

Suzanne and I wrote *Smart Moves* because there's a black hole of ignorance between graduation and career success. You've read in the media what's out: a commitment to a single career, a continuous upward financial trajectory, and lifetime employment. You probably even know what's in: managing your career, moving frequently, and seizing opportunities. Much less clear is how a liberal arts graduate actually identifies and follows his or her passion. With so much personal happiness riding on this seldom studied but quintessential career imperative, we thought we'd search for answers by looking in depth at the lives of a small but very diverse group of liberal arts graduates.

The stories and voices of twenty-three graduates fill most of this book. Their lessons are not prescriptive, and they don't come with a money-back guarantee. We can't tell you a fail-safe formula to conjure up career readiness or a six-figure salary. There isn't one. So much depends on interests, talent, personality—and luck. But the collective smart moves of our graduates do provide a framework for success. As you consider career realities in the twenty-first century, you may be surprised to learn that:

- A major doesn't equal a career.
- Graduate or professional school may not be the best choice immediately after graduation—if ever.
- Your son or daughter will probably not get his or her first job through on-campus recruiting but may still benefit greatly from career office resources.
- Internships may prove more valuable than a second major or summer school—and often the most valuable internships are unenjoyable ones.
- What happens outside the classroom is just as important as what happens inside.

- The best first job after graduation doesn't have to be the most prestigious or the most lucrative; ditto the second job and the third.
- There truly is a career value to a liberal arts education.

The last five chapters of this book are devoted to stories from some of the most interesting liberal arts graduates you'll ever meet. Liz, an American studies and art history major, is now the cheese buyer at one of America's most celebrated cheese shops. Theresa, a philosophy major, runs her own small nonprofit organization providing technical support to other non-profits that can't otherwise afford it. Brad is a human biology major who's combining his work in finance with his interest in third world health issues.

And speaking of you, perhaps now, a generation out of college, you'll discover this book is helpful to you as well as your children. We strongly believe that you're never too old to learn—or to change jobs. You may not be able to go back and relive your college years, doing everything right this time around. But there are plenty of tips and insights in

> **You're never too old to learn—or to change jobs.**

these stories to inspire you to action, whether you're contemplating a new job or career change or battling a full-blown midlife crisis.

Perhaps you intend to give this book to a son or daughter in need of career direction. Or you may discover, like me, that your wonderfully smart and charming second son has no intention of reading this or any such book until after he's made his postgraduate career mistakes. If that's the case, recognize that the best you can probably do for now is to ask the right questions and steer him in the appropriate direction for advice, support, and knowledge.

Career planning is like learning to walk and talk. Everyone does it in his or her own time. Those who walk first don't necessarily grow up to be dancers and sprinters. And those who talk late—well, some of them grow up to be actors and newscasters and virtuoso mezzo-sopranos. Read this book for your sons and daughters and read it for yourself. There's enough inspiration to go around.

—Sheila J. Curran

1

Smart Moves

Can You Get There from Here? The Road and the Map

Go ahead and make your plans, pursue your chosen fields and don't stop learning. But be open to the detours that lead to new discoveries, for therein lie some of the spice and joy of life.

—Kofi Annan, secretary general of the United Nations, written for Commencement 2004, Duke University

⎯⎯⎯◄•►⎯⎯⎯

Think of your career as the trip of a lifetime. Nowhere is it written that you have to start the trip at twenty-two. No one says it has to end at sixty-five. And only you can decide the places you'll stop. It's daunting, but all the more exciting, because you have a critical advantage: your liberal arts diploma. This tangible result of years and years of hard work is like a key that fits in the ignition of a new car that will take you anywhere you want to go.

Are you bound for the on-ramp of the interstate, already speeding toward a promising first job in an appealing career? Or are you headed for a so-called blue route, a forty-five-mile-per-hour, two-lane, scenic road, with only a general idea of what you might want to do with your life? Maybe you're still stuck at the curb, altogether clueless about what to do with that religion degree of yours or the psych degree you worked so hard to earn.

> Nowhere is it written that you have to start the trip at twenty-two. No one says it has to end at sixty-five. And only you can decide the places you'll stop.

What you need—whether heading for the highway, for the country road, or still stuck in neutral—is a new kind of map. And we're not talking MapQuest or GPS, some high-tech one-route-fits-all set of rigid directions. These tell you how to go from point A to point B, but neither accounts for bad weather, traffic-snarling accidents, or the personality or preferences of the driver behind the wheel. You're holding this new map in your hands, a different kind of careers guide for the quarter million or so annual liberal arts graduates of America's colleges and universities.

Students and graduates need examples, not of specific careers, but of ways to position themselves for the kind of work *they* want.

Consider it a road map for your life. It's a new and different kind of map, and a low-tech one at that. In *A Whole New Mind: Moving from the Information Age to the Conceptual Age*, Daniel Pink includes this observation from a cognitive scientist named Roger C. Schank: "Humans are not ideally set up to understand logic; they are ideally set up to understand stories." That's our route here: stories. Who better to lead the way than liberal arts grads who have already put the key in the ignition and driven off in search of their life's work? They've already encountered potholes and detours, veered off on wrong turns, and discovered shortcuts and scenic routes on their journeys to career happiness.

Unlike an ordered set of directions—do this first, then that—to guide you on your journey, our career map isn't nearly so neat and simple. Life isn't neat and tidy. Careers can't simply be downloaded. No one is going to hand you a career. There are just too many variables. We discovered these realities through decades of working for colleges and universities. Experience tells us that students and graduates need examples, not of specific careers, but of ways to position themselves for the kind of work *they* want. How can you best break into a tough industry like radio or theater? When does it make sense to work for free? Are two simultaneous careers the answer? Who better to provide answers than liberal arts graduates like yourself, notably graduates well into their own career journeys?

3

We don't expect that you'll blindly follow the stories of our guides. Every story is influenced by personal experiences, interests, values, and circumstances. You may have a significant other who's pulling you in a particular direction. Or perhaps the bright lights of the big city obscure other routes for you. And some of the liberal arts graduates whom we've profiled have made occasional "not so smart" moves that you'll want to avoid. But they're real people who are following their passions. They've taken both the car and the map and made their way to places they did not imagine at twenty-two.

Are you interested in becoming a stunt actor? Probably not. But you'll be fascinated to discover how **Ray** navigated not the proverbial three career changes, but *five*, within his first ten years of graduation. Likewise, there is much to learn from **Judith**'s career odyssey, moving from a rising manager in a major U.S. chemical company to job hunting in Istanbul. Lives and careers can take some curious—and instructive—turns.

If you flip through the demographics of our stories, you'll notice that our liberal arts graduates have some interesting titles: playwright and actress, venture capitalist, entrepreneur, journalist, Peace Corps volunteer, nonprofit director. Did we go out in search of unusual occupations? No. These are simply people we've met with interesting career stories. The fact is, as a liberal arts graduate, you have access to thousands of different occupations and titles—and most of them bear little resemblance to the title of your major.

Those of you panicking about starting the trip for fear you'll end up on the wrong route will be elated to discover this not-so-secret bit of career advice: your first job may have absolutely nothing to do with where you end up in midcareer. **Adelita** started off as a secretary for public television station WGBH. She is now director of the Department of Labor and Training for the state of Rhode Island.

> **Y**our first job may have absolutely nothing to do with where you end up in midcareer.

Jennifer held an internship with the United Nations. Her subsequent career led her to teaching. **Warren**'s first paying job was as a reproductive-health educator. He's now in business for himself, baking cakes. Take heart. If you're not ready to start an epic journey, you may want to start with shorter ventures.

In fact, very few of our graduates headed straight for the interstate, knowing what they wanted to do as they accepted their diplomas. Sheila

If you're not ready to start an epic journey, you may want to start with shorter ventures.

often makes this point with college seniors by throwing out a list of jobs: assembly line worker, cruise ship assistant, day care worker, secretary, employment director. Her question to the group is "What do these positions have in common?" Few get the right answer: all are positions that she has held. Is being an assembly line worker a recommended step on the road to being a career director? Hardly. But it did teach her that she wanted to work with people, not widgets!

In the course of writing this book, several of our candidates changed jobs, locations, or careers. Their stories—and their lives—are still evolving and unfolding. And so is yours. You can't follow their routes precisely. But you can collectively use their stories as a mental compass to guide you.

In this chapter you'll learn about career realities for today's graduates. You'll discover why a liberal arts education can be the best possible background for a career—whatever you choose to do. And you'll discover the kinds of smart moves that you can employ in pursuit of your life's work.

This is not a book about the destination. It's about the journey. Welcome to the driver's seat.

Careers are dynamic. If you remain static, you may have a stable job, but it's unlikely that you'll have a career.

Liberal Arts Students: Stepping into Your Own Career Reality Show

In thirty-five years of teaching, I have never seen a student who really wanted a job fail to get one after graduation, regardless of his or her major. . . . But I have seen many students fail to get an education because they were fixated on the fiction that one particular major or another held the magical key to financial success for the rest of their lives.

—Marshall Gregory, professor of English, liberal education,
  and pedagogy at Butler University

------- ◆•▶ -------

Graduation day: You've gathered the family from far and wide, and there's an air of excitement on campus. You may be the one receiving the diploma, but it's your parents who sport the biggest grins (and not just because they've written—or think they've written—the last of your tuition checks). But one thing tempers their elation when they give you a congratulatory hug. You may have a newly minted degree in public policy, but you don't have a job.

Talking with neighbors and friends—not to mention with their own parents—parents of recent liberal arts graduates employ many euphemisms to cover for their children's idling careers and not-quite-secured futures. "Julie's going to Europe." "Jonathan's coming home for a while." "Juan's thinking about law school." "Dave's going to Hollywood for his acting career." What these parents can't bring themselves to say is that after twenty-one years of always knowing the next step in their children's lives, they're now in the dark.

No one wants to discuss the elephant in the room. But here's the reality: close to half of all graduating seniors who want a job are likely to leave college without one.

Unemployment at graduation says nothing about your future prospects.

Luckily, unemployment at graduation says nothing about your future prospects. After all, if you simply needed a job, you could be working at a restaurant. It doesn't mean you're a failure or that you should be awarded your first D for poor career planning. A few students—the ones who decided to set foot in the careers office for the first time in April of their senior year—they may actually derserve that D, but fortunately life offers the equivalent of "make up exams." This section of chapter 1 will talk about the realities of work for today's graduates, the job market and how to best prepare for your career.

The Job Environment: A Rude Awakening to Life and Career

Before you dip your toes in the career pond, you'd best prepare yourself for a very different lifestyle from the one you've been living in college. Are you ready for the "real world"? You might ask yourself that question as you rise at noon after two consecutive all-nighters. Unless, perhaps, you go on to become a video game designer, you'll likely face a major lifestyle adjustment upon entering the workforce.

In college, you worked hard, but in your own way and in your own time. One of the shocks of entering your new workday world is discovering that people actually get up at 6 or 7 A.M. And often they're required to be at their desks at 8 A.M. *You* might want to do your work at 10 P.M. when you're mentally "in the groove," but unless you find a very understanding boss, that's unlikely to be an option. Nor should you count on a few hands of video poker between job assignments, as between classes. Understand, too, that failing to perform an important assignment no longer means a bad grade on a paper; in the working world, unsatisfactory work can cost you your job. It's enough to send you back to bed, to bury your head in the pillow.

Let's face it. Entering the real world requires quite an adjustment, and finding a job—let alone a career—is difficult. It's particularly hard when you're trying to study for finals or write a thesis. Take heart. Reading this book will prove that you don't have to have a high-paying, prestigious, or even professional job right out of college in order to succeed in a career. But it does help to know where you want to go and how to get there, especially in a world where the notion of "career" has changed.

The New World of Careers

The world of careers has been evolving so subtly over the past twenty-five or thirty years that few people have paid significant attention. But ask "boomer" parents to describe *their* postgraduation career realities and you'll notice how much is different. The changes fall into five categories: attitudes toward work, growth of the service industry, changes in the on-campus recruiting cycle, the rising prominence of internships as a recruiting tool, and the increase in one- to two-year positions.

September 11, the stock market crash of 2001, and corporate malfeasance have all affected attitudes toward work. Gone is the expectation of a stable position for life. Gone is the expectation of loyalty from a company or to a company. In 2001, some students were made offers that were subsequently withdrawn due to the failing economy. Five years later, trust remains an issue, and that is reflected in the fact that significant numbers of students believe it's appropriate to accept a position and then renege on the acceptance if they find a better offer. (It isn't!)

The bright side of the new world, however, is that it's now perfectly acceptable to change jobs—and even being laid off or fired needn't be disastrous. Many of the stories in our book profile liberal arts graduates who've changed not only positions, but also careers multiple times, and some, like **Warren**, **Theresa**, **Alison**, **Cara**, and **Todd**, have gone into business for themselves. The opportunity to be your own boss is extremely attractive if you're pursuing your passion. But even if you're vying for jobs in the conventional economy, you're likely to find a significant number of new opportunities.

According to the U.S. Bureau of Labor Statistics (BLS), total employment between the years 2002 and 2012 is projected to increase by 21.3 million jobs. BLS expects that professional and service occupations—areas of prime interest to liberal arts graduates—will account for more than half the total job growth over the 2002 to 2012 decade. There will be not only more jobs,

Careers exist now that few could imagine ten years ago.

but also new types of positions. Careers exist now that few could imagine ten years ago. Who could anticipate, for example, the need for a "usability specialist"—a job well suited to a liberal arts graduate who can translate technical language into words and concepts that the layperson can understand?

Careers offices have already seen an increase in service industry recruiting—particularly in consulting and financial services. One of the easiest ways to find positions in these companies, and in other organizations that recruit large numbers of entry-level liberal arts graduates, has traditionally been to go through on-campus recruiting, which is run through your campus careers office. What's changed over the past decade is that companies are coming on campus earlier and earlier. Most interviewing for full-time jobs now takes place during the fall, rather than the spring, of senior year. Consequently, prime time for exploring your interest in these types of opportunities may come earlier than you might think. If you're studying abroad during your junior year—like a significant proportion of college juniors—you may need to do some serious career investigation before you leave campus.

Companies not only recruit earlier than they used to, they're also changing hiring methods. More and more, companies now look to their internship programs as a talent pipeline, and they're interviewing for interns on campus during their second semester of their junior year. According to a May

2005 Monster.com survey of almost a thousand recruiters, more than half of the employers who responded had a formal internship program. Savvy students know that employers are increasingly using this "rent to buy" philosophy; they want to identify talent early, to try you out before hiring you permanently. Using interns is a smart move for employers: companies cut recruiting costs while ensuring that their hires will be a good fit with their organization. But

More and more, companies now look to their internship programs as a talent pipeline.

internships are also good for *you*. They allow you to really test a job and an environment to ensure they match your interests, aptitudes, and values.

The urge to explore options (and not commit to a particular direction!) often continues way beyond graduation. For evidence, consider this startling statistic: the number one employer of Duke University graduates in 2005—by far—was Teach for America, through which graduates undertake a two-year teaching assignment in an underserved area. Many graduates accept such assignments because they want to give back to society while also figuring out what they *really* want to do with their lives. Teach for America is an example of the rapid growth in one-to-two year positions, after which students often go on to further education or accept very different types of jobs. Another popular, short-term option is the Peace Corps. Some students even look at highly competitive investment banking positions as short-term learning opportunities because they are designed as two-year assignments.

We have chosen to focus this book on the stories of liberal arts graduates who have not followed a well-defined path, because their smart moves are more instructive and their careers—in all their complexity—are often more interesting. If you're reading this book, you've already taken the first step to finding your future. But discovery won't happen automatically. You're going to need some stamina on this journey of a lifetime, and more than a little help along the way.

The Blessings and Curses of Parents

To whom will you go for help? If you're like most of today's students, rather than using campus resources, your parents may be your first port of call. After all, parents of "millennial" students—those born after 1982 according to authors Neil Howe and William Strauss—are often their best friends. They're the ones who'll listen to you, help you, and solve your problems. The ones who are hardwired to you via an ever-present cell phone.

According to a Monster.com survey of students and graduates from across the country conducted in February 2005, three-quarters of all college graduates intend to spend at least one month living at home. Almost half of the 2004 graduates were still living at home more than six months after graduation. Unless living at home is a financial necessity, though, our advice is very clear: for the sake of your career, move on. Only one of the successful liberal arts graduates profiled in this book spent significant time at home after college. The rest were too busy taking active control of their futures.

> **U**nless living at home is a financial necessity, our advice is very clear: for the sake of your career, move on.

Parents are both a blessing and a curse. They probably think you are, too!

Independence, of course, means largely forgoing having your parent partner in your career search. Many parents do significant amounts of career research on behalf of their children. On the surface it looks great, but often parental involvement comes at a price. In an April 2005 *Wall Street Journal* article entitled "Not Your Father's Job Market," reporter Erin White notes, "Often the advice parents give is outdated, irrelevant, or just plain lousy. Even parents with successful careers aren't necessarily expert job hunters. And many parents don't have much experience in hiring or recruiting. So they sometimes pass along the mistaken assumptions they have made over the course of their careers. Or they suggest things that might be appropriate for their own industry or level of seniority, but that aren't right for the jobs their kids are pursuing."

> **O**ften parental involvement comes at a price.

Your parents may love you dearly and know you nearly as well as you know yourself, but few parents know the true breadth of opportunities available to millennial graduates. Moreover, if you involve your parents too heavily in your career search, you may find them also assuming responsibility for your career choice. And *their* choice may be very different from yours! Inevitably parental values creep into their advice, as that given to **Adelita**, whom you'll meet in chapter 3, A Life of Service. Her parents, not uncommonly, defined success for a talented liberal arts student like their daughter in terms of two prestigious careers: doctor or lawyer.

Parents often feel very insecure not knowing exactly what their children will do with their lives. So they latch onto careers, like law, that command high compensation and perceived status and stability. What today's parents fail to realize is that much has changed since they were of college age, notably the cost of professional education.

Parents may erroneously believe that there are only a handful of careers that define success for a liberal arts graduate.

Despite their limited knowledge of options available to liberal arts graduates, some parents still try to direct their children's careers. Not surprisingly, the resourceful student will usually find a way to thwart such parental pressure. A couple of years ago, a student showed up wearing a designer suit and flip-flops to an interview with an investment bank. Clearly, he didn't want the position. The dialogue between him and his parents probably went something like this:

Parents: "How did the interview go?"
Student: "Not so well. They didn't seem to think I was a good fit."
Parents: "You *did* wear that nice suit we bought you, didn't you?"
Student: "Of course!"

If you're being pressured into a particular career, resist the temptation to give in. Happiness and career passion do go hand in hand. But only if the career passion is yours, not your parents'.

Happiness and career passion do go hand in hand. But only if the career passion is yours, not your parents'.

Getting parents to back off may be tough, so it's worth remembering one of their primary goals: your career happiness. Making the following four points may help.

First, ask your parents to trust that you will get there in the end. Many parents feel that unemployment at graduation is an embarrassment. It shouldn't be—and the reasons will become clear when we talk about "just-in-time" hiring. Most graduates eventually fall on their feet—some sooner, some later.

Second, let your parents know that you're taking responsibility for your career. Choosing a career direction is an intensely personal matter. Values, interests, and personal preferences all factor in. However much your dad wants to help, there's no substitute for doing your own job search, researching organizations, and contacting alumni and employers. Since careers and jobs change so frequently, you need to practice figuring out how to achieve your objectives—not to mention how to get off the family payroll.

Third, ask your parents to support your career choice. This isn't easy if the choice seems unusual or just plain crazy. **Thad**, whom you'll meet in chapter 6, Offbeat Passions, had to explain to his parents why he was passing up an attractive job at Coca-Cola in order to look for an off-the-field job in major league baseball. Initially, they couldn't understand why he would pursue something so risky. But once they understood the depths of his passion, Thad's dream became the family's dream. Get your parents to buy into *your* dream.

The ability to learn from failure is a critical life skill—a prerequisite for developing career resilience.

Fourth, ask your parents to support your successes and your failures. Almost all highly successful individuals have experienced failure. The ability to learn from failure is a critical life skill—a prerequisite for developing career resilience.

If someone else always solves your problems, you can't build the kind of flexibility and self-confidence necessary to function effectively in the work world of the twenty-first century.

Making the Most of Your Careers Office

So if not your parents, to whom will you go to for advice? One often overlooked source of support, inspiration, and knowledge—not to mention connections—is your careers office.

In chapter 3, A Life of Service, you'll meet **David**. David is currently a senior executive of a major nonprofit organization that facilitates volunteers addressing social problems. But he wasn't always so focused. Fortunately for him, he pushed open the door of his careers office freshman year, and he ended up with not only a career counselor, but also a mentor. The counselor helped him discover his passion in life as well as ways to find jobs that aligned with his passion. What David realized, with the help of his mentor, was that the career process—from interest identification to actually finding a position—doesn't happen overnight. No one will simply find a job and say, "It's yours." Finding a job, and ultimately a career, is hard work.

> No one will simply find a job and say, "It's yours."

If you don't use your campus careers office, you've wasted part of your tuition bill.

Starting early can make a huge difference. When Sheila does a careers presentation at Parents' Weekend, she is invariably greeted with some version of "My daughter's only a sophomore. She still has a long time to go before she needs to come and see you." Nothing could be further from the truth. Wait till senior year to meet with a career counselor and you'll squander much that a good college careers office has to offer. Most careers offices seek not just to help you explore, prepare for, and obtain a job after graduation, but also to help you make the most of your entire college experience. In the process, they better prepare you for a lifetime of changing jobs and even careers. To avoid the careers office is to miss out on some important ways to integrate your academic education with your career aspirations.

No one expects a sophomore to know what he or she wants to do after graduating. In fact, an open mind and curiosity are more important than any specific career objective. These are, of course, precisely the characteristics that also help you make the most of your liberal arts education. Often, students enter college overly influenced by their families' expectations. Our most important piece of advice to younger students is this: forget your

Start from scratch, and dream your own dreams.

pat answer to the question "What are you going to be when you grow up?" Start from scratch, and dream your own dreams. Only when you really examine what you want to do in the context of available options can you say, "That's what I'll be when I grow up."

If you're throwing up your hands and saying, "How do I do that?" the simple answer is look around you! Most liberal arts campuses are full of opportunities to educate yourself about your future. Sometimes you'll hear about these opportunities from friends, sometimes electronically. Maybe, like **Ray** and **Brad,** you'll spot a flyer tacked on a campus bulletin board. Ray saw a notice of an upcoming presentation on careers in Hollywood. The flyer that caught Brad's eye announced a presentation by a nurse talking about her work with Doctors Without Borders. In both cases, the presentations awakened interests that would ultimately lead to a step in their careers.

When most students think about a careers office, they're thinking about jobs. Jobs for the summer, jobs during the school year, and, especially, jobs after graduation. For many students, the most visible manifestation of employment is, of course, your school's on-campus recruiting program. Typically, dozens of employers will come to campus looking specifically for liberal arts grads, offering an easy way to identify opportunities and interview for a position. While a fantastic resource for many, on-campus recruiting often disappoints because the types of employers you want to see may not be represented.

You never know when career inspiration will strike. Just take advantage of events and presentations that interest you.

Fewer than 30 percent of all graduating seniors are likely to find their jobs through on-campus recruiting efforts.

Two little-known facts may surprise you: First, fewer than 30 percent of all graduating seniors are likely to find their jobs through on-campus recruiting efforts. Second, on-campus recruiters represent only a fraction of the organizations that may be interested in you. Why the sparse representation of such organizations? To successfully recruit on campus, a company needs to accurately predict a year in advance how many entry-level professionals it will need. Many for-profit companies, and even more nonprofit companies, typically run with leaner staffs and small hiring budgets. They don't know how many new employees they will need because they hire only to replace someone who is leaving. The small number of entry-level graduates they seek doesn't justify a full-blown campus recruiting effort.

When the recruiting season starts in the fall, students often find themselves psychologically intimidated by their friends, whose interview attire reminds them of that vexing "employment" question, "What are you going to do when you graduate?" Many seniors don't realize that if they're not interested in the on-campus recruiters, they haven't missed the boat. Most employers who are interested in liberal arts graduates won't be recruiting until much later in the school year, and you can bet they won't be advertising in the school newspaper. You're going to have to seek them out.

Employment Realities for Liberal Arts Graduates

If you're a top student, it's tempting to put aside your true passions and flock to the campus recruiters from investment banking and consulting firms. Entry-level salaries can exceed fifty-five thousand dollars per year, often with substantial performance-based year-end bonuses. It's really tempting to follow the money. Unless you understand and are passionate about the type of work, resist the pressure. Many recent graduates find themselves working hundred-hour weeks in New York with no time for family or friends. Their lives have disappeared into their jobs.

Lucrative positions in high-profile industries actually make up a relatively small proportion of the job offers to graduating seniors. According to the National Association of Colleges and Employers (NACE), liberal arts graduates in 2004 received the greatest number of job offers from the educational services sector. This is a very broad category that includes teaching at all levels, working for testing agencies like Kaplan, or doing administrative work in a college or university. NACE lists other top choices for liberal arts grads as federal, state, and local government; retail; and social assistance. Clearly, these are not career fields usually associated with a high income. They don't come with perks, like a nice car or a year-end bonus. In fact, according to NACE, average entry-level salaries tend to pay less than thirty thousand dollars.

In all likelihood, you'll find your first full-time position through a just-in-time hiring process. You'll be hired because someone has quit. Even a month ago, they probably couldn't have predicted they'd need you.

Assuming that you get one of these just-in-time positions, it's still hard to grasp why your entry into a flagship state institution, a selective liberal arts college, or an Ivy League institution wouldn't have a greater immediate economic value. Unfortunately, many employers neither understand nor appreciate liberal arts graduates despite the fact that significant numbers of such graduates populate the higher echelons of Fortune 500 companies. Company recruiters often don't see the relevance of the degree or how the graduate can contribute to the organization.

If you want the opportunity to get your foot in the door and prove yourself, you'll need to redefine for your future employer what you've really learned over four years.

Sadly, liberal arts graduates have an image problem. Too often they are stereotyped as coddled on campus, writing papers on esoteric subjects with no practical application. If you want the opportunity to get your foot in the door and prove yourself, you'll need to redefine for your future employer what you've really learned over four years. In later chapters, you'll read the stories of liberal arts graduates who did just that.

Getting the Attention of Employers

It doesn't seem fair. In high school, you were bestowed with all kinds of honors. In addition to your academic prowess, you were a success outside the classroom. Maybe, like **Mike**, you made a name for yourself on the gridiron, or, like **David**, you excelled as news editor of the school paper. Maybe, like **Adelita**, you starred on your high school debate team. You were the go-to person, the student who demonstrated leadership skills, and the one voted most likely to succeed. While your classmates looked on in envy, you received fat packages announcing invitations to matriculate at selective schools across the country. Once so heavily recruited by colleges, why don't employers want to hire you now—especially now that you're older and wiser? And why don't they want to pay you what you think you should be worth?

To get into a good college, you needed the whole package: smarts and extracurricular success. Not surprisingly, employers want the whole package, too. They don't just want someone with a 4.0 GPA. Employers are looking for new recruits with intelligence but also with certain attributes. And they don't care which part of your liberal arts education helped you develop the skills. High on the list of what hiring managers want to see in new employees, according to the NACE (*Job Outlook,* 2005) are teamwork, interpersonal skills, and a strong work ethic. Completing the employers' list of desired characteristics are analytical skills, motivation and initiative, flexibility and adaptability, computer skills, attention to detail, leadership skills, and organizational skills.

There's no shortage of ways to demonstrate transferable skills through your liberal arts education.

Luckily, there's no shortage of ways to demonstrate transferable skills through your liberal arts education. Your curriculum undoubtedly offered rich opportunities to research, evaluate, and synthesize vast quantities of information. All those papers probably helped you hone your writing skills. And maybe a few seminar classes called for oral presentations that have made you a more polished public speaker. You've probably also developed key skills outside the classroom. **Jennifer** certainly learned flexibility and adaptability through her study abroad. **KC** benefited greatly from her relationships with administrators and faculty as class president.

To better stand out from the pack of other applicants, try taking the employer's point of view and figure out how you can meet their needs. You don't need to wow an interviewer with a show-and-tell array of documents.

> To better stand out from the pack of other applicants, try taking the employer's point of view.

But you do need stories: stories about the experiences that have helped you develop skills, stories that demonstrate that you understand the employer's needs, stories that portray you as someone who can do the work, who'll be fun to have around, who'll be a good addition to the team.

Ever heard of the 2 A.M. in Japan test? That's the interview question employers never ask aloud, but pose mentally to themselves. Essentially, they're questioning whether you're somebody they'd want around, not only in the office, but one-on-one if they were stuck with you in an airport in Japan at 2 A.M. They're never so blunt as to raise this scenario, but they typically zero in on this important, less tangible part of the hiring process by inquiring about your passions. Now's the time when you *can* talk about your fascination with the fruit fly—or anything else in which you're genuinely interested. **Thad,** whom you'll read about in chapter 6, Offbeat Passions, identified his passion as baseball when interviewing for an internship at Coca-Cola. Thad's version of the 2 A.M. in Japan test got tossed right back at him in the form of a baseball trivia question. Want to see how he did? Turn to his story.

Valuing a Liberal Arts Education through the Career Lens

If you are concerned that your liberal arts education isn't going to train you for a specific career, you're missing the whole point. The value is that it's preparing you for any career.

—Jennifer Floren, CEO of Experience, a company that has provided innovative recruiting services to colleges, students, and employers since 1996

◄ • ►

Many recent graduates lament that their first professional jobs have little intellectual content, aren't challenging, and require little more than an eighth-grade education. You would expect then, that some of these graduates would question the value of a liberal arts education. In our experience, that rarely happens. And if you asked the twenty-three graduates we've profiled in this book, none of them would choose to replace their degrees in philosophy, history, or music with something more practical.

But ask the same question of many members of the general public—including parents—and you'll find a great deal of ambivalence about the value of a liberal arts education. The difference has to do with how liberal arts graduates and non-graduates perceive the purpose of such an education. While liberal arts graduates see value in the breadth and depth of their education, those without such an education—eyeing more tangible results—often question the value. Indeed the most often cited reason for a college education, according to a recent survey of readers by the *Chronicle of Higher Education*, was the ability to get good jobs—the kind that pay well. In other words, a money-in, money-out equation—and one that values prompt repayment of education "stock" dividends.

> Most entry-level jobs don't really need the education of a college graduate, but you have to take them to get the jobs that do.

What do we, *the authors*, think about liberal arts education? We will go out on a limb and say that a liberal arts education is the best investment you could ever make. Pursued with an intellectual curiosity, ideally in pursuit of a passion or two, a wide-ranging roster of college courses endows you with an open-ended ticket for your life's journey. Used wisely, it allows you to go anywhere and do anything. Put in the terms of humanistic psychologist Abraham Maslow, a liberal arts education makes "self-actualization"—the pinnacle of human needs—not only possible, but also probable.

> A liberal arts education endows you with an open-ended ticket for your life's journey.

This section will lay it all out: the common misunderstandings about a liberal arts education, its relationship to a career, and the ways to take advantage of it. And we'll let you in on a secret: The benefits of a liberal arts diploma typically don't come from the subject matter of your degree, whether it's Spanish, anthropology, or even economics. It's *how* you spend your time in college that counts.

Myth #1: Paying for a Liberal Arts Education Is a Lousy Investment

The cost of higher education in the twenty-first century epitomizes the expression "sticker shock." Attend a highly selective liberal arts college today, and you're looking at a tuition bill that's equal to a hefty down payment on a very nice house. And the cost is skyrocketing. According to the College Board, from 1995 to 2005, average tuition and fees, after being adjusted for inflation, grew by 36 percent in private four-year institutions and by 51 percent in public four-year institutions. Even in-state tuition at public universities—which, incidentally, has grown at a much faster rate than the cost of private education—may set you back close to forty thousand dollars. So the obvious question is, whether your liberal arts education is really an investment?

It's clear that for most people, there's an economic advantage to a college degree. As Katherine Haley Will, president of Gettysburg College, reasoned in a 2005 interview with National Public Radio, "Tuition remains a significant investment, but there are few better investments. Twenty years ago, the average college graduate earned 1.5 times more than those who did not graduate; today, the average college graduate earns almost twice as much as nongraduates." The economic advantage, however, may not be apparent at the beginning of a liberal arts graduate's career. And if you believe the only acceptable investment result is a high salary, you may be disappointed.

What your investment buys you is opportunity.

What your investment buys you is opportunity: opportunity for prosperity, and—something much more important—opportunity to follow your passion, wherever it may lead.

Myth #2: A Career Is Something You Do If You Can't Get into Graduate School

Ask any group of liberal arts students what they intend to do when they graduate, and it won't be long before you'll hear some of them say they're going to law school or medical school. Given the financial rewards and the media's glamorous depiction of these occupations, who could fault them? Well, we will—at least in some instances. Because in making your decision so early, you're often closing off opportunities that may better suit your values and interests. Fewer than half of those who originally intended to go to law school or medical school actually end up doing so.

The truth is, you don't have to make up your mind so early about medical school or scramble to try to get your requirements out of the way. A liberal arts graduate, Mark, who is now a prominent physician, recently commented, "I was not pre-med in college (got scared out of it during my first year), and only started taking pre-med courses a few years after I had graduated. So I tell anyone who has a career to which he or she aspires to hang in there; if you really want it, you can and will do it."

And there's the crux of the matter: You have to know what you want to do and *then* find a way to do it, rather than commit to professional education and then figure out whether it's a necessary step toward your current career objectives. Too often, graduate or professional school is seen as a default when you can't think of anything else to do. It's the acceptable option. The one that will make you seem successful in the eyes of your family and friends. You may also have the erroneous notion that a law degree makes a great canvas for most any career dream. Law school will probably make you a better writer and a more logical thinker. It may also help you with some aspects of business. But if you don't plan to practice law, you may not find the additional financial reward that you expect.

> Too often, graduate or professional school is seen as a default.

Our best advice is, if you don't know for sure that you need a law degree, or any advanced degree, hold off! But by all means, pursue it if you're certain it will help empower your dreams. **Ally**, whose story you'll read in chapter 4, Fulfilling Creative Passions, headed straight to graduate school out of Wake Forest University. She describes her master's in fine arts as a "three-year root canal," but she found it invaluable in broadening her career options. Even if you know you'll need an advanced degree, there may be some financial benefits to waiting to enroll—particularly if the degree you need is in business: some companies offer to pay tuition and expenses. In return, they expect the employee to commit to additional time working for them. Two years out of graduation, **Judith** found herself in exactly that situation with her employer. It's worth looking around for organizations that will support your professional development needs.

Myth #3: A Major Equals a Career, and More Majors Equals Better Careers

The urge to gather credentials, whether they be professional degrees or college majors, is endemic on college campuses. It seems to be a badge of honor to accumulate as many majors and minors as possible. But does it do any real good beyond bragging rights and resume padding?

Most employers, if you press them, will tell you they don't care how many undergraduate majors you have. Moreover, if they're seeking liberal arts graduates, they also don't worry about what subject you specialized in. How is it, then, that most of the top investment banking positions and consulting positions, for example, tend to go to students with backgrounds in economics? Employers of liberal arts grads look for interests and skill sets much more than majors. In this case, economics majors tend to be more interested in business than art history majors.

> **Most employers don't care how many undergraduate majors you have.**

What if you're a philosophy major who wants to get a highly competitive position in an unrelated field? No, you haven't studied your way out of that job, but you must make a few strategic "amends". First, you have to educate yourself, including quizzing all the alumni you can find in your chosen field. Second, you need to build experience, usually through internships. Finally, you need to prepare well, so that you can demonstrate your relevant knowledge and qualifications both in writing and interviews. It's worth noting that when your major is in a different area from the type of position you seek, a cover letter can make all the difference—*if* you use it to connect your educational background and skills to your desired goal.

Resumes resonate, but cover letters convince.

Use your career office to get practice interviewing, and do so well in advance of your interview. It can make all the difference.

Myth #4: **GPA Is Everything**

If you were admitted to a top liberal arts school, you're probably someone who did well on your SAT or ACT exams. So you don't expect, with a good math SAT score, to struggle in college calculus. But college isn't high school, and many liberal arts classes can be challenging, particularly if you have to, or choose to, take courses in your areas of weakness. Even in these days of grade inflation, you're unlikely to end up with a string of As. So what's the truth about GPA? How important is it?

GPA is a key factor in admissions to graduate and professional school, so if you're going that route, you'll need to put extra time and effort into your studies. And according to the *Job Outlook 2004*, produced by NACE, almost two-thirds of employers screen for employment by GPA. But if you don't have a stellar GPA, don't be discouraged. Even though highly competitive positions usually (if unofficially) require a GPA of 3.5, some employers only look for a GPA of 2.5 or more. And many are only concerned that you have a college degree.

It's important to note that a high GPA—if it's needed at all—only matters for a first job. After that, your future depends on your performance. (Readers take note: we didn't ask any of the successful people profiled for this book for their college transcripts.) We all know smart people, who—for whatever reason—didn't do well in school but blossomed later in life. If you want to overcome a poor GPA, get an internship—paid or unpaid— and prove what you can do.

> A high GPA—if it's needed at all— only matters for a first job.

The true value of a liberal arts experience has little to do with GPA; it resides in all aspects of your college education—extracurricular activities, summer internships, study abroad, and even late-night debates, be they political or a partisan rehashing of that night's Red Sox–Yankees game. And it's from all areas of your liberal arts education that you'll gain the transferable skills that will make you a desirable candidate for employment.

Myth #5: A Liberal Arts Education Occurs Only in the Classroom

Education happens in *and* out of the classroom, but the most useful education requires you to take some initiative.

It's tempting to plan your academic curriculum around the areas with which you're familiar and where you know you excel. Don't! Stretching yourself and pursuing the unfamiliar can give added value to your liberal arts education. The career advantage shows up in two ways. First, without exception, higher-level professional positions will require you to learn new knowledge and new tasks. Trying classes in subjects you'd never even heard of in high school will give you the confidence to tackle unfamiliar career assignments later on. Second, you may find that exploring different fields leads to new interests, new experiences, and new skills. **KC**, in chapter 3, A Life of Service, took a calculus class at the suggestion of

Stretching yourself and pursuing the unfamiliar can give added value to your liberal arts education.

a professor. She remained an American studies and history major, but the math course sparked an interest. KC now spends a lot of her time working with numbers as chief financial officer for the Andy Warhol Foundation for the Visual Arts.

Another way to step outside your comfort zone and build invaluable skills is through study abroad. **Jennifer,** who is, not surprisingly, in chapter 5, Taking Your Degree Abroad, could be the poster child for foreign study. She spent several semesters of college in Costa Rica, Kenya, and Italy. Unlisted in her course syllabi was one of the biggest lessons she learned in her foreign travels—the ability to relate to all kinds of people in any situation, surely a valuable skill in a global age. By constantly putting herself in new environments, Jennifer developed an equally valuable characteristic: the confidence to do anything.

Here's an additional piece of advice for liberal arts students considering going abroad: don't take the easy route. Hundreds of students hardly know they're actually studying abroad because they spend all their time with their classmates and professors from home. On the surface, it may seem very attractive to go abroad to a place where the natives speak English and where you can while away your time and newfound freedom in the local pub. Resist the temptation. If you follow this path, you may have a fun time, but you will gain little knowledge about yourself or the world.

If all you do is study, you may have attended a liberal arts institution, but you haven't been liberally educated.

According to a survey by international executive search firm Spencer Stuart, in January 2005, over 30 percent of CEOs in S&P 500 companies had international experience.

You don't have to go abroad to enhance the value of your liberal arts education. Many times you can do so simply by being actively involved in extracurricular activities, as most of the stories in this book so vividly demonstrate.

Myth #6: **A Liberal Arts Education Is a Solitary Affair**

There's one secret advantage to virtually all residential liberal arts institutions, and that's people. If you start to truly engage these on-site resources, along with the alumni, you will reap untold rewards.

We encourage students to build at least one strong connection with a faculty member and administrator each semester. Doing so gives you at least eight people at graduation who know you very well and can support your dreams. Every college has dedicated teachers—whether they be faculty, administrators, or even peers. Seek them out. Invite them to lunch. Let them get to know you without a notebook open in front of you.

Often, the learning that comes from those out-of-classroom conversations is the learning that endures. That's what you remember when you think back on your four years in college. The true legacy of a liberal arts education is what remains with you after you've forgotten 90 percent of the specific information you were taught.

> The true legacy of a liberal arts education is what remains with you after you've forgotten 90 percent of the specific information you were taught.

> One of the secret advantages of a residential liberal arts experience is the opportunity to engage with all the members of that community—faculty, staff, administrators, and alumni.

The Smartest Moves on the Road to Career Success

Don't ask yourself what the world needs, ask yourself what makes you come alive. And then go for that. Because what the world needs are people who have come alive.

—Harold Whitman, philosopher and theologian

＊＊＊

> Navigating your career is a challenge for anyone, at any stage of life. No book can reliably tell you which step to take first, then next.

This book tells the career stories of nearly two dozen individuals who have truly taken advantage of their liberal arts education. They've married their educational and experiential learning in ways that have helped them discover and follow their passions—very different passions. Even so, many of these graduates share some very smart moves. That's what this section is about: pulling all the smartest moves together and assembling their collective wisdom.

At some point in their lives, most of the graduates we showcase here spent considerable time figuring out not only what they wanted to be, but also who they wanted to be. In other words, they not only thought about the nature of their career, but also about what they really valued in life. It usually didn't take them long to decide that passion trumps money, even if it means starting on the bottom rung of the ladder with no guarantee of being granted the next step upward. Almost to a person, they believe in building networks and social relationships, not just for support but also for something even more valuable: an honest critique of plans and strategies. These graduates didn't leave learning at the classroom door. Instead, they have experimented and experienced life, often through internships, and in the process they fine-tuned their careers. Our graduates have never been bound by their lack of a particular skill or knowledge of a subject.

After identifying their competence gaps, they've taken classes, read books, and researched whatever they needed to know. A great many of them have also shared an additional helpful career strategy, the ability to find a hook—something special that would make someone want to hire or promote them, or possibly suggest them for another job.

It usually doesn't take long to decide that passion trumps money.

Should you skip to the final pages of many of the stories, you'll see individuals happily hitting their stride in jobs they find rewarding and challenging—career nirvana. But to peek in on them five, ten, fifteen years out of college is a bit like watching a near-perfect Olympic gymnastics performance and thinking, "She sure made that look easy," without considering all the hard work, the coaching, the practice, and the missteps it took to reach that high level of achievement. None of the individuals portrayed in this book soared straight to career happiness. Collectively, they had to overcome false starts, bad choices, tough job markets, parental pressures, bosses from hell . . . The list goes on.

It helps to remember that no one talks about all the positions for which they didn't get hired or the dead ends they pursued. Luck plays a big part in anyone's life and, paradoxically, more often in the lives of the successful. Why? Because they're primed for serendipity and seize the inevitable moments when opportunity knocks.

If we had kept a running count, that would be one of dozens of the smart moves made by the twenty-three liberal arts graduates profiled in this book. We have grouped these smart, career-enhancing moves into five key, smartest lessons, if you will, that put them on the track to success:

- Discover who you are and where you want to go.
- Get experience.
- Build social and networking relationships.
- Identify your competence gaps.
- Find your hook.

Smartest Move #1: Discover Who You Are and Where You Want to Go

If you thought *finding* a job after graduation was the most difficult thing to do, think again! Far harder than the initial job search is figuring out exactly what you want to do. We're talking about self-assessment. Self-assessment is hard for most college students. For one thing, it takes a significant amount of time, a commodity in short supply for overprogrammed millennial kids. But it also takes introspection and the willingness to jettison preconceived notions about success. There's no guarantee that if you take the instruments commonly offered in your careers office (for example, the Strong Interest Inventory or the Myers-Briggs Type Indicator), you'll magically find direction, but they're worth doing as step one in your career search.

Far harder than the initial job search is figuring out exactly what you want to do.

Planning your future only makes sense when you're willing to think about yourself. And thinking about yourself takes time and a lot of skills seldom taught in college.

Warren went to law school "by default" because he couldn't think of anything else to do. Only after he became a government lawyer did he search within himself for his passion—and make the kind of 180-degree career shift that occasioned a feature story in the *Washington Post*. Introspection, if sometimes late, is a hallmark of many of the people profiled in this book. They are constantly looking at their lives (not just their careers) and asking these questions: "Is this what I want?" "Where's my next step?" "Is this good for my family?" "Do I need different types of experiences?" "Am I happy?" Some of our liberal arts graduates have developed a formal process like KC, who has a checklist of questions that she asks herself on a regular basis. Others, like Adelita, take a less formal approach; she uses her husband and trusted friends to give her honest feedback on her career direction. Theresa keeps a journal of thoughts and observations, especially as they apply to her career.

It sounds obvious—but it's your life, your career. Don't be swayed in your career direction by those around you as graduation nears. Resist the temptation to follow the pack and forget who you really are. Often that means remembering who you were, what you loved as a child, as many of the stories in this book inform us. **Sharon** filled second-grade notebooks with sketches of fashion design. They foreshadowed her current-day freelance journalism career, researching and writing fashion stories, as well as her full-time work in retail. **Beth**'s early interests were in writing. She applied that love in her communications career. Baseball defined **Thad**'s boyhood. How fitting that he now reports to work in the executive offices at a major league ballpark. Still, it took considerable courage and determination for him to slide safely into home. Don't ignore your early passions. See if they still fit.

No *successful* liberal arts graduate goes through his or her career on autopilot. They all make informed choices. Find out who you are and what you really want. Success follows informed choices.

> Look at your life. Ask these questions: Is this what I want? Where's my next step?

Smartest Move #2: Get Experience

One of the key reasons students don't follow up on the information imparted by self-assessment instruments is that they simply don't know how. The Strong Interest Inventory, for example, provides lists of job types that fit with your profile. But just because a self-assessment exercise identifies potential positions doesn't mean those positions fit with your personality.

If a particular opportunity sounds intriguing, there's no substitute for trying it out. That means internships, co-ops, or other kinds of learning opportunities. Without exception, all the people profiled in this book have had early work experiences—paid and unpaid—that helped them figure out both what they wanted to do and what they *didn't* want to do. **Chris C.** had several internships, two in Washington that foreshadowed his ultimate career direction—foreign affairs—and one in a high-powered law firm where he saw enough to convince him that he never wanted to be a corporate attorney!

Sometimes, internships and low-paid clerical or service jobs offer the only way you can get your foot in the door. Parents hate to see their children in jobs they could have gotten without going to college, let alone an expensive liberal arts college. But patient parents understand what their career-savvy offspring have come to realize: sometimes the only way to get your foot in the door is to start at the bottom. Does that mean the education was a waste? Not at all. Liz, an Ivy League graduate, would never have made it to director of wholesale and importing at one of the country's top cheese shops had she not started behind the cheese counter, working weekends and making minimum wage. But it was her college-honed ability to synthesize information, her writing ability, and her broader people skills that made her right for the higher-level job.

> **S**ometimes, internships and low-paid clerical or service jobs offer the only way you can get your foot in the door.

Smartest Move #3: Build Social and Networking Relationships

The more outrageous your ambition, the more likely it is you'll need help getting there. If you want to be a doctor or a lawyer, helping hands abound. If you want to work in publishing, work on Capitol Hill, or teach abroad, there are counselors and alumni to advise you. But what if you want to venture totally off the beaten path? If you're trying to make enough money to live while following your passion for performing stunts, climbing mountains, or writing plays, you're going to need guides who are unlikely to be found on any college campus. Not surprisingly, the people in these pages who hold off-beat passions could write their own book on networking. However, building social and networking relationships is one of the hardest skills for any young person to master.

> **T**he more outrageous your ambition, the more likely it is you'll need help getting there.

Here's a tip to get started: In your career toolbox, you need two items. The first is an elevator speech, and the second is an eyeball paragraph. Both seek the same goal, namely, to convince the person you're talking with or writing to that they should spend more time with you. In the case of the elevator speech, you need to prepare a thirty-second response (the brief window of time you might have with someone going from a ground-floor lobby to the fifteenth floor) to the question "Who are you and what are you looking for?" Of course, you may never get that exact question, but you'll be ready with a concise personal message that you want to convey. In the case of the eyeball paragraph, you need to write a concise statement that the recipient can simply eyeball. Many emails are trashed because of rambling and unfocused messages. It's essential that yours tells the recipient immediately who you are and what you want and need.

You want to have these personal summaries on hand and firmly in mind because you never know when you'll need them. **Sharon** used her elevator pitch on the subway. She knew she wanted to venture into journalism. One day, speeding below the streets of New York, she noticed a woman wearing a jacket bearing the logo of one of the city's four major newspapers. Sharon boldly struck up a conversation, and she quickly shifted to her elevator speech. She made the most of this serendipitous encounter, which soon led to a job writing articles for the paper's online edition as a freelance intern. Most of the conversations you have with people won't have such an immediate and positive result, but the more you share your passion with others, the more likely you'll find personal supporters and boosters.

Building your network is a key skill for any liberal arts graduate, whether you're starting out or moving up. Whether they're former bosses, friends, business acquaintances, faculty, or advisors (or in **Ray**'s case, the stylist who cut his hair), people in your corner can make all the difference. They're great sounding boards, wonderful confidence builders, and above all, probably your best source of job leads. Don't hide your passion. Let everyone know your career destination, and you won't travel alone.

Smartest Move #4: Identify Your Competence Gaps

The higher you move in your career, the more likely you'll be confronted with tasks and responsibilities with which you're unfamiliar. Knowing what you don't know is important. But far more important is figuring out how to acquire the knowledge or skills that you lack. In other words, you need to identify and fix your competence gap.

Assessing this shortfall, you need to ask two key questions: "Is the skill necessary for a field in which I want to stay?" and "Would the skill help me to achieve my future goals?" If the answer to either question is yes, you need to find a way to close the gap.

> **I**dentify and fix your competence gap.

Don't just identify the competence gaps for your current position. Identify your competence gaps for the position to which you aspire.

Harpreet knew that if she ultimately wanted to become the head of a nonprofit organization, she'd need business skills—skills she didn't possess. She could have headed off to business school, but that's expensive. Harpreet chose to meet her needs a different way—a way that would allow her to gain the skills and mentoring she needed while earning a handsome salary. She applied for a job at a top nonprofit consulting firm. Making a lateral move into a highly competitive area like consulting is difficult, particularly since consulting companies typically use the "case" interview to select new hires. Harpreet, like most people, had never experienced such interviews. Another competence gap uncovered! True to form, Harpreet prepared herself for the interview, this time by using the online resources of Vault.com. She got the job.

A large proportion of liberal arts graduates find their passions lie in an area that requires some knowledge of business. After all, business skills are required whether you're running an international nonprofit like **Alison** or are starting your own marketing company like **Cara**. Since few liberal arts colleges offer a business curriculum, graduates commonly identify business savvy as a competence gap. Four of the people we've profiled decided to go the formal route and get an MBA. But **Theresa**, who needed business advice to set up her own nonprofit company, tried a different and just as valuable strategy: she was able to find the counsel she needed through volunteer advisors in her alma mater's alumni network.

Help is, in fact, all around you—in the form of bosses, peers, and connections from college. Get in the habit of an annual career review

> **Get in the habit of an annual career review and competence checkup.**

and competence checkup. Identify the kind of learning you need, and think broadly about where you might get help. Look where you've been, see where you want to go, and make a plan to marshal all your resources to get there. What often distinguishes those who achieve their career goals from those who don't is the passion to keep learning—even in the absence of an immediate reward.

Smartest Move #5: Find Your Hook

We hang our final smartest move on finding your hook. If this is a term with which you're unfamiliar, think back to your college application. Competitive colleges have tremendous difficulty in selecting a well-rounded group of students. Too many people look identical: stellar

> **To get your foot in the door, you need to find a hook—a way to distinguish yourself from the pack.**

grades, great extracurricular activities, solid citizens. To get your foot in the door, you need to find a hook—a way to distinguish yourself from the pack. In the case of college, a hook could be acing the verbal SAT, becoming a black belt in karate, or—in one case at an Ivy-League university—showing up in the admissions office every day

after school and sitting quietly in the waiting room doing your homework. When you're looking for your first professional job, you're going through the same admissions process all over again. It's not easy, so you need a hook.

Almost all the liberal arts graduates in this book found a way to differentiate themselves from other job seekers. But having a hook is not enough. Like a good fisherman, you must cast it deftly. It needs to hit the mark—and stick. When you've decided on your hook, make sure it's part of your resume, cover letter, and interview.

Sharon's hook was her commitment to the field of fashion and retail *while she was still in college.* By the time **Sharon** left the University of Michigan, she'd racked up no fewer than four internships, one of which she designed herself. Those internships bespoke a passion and focus that employers rarely see in new graduates. She had her choice of job offers.

The more you know about what you want to do, the easier it is to find and employ a hook. **Chris C.**'s passion is foreign affairs. He knew, from his failed first application, that becoming a diplomat is extremely difficult. So he crafted a strategy that would give him an edge. Knowing that extra credit would be given for skills in essential foreign languages, he shrewdly accepted a Peace Corps assignment to Morocco, where he could learn Arabic, a language of growing global importance. His fluency in Arabic, in the end, opened the door for him.

So how do you figure out your hook? You need to adopt your potential employer's point of view and identify ways that you can add value. **Todd** approached the dean of the School of Music and proposed that he repair and restore the school's collection of musical instruments. In Todd's case, he simply identified the school's existing need and had the confidence and the background to present himself as someone who could fix the problem.

Here's the best news: Even if you have no unusual skills or talents, you can set yourself apart from other graduates and find your hook by simply doing your homework. Sounds obvious? It is. But it's amazing how rarely candidates go beyond a cursory glance at a company website. The type of job **Brad** found at Genentech required someone with an MBA or significant related learning experience, qualifications he didn't have. But he landed a job because he knew enough about the company, the job, and the challenges to act like a much more seasoned candidate. Do your research. It will help set you apart from other job candidates.

Final Words

Finding your first professional position is probably the most difficult task you'll accomplish after applying for college. (At least until you decide to make a dramatic career shift, like **Warren** or **Liz** or **Beth**.) Fortunately, this first occupational line on your resume does not determine your future career. In fact, a career is something that is defined over time, rarely conceived from the start. **Jennifer** arrived at her current career as a middle school teacher via a seemingly unconnected string of exotic overseas jobs, which she eventually determined to all have a foundation in education.

> **A** career is something that is defined over time, rarely conceived from the start.

Sometimes it's only in retrospect, looking through life's rear window, that you see the overarching themes. Of course, your gaze now extends out the front windshield. It's the road ahead that concerns you. Where will it take you? How will you know when you've arrived at your career destination?

You'll know, or certainly have a much better chance of knowing, if you learn from our collection of compelling career stories. The point is not necessarily to end up in the professions of any of those profiled in this book. Their backgrounds, their talents, their passions no doubt differ from yours. Think of this book like your liberal arts education. Remember, it wasn't so much what you studied that matters, it's that you learned how to learn.

Which explains why we titled our book *Smart Moves*. It's not the names, or colleges, or majors, or occupations that matter. You needn't remember that **Jonathan** graduated from North Carolina State University. Or that **Emily** studied Chinese language and civilization at the University of Chicago. Or that **Beth** left a career in public relations to join an international nonprofit organization. Or that **Liz** was bored silly in her first job at a dot-com. Moreover, unless you want to be a cake maker or a stuntman, start your own marketing company specializing in the arts, or land in any of the many professions described in this book, you won't be able to specifically follow in the footsteps of any of these people.

But you will be able to follow many of their smart moves—perhaps taking a gap year like **Harpreet**, setting aside quiet moments for soul-searching like **Beth**, or following your heart like **Thad.** You can tease out the relevant advice and strategies while taking inspiration from those whose hard career work has paid off. Smart moves may not always pay off in high salaries, mind you, but they will reward you with a more precious commodity: happiness.

So don't panic. Relax. We give you your career guides and this last bit of advice: enjoy the journey.

2

Up,
Down,
and
Sideways
in the Business World

You've Got to Run Your Own Race

COLLEGE: Brown University, 2000

MAJOR: human biology

PASSION: alleviating unnecessary suffering

EARLY EXPERIENCES OUTSIDE THE CLASSROOM: Doctors Without Borders

EARLY WORK EXPERIENCE: Internet start-up, biotech company

CURRENT JOB: investment analyst at a health-care private equity fund

It's a rare high school student who, at age seventeen or eighteen, has already identified a passion in life, thereby orienting his or her path through the ensuing decades like the needle on a compass. But then most teenagers don't watch a close friend succumb to cancer. Brad Mak articulated his passion in a speech to his fellow graduating seniors at Choate Rosemary Hall, the Connecticut prep school he attended, when he spoke about a dorm mate and fellow running back on the football team, a classmate he'd watched die from the ravages of leukemia.

"Why is there suffering in the world?" Brad asked. He had to admit he had no answer for that question. But he went on to promise, "I'm making a commitment to myself that, whatever I end up doing in this world, I'll always have an obligation to try to alleviate unnecessary suffering."

That he would think of becoming a doctor was not surprising. His father was a physician, and for many years his parents had been suggesting medicine as a potential career. Though he went to prep school in the East,

Brad's family lived in Los Angeles during his childhood. He's first-generation Chinese American. Both of his parents emigrated from Hong Kong. Before switching to real estate, his mother worked for many years as a physicist at the Jet Propulsion Lab, helping send NASA rockets into space. "I grew up with very hardworking parents as role models," he says. "I always thought if they are working hard, I should be too."

Brad says he never felt pressured, certainly not as in the stereotypical Asian American "play the violin and go to medical school" household. Still, there's this memory from his childhood: "If I wanted to go to the store on a Saturday morning to buy a toy, my mom might say, 'Do fifty math problems first.' If I did them, I could go. It was always work hard, get a reward."

Brad's grades, mostly in the A-minus, B-plus range, and 1400s on his SAT scores helped get him into Brown University, where he embarked on the pre-med track and lined up a related experience the second half of his freshman summer. A lover of the outdoors, he headed to Aspen, Colorado, and waited tables at a restaurant the first half of the summer, then took a monthlong EMT search-and-rescue course, which included a rotation in an emergency room. Already, Brad, was envisioning his medical school application. Professors and fellow students were advising him to go work in a lab; that was the way to get into medical school. "But I wanted to do something I liked," he says, "something that was still going to help me. I was also thinking [the EMT course] might help differentiate me from all the others."

Fall semester of his sophomore year, Brad took a course that changed his life. The course was called The Burden of Disease in Developing Countries. He was surprised to learn that diarrhea is the number one cause of death of children in much of the world. "I had seen my friend die of cancer. This broadened my concept of unnecessary suffering to the entire world," he says, adding, "I really hit my academic stride with that course. The material was so engaging. I was passionate, full of energy. I knew what I wanted to do. I had found my calling."

Brad realized, however, he was discussing troubling health conditions from the comfortable, distant vantage point of an Ivy League college campus. Believing he needed to step away from his ivory tower and into the real world, he decided to go overseas to witness third world poverty and health problems firsthand. When he read about severe flooding in Somalia in November 1997, he called the local Red Cross office in Providence, offering to volunteer in the flood relief efforts over his upcoming winter break. They told him sorry; he didn't have any experience working overseas. They only took doctors and nurses. Brad's EMT training wasn't enough. Could he repair automobiles? They could always use mechanics.

Over the next two months, Brad cold-called more than forty other organizations, most of them overseas relief organizations, stressing his EMT training in both urban and wilderness settings. Always, the same question stopped him cold: "Have you ever worked overseas before with a relief organization?" Frustrated, he'd ask, "But how does one get overseas experience if no one is willing to provide me with an initial opportunity?"

Brad discovered a possible way around this catch-22: Peace Corps–like organizations that offer overseas experiences on a "pay to volunteer" basis. He was about to try this route when he spotted a flyer on campus. The flyer announced that a nurse with a nonprofit organization called Doctors Without Borders would speak on campus about her organization, which brings medical care to needy corners of the world. Brad saw an opportunity—not just to attend the lecture, but also to make a personal connection with someone in the organization.

He first tracked down the medical student who'd organized the talk, then he offered to welcome the Doctors Without Borders nurse when she arrived on campus. Brad arranged to meet her taxi and escort her to the medical school for the talk. He had a cup of coffee with her before the event, telling her he was writing a research paper on the effects of malaria in the developing world. He demonstrated his enthusiasm and hunger for real-world exposure to such ailments.

> Don't miss an opportunity to make a personal connection whenever possible.

> **"I really hit my academic stride with that course. The material was so engaging. I was passionate, full of energy. I knew what I wanted to do. I had found my calling."**

When she later shared with him the inevitable offshoot of her visit—dozens of students like Brad, all eager yet unqualified to work for Doctors Without Borders—Brad offered to help. Through his own research, Brad had amassed a database of nearly fifty volunteer organizations. He'd be happy to act as a liaison for Doctors Without Borders on the Brown campus, relieving her of much of the student follow-up. "I created a relationship with her," says Brad. And in doing so, of course, he separated himself from all the other interested candidates.

His strategy and effort paid off a few weeks later. The Doctors Without Borders nurse informed him that her organization's Los Angeles office could use an office intern over the winter break. Brad commuted from home, cold-calling other nonprofits in the metropolitan area, learning about their overseas missions, asking the names of their key executives, and preparing a guide to international development opportunities. Between calls, stresses Brad, "I'm like reading everything in their office. You have to be like a sponge, get to understand the dynamics of the organization, how everything works."

Back at Brown that spring, Brad called the woman for whom he'd worked over winter break, reiterating his desire for overseas experiences. He was no longer just some faceless student calling from three thousand miles away. She'd witnessed his hard work and enthusiasm. She offered a possibility, explaining that one of her friends was director of disaster preparedness for all of Latin America. Brad could work that summer as a field intern in Costa Rica and Peru and write up his experiences for Doctors Without Borders—but he'd have to pay his own way. Thrilled that his networking efforts had paid off, Brad turned to the careers office at Brown. With his advisor's help, he applied for a $2,500 fellowship to pay for his Latin American trip the summer after his sophomore year.

The highlight of Brad's summer internship came when he went beyond his assignment to suggest and help build a latrine—the first sewage control in a fifty-year-old remote mountain village in southwestern Peru. Retelling his experience in the Brown alumni magazine, Brad wrote, "Okay, so this wasn't the most dignified part of my pre-med education. But it did teach me something I could have never understood in the comfort-

When you're interning, act like a sponge.

Don't underestimate the value of campus resources to help find advice and funding to pursue your interests.

able, air-conditioned classrooms of Brown: international medicine is as much about fighting poverty as it is about treating illnesses."

He continued to press for more overseas experiences, leveraging whatever connections he could find. After meeting a classmate whose father worked for the World Bank in Bangladesh, Brad asked, "Can I go there with you over winter break?" Brad went, and he spent the three weeks meeting with doctors, scouting for a summer opportunity that focused on treating communicable diseases. Once again, with the help of the campus careers office, he secured a fellowship, this one for five thousand dollars, which funded his summer research on evaluating the impact of a community health program in rural Bangladesh. Brad returned with a much deeper understanding of the political, economic, and social challenges associated with international health and development—and a sense of how much well-intentioned aid and medicine is lost to graft and corruption before ever reaching the intended recipients.

Indeed, Brad's overseas experience weighed heavily on his mind during fall of his senior year, when he sat in his first MCAT class, a crash course favored by many pre-med students as a way to prepare for the upcoming MCAT exams necessary for medical school applications. Brad lasted ten minutes, then he walked out of the class—deciding then and there that he didn't want to be a doctor after all. He'd take a different path to alleviate suffering.

Brad didn't know exactly what path he might take, but he sensed that he needed to know more about other, broader aspects of health care, especially the financial end. So he filled his class schedule with accounting, corporate finance, and macroeconomics courses. In advance of winter break, Brad returned to a familiar place on campus: the careers office. "They put me in contact with the head of the Brown alumni association in San Francisco and helped me craft an email blitz to alumni who were working at twenty-five Internet companies," Brad says, explaining that the strategy helped him set up early stage job interviews and learn about the then still-flourishing dot-com world.

He wasn't shy about pressing friends and people he met for leads. Brad got hired at a San Francisco Internet start-up called eFrenzy because one

Medical school is time-consuming and expensive. Don't wait until the MCATs to decide whether you want to be a doctor.

of the founders was the older brother of a friend of his from Choate. The company faltered, like many dot-coms in the new millennium bursting of the Internet bubble. Brad left the prophetically named eFrenzy in the spring of 2001.

"My new job," he recalls, "was to find a job; every day, eight to five, all I did was job search. I had what my dad calls a Ph.D. mentality—poor, hungry, and determined."

> **"I** had what my dad calls a Ph.D. mentality—poor, hungry, and determined."

Yet again, Brad networked his way to a job offer. His sister, who worked at an investment bank, knew a former co-worker who had left the bank to work for a California biotech firm called Genentech. Brad called him, learned of an opening in the company's strategic planning group, and sent in his resume.

"I'm home doing my eight-to-five job search when the phone rings," he says, explaining that the caller identified herself as being from Genentech. "She started conducting the job interview right then, on the phone. Fortunately, I had Genentech in a database of biotech companies that I had compiled, which listed the company's key products, allowing me to speak more intelligently about the company and industry."

Brad got the job and moved up quickly from associate manager to manager, where he was responsible for strategic planning, market research, and sales forecasting for a drug approved to treat lung cancer. In this role he learned about the long, arduous, and expensive drug development process, from research to dealing with FDA regulations. In his office Brad hung a motivational sign that he took to heart: "Don't be afraid to innovate. Be different. Following the herd is a sure way to mediocrity." Outside work he pursued two major interests: philanthropy and athletics.

Eager to stay true to his goal of alleviating human suffering, Brad volunteered at a venture philanthropy organization called the Full Circle Fund, which supplies innovative nonprofit organizations with badly needed grant money and operational support. Identifying, funding, and working with organizations that address the needs of low-income families in San

Build a system to organize your job search. That way you'll be ready when your future employer calls.

Francisco, Brad expanded both his understanding of the nonprofit world and his network of contacts.

In his remaining free time he trained for and competed in grueling adventure races as a member of Team ATP (a biological term for energy). An apt name, for these high-altitude mountain biking, trail running, and kayaking races sometimes went on for as many as eighty-five miles. "Pushing yourself for twenty-five hours nonstop with no sleep sounds impossible," Brad says. "And then you go and actually do it. You extend your comfort zone." He secured sponsors for Team ATP and even persuaded the Outdoor Life Network to feature his squad in its cable TV coverage of an actual adventure race. Such promotional skills, he noted, will come in handy should he ever start his own business.

"Things were going well at Genentech," he says. "But I realized in the fall of 2003 that it was time to look for another job."

Why? Why look elsewhere soon after your contributions have been rewarded with more money and more responsibility? Brad answers with a metaphor that he's found helpful for taking stock of his life's journey. He pictures a dashboard. His dashboard has four gauges. One is for career. Another monitors his nonprofit or volunteer work, which he considers an important part of how he wants to spend his time and who he wants to be. A third gauge tracks athletics—sporting and physical pursuits that help keep him healthy and balance his days. The fourth gauge, not yet activated, "is for getting married and having kids."

At twenty-four, Brad had became the youngest manager in his fifty-person department at Genentech. He could tell that the next jump, to senior manager, probably loomed several years down the road. A lateral move within the company, to marketing for example, didn't really interest him. Brad was itchy. Eying his career gauge, he saw the needle dropping out of an optimum range. He really wanted to expand his knowledge of health care—especially the financing of companies—so he started putting out feelers through some of the contacts he'd made at the Full Circle Fund, many of whom worked in venture capital.

After a headhunter suggested that Brad interview for an analyst position at a health-care private equity firm in New York City, one of his Full Circle

Fund contacts provided a key reference. Thus, Brad switched jobs and coasts, signing on with Paul Capital Partners, a New York private equity firm that manages five billion dollars in capital investments. He started in the fall of 2003, helping his twelve-member health-care team decide when to invest millions of dollars in various drug companies, typically to help fund clinical trials and commercial development of promising new medicines.

"Genentech provided me with an understanding of how to develop and market drugs," he says. "Now I'm on the financial side, learning how to fund life science companies that are developing innovative drugs." He's watched the needle on his career gauge rise accordingly. Although Brad does not have a clear picture of how he'll someday have a hand in alleviating suffering in the developing world, he is very aware that to realize his goal he needs to acquire a wide range of skill sets.

"I'm now working with people in their fifties and sixties who have experience starting companies and running companies," he says, admitting that he's picking their brains and absorbing everything like a sponge. And as before, he's expanding his network through volunteer work, signing on with a New York nonprofit consulting firm called the Community Resource Exchange, which provides expert help and influential connections to all manner of needy organizations. "Right now," he says, "I'm working on a business plan for a Harlem charter school."

Always looking to expand his skill set, and noting that everyone above him at Paul Capital Partners possessed either an MD, a Ph.D., or an MBA, Brad started applying to business school in the fall of 2004. The essay writing cut into his training for the New York marathon, until, suddenly, his plans changed.

His company offered him a job as employee number two in its new satellite office in London. Come summer of 2005, they wanted him to join the pioneering investment manager, a former managing director of a big European pharmaceutical company. The new job appealed to Brad on several counts. "I can learn directly from him, and it will be just the two of us who meet with the CEOs and CFOs of companies to pitch our investment model," he says, explaining that as the junior member of the health-care team in New York, he generally stays at company headquarters. Overseas,

Career growth depends on continuous learning. Find people who can teach you what you need to know.

his base will be London, but the focus will be Europe. In short, his contacts and health-care knowledge will spread internationally.

With business school still off in the near distance, he's thinking of an innovative course load, of setting an untraditional course, of striking off on his own, away from the herd. "At some business schools you can take courses in the school of public health and the school of government," he says, explaining that he may want to sign up for fewer traditional courses like marketing, and instead, "enrich myself about Indian and Chinese foreign policy and the health-care industry in these countries. And then maybe use my summer internship to work at a biotech company in China, to really get my feet on the ground."

On Christmas Eve 2004, on a hiking vacation with a close friend, Brad's feet were spectacularly grounded 19,340 feet above sea level. He'd made it to the summit of Mt. Kilimanjaro, the so-called roof of Africa. The day was clear. The view was breathtaking—the African plain stretching to the horizon.

A continent in need of health care—HIV drugs, malaria medicine, clean drinking water—Brad had thought on the long hike up, knowing he'd made the right career choice. Had he followed his original career path, studying medicine and becoming a doctor, he would have had a profound impact, patient by patient, on a small number of individuals. But on his current, ever-evolving path, with his mission of alleviating human suffering on "a more macro scale," Brad saw more clearly, hiking up Mt. Kilimanjaro, that he's preparing himself to help far more people. He's not yet sure how. Maybe he'll start a biotech company that will specialize in developing or distributing "orphan" drugs—those used to treat diseases affecting less than 200,000 Americans—in the Third World. Perhaps he'll head up or serve on the board of an innovative nonprofit organization. Maybe, he says, he'll start his own foundation. Could be, he'll need to shift careers for a time to delve deeper into the politics and economy of a country that he targets for his efforts. Brad doesn't know exactly how he'll eventually zero in on his life's mission.

"I know it's a question that might take me thirty years to figure out," he says, explaining that when he next finds himself at an important career crossroads, he'll ask himself the same questions he has up till now when making key career decisions: How does this fit with my life story? Does this new job, this new direction, fit the person I'm trying to be? Is it aligned with my life's passion? Brad has learned much by his midtwenties, but perhaps nothing as important as this: "You've got to run your own race."

Brad's Smart Moves

- He pursued opportunities and added experiences to his resume to differentiate himself from other candidates. He even put winter breaks from college to good use.

- He's learned many of his most important lessons outside the classroom and off the job.

- He became a familiar face at the campus careers office, which helped him identify and secure fellowship money to help pay for foot-in-the-door unpaid internships.

- He diligently networked his way to connections that led to career-defining experiences and job interviews.

- He sought his second job with a Ph.D. (poor, hungry, and determined) mentality and tenacity.

- In making career decisions, he always asks himself, "Does this fit my life story?"

Testing Many Waters

COLLEGE: Auburn University, 1993

MAJOR: marine biology

PASSION: discovering or creating a career at the crossroads of science and business

EARLY EXPERIENCES OUTSIDE THE CLASSROOM: scuba dive intern at the Living Seas Pavilion at Epcot at Walt Disney World, marine science instructor at Seacamp in the Florida Keys

EARLY WORK EXPERIENCE: marine science education program coordinator at the Harbor Branch Oceanographic Institution, regional conservation program coordinator for the National Fish and Wildlife Foundation

CURRENT PURSUIT: MBA student at Duke University

Christopher Nordstrom, who views his zigzagging career path as hopping from stone to stone in life's river, had just leapt to another stone in the fall of 2000. It was a big leap. Chris, who had never lived in a major city or in the "cold" north, accepted a job in Washington, D.C., with the nonprofit National Fish and Wildlife Foundation, which kept him mostly behind a desk. He lived in a windowless basement apartment, commuted on crowded subway trains, and, as winter set in, headed off to work in the dark and returned home in the dark.

This was quite a change from his former life in Florida, where he enjoyed a condo on the beach and a job at the country's third-largest oceanographic institution, a job that often found him working in flip-flops and a bathing suit. A lover of fish since boyhood, Chris had earned an undergraduate degree in marine biology and a master's focusing on fish ecology. So why would he leave a job he liked, one that kept him in close contact with a lifelong interest? He did so because he understood the difference between a job and a career. To borrow his metaphor, Chris had begun to look more than one rock ahead in the river. Counting internships, he'd already jumped on and off a half dozen rocks since leaving his boyhood home in Oviedo, Florida, not far from Orlando.

The house he grew up in sat on three wooded acres. The youngest of three children, Chris roamed outdoors freely, exploring nature, but always making it home by 7 P.M. on Saturday nights to watch oceanographer Jacques Cousteau on TV. "We'd put a man on the moon, but we hadn't been to the bottom of the ocean yet," he says. "Every week was a new adventure, a new species, a new exotic location. It was constant discovery."

When he was still in grade school, a family trip to Chicago further hooked him on fish. He recalls walking up the steps of the templelike Shedd Aquarium on a cold, sunny day and stepping into "the dim, dark underwater world with all the amazing creatures—the shapes, the sizes, the colors."

Not long afterward, Chris filled an aquarium of his own, a ten-gallon tank he found in the attic that had belonged to his older brother. Years later, while working part-time in an aquarium shop, initially selling fish and maintaining tanks, then stepping up to such management tasks as inventory control, he added to his own collection of freshwater and marine aquariums. By the time he topped out at fourteen tanks, he'd moved into his brother's vacated bedroom. The noise from the accumulating aquarium motors had grown so loud, Chris could no longer sleep in his own room.

In high school he got mostly As and Bs, enjoying math and science courses and especially biology. Most of his college-bound classmates headed off to Florida State or the University of Florida. Chris chose Auburn University. "I wanted to break away, get a fresh start," he says. "I walked onto a campus of twenty-five thousand students and didn't know anyone. That's what I wanted."

He started as a business major the fall term of his freshman year, relegating his aquatic interests to hobby status and joining the campus marine biology club. His choice of studies soon seemed wrong. "I didn't feel like I fit in with the business majors. The material, the people, the classes . . . I didn't feel comfortable," Chris recalls. After two quarters, he reversed his emphasis, switching his major to marine biology while remaining a member of the management club. In addition to his heavy load of zoology and marine biology courses, he looked to broaden his skills with an advanced writing course, a communication course, and two quarters of Spanish.

"I was thinking if I did go with marine biology as a career, the oceans circle the globe and language skills would certainly be beneficial, as would communication skills," he says, explaining that he faced his fear of public speaking head-on with classes that required him to do just that.

During vacations as an undergraduate, Chris expanded his aquatic range by learning to scuba dive. This enabled him, the summer after his junior year, to assist an Auburn professor with an underwater geologic research project in the Bahamas on wave energy and sedimentation rates. "I loved it," Chris says. "Driving the rubber Zodiac along the coast, heading out to the reef, I could almost close my eyes and feel like I was Jacques Cousteau."

Chris had yet another early career epiphany the summer of 1993. Eager to immerse himself in a new aquatic ecosystem, he opted to fulfill his summer marine laboratory requirement not on Alabama's Dauphin Island, as did most Auburn marine biology majors, but at a University of Oregon facility in Coos Bay. "Walking at low tide out there, the biodiversity of marine life was unbelievable," he says.

> **"D**riving the rubber Zodiac along the coast, heading out to the reef, I could almost close my eyes and feel like I was Jacques Cousteau."

Face your fears head-on and don't be afraid of failure.

Back on the Auburn campus that fall, headed toward a December graduation, Chris was already eyeing the next couple of rocks in the river of his life. Looking to someday continue his marine biology studies in graduate school, he took the GREs. Meanwhile, he received word that he'd been accepted for a dream internship he'd applied for the previous spring.

So after Auburn, Chris began a six-month stint at the world's largest aquarium, the six-million-gallon tank at Epcot's Living Seas Pavilion in Orlando, Florida. He served as one of three paid dive interns, assisting with dolphin research studies, underwater feeding of the animals, and tank maintenance, but he spent much of his time broadening his diving experience with various scuba certifications, such as dry suit, photography, and navigation.

Early in the internship, looking ahead to grad school, he made an appointment to meet with Dr. Franklin Snelson, a renowned stingray and shark expert in the biology department at the University of Central Florida. His advice to those considering a graduate degree in the sciences is to "go out and find a researcher who's doing research you're interested in, one who has lab space, and funding, and the time to devote to you. Once you've established a relationship, you have a champion."

This meeting also boosted Chris's chances of being accepted to the graduate ichthyology program at the University of Central Florida in another way. Because Chris brought his college transcript with him, he had the opportunity to show it to Dr. Snelson, who spotted a gap in his undergraduate education. He counseled Chris to take a statistics course. Chris did just that.

In the spring, looking to start graduate school in the fall of 1995, Chris got rehired at the Living Seas as a short-term full-time employee. "I couldn't have been more excited going to work every day," he says. "As I walked toward the building I'd see the giant pumps outside, and walking in, hear the water splashing. Then I'd round the corner and be greeted by two Florida manatees as I went to my locker. I'd put on my wet suit, open the door, and there'd be the excitement of all the people, the noise, kids screaming. And I'd jump in the world's biggest aquarium. I never got tired of it."

Now only a couple months from beginning graduate school, Chris followed his Living Seas position with another enjoyable, short-term aquatic job. He'd seen a flyer on a bulletin board at the Living Seas Pavilion calling for marine science instructors and counselors at Seacamp, a summer marine science camp located in the Florida Keys. He taught some classes in the lab and drove a boat out to the reefs to lead snorkeling sessions or assist a dive instructor. He even taught a marine aquarium class, helping the kids collect fish, teaching them about the fish they caught, and then explaining how to care for them in an aquarium. In the process, Chris learned too. He discovered how much he enjoyed teaching.

If you love what you're doing, you'll never tire of it.

The boy who had filled his bedroom with aquariums, now with a degree in marine biology, had seemingly hit the jackpot. Why leave paradise? "Why go to grad school if I'd found such a good place?" Chris echoes. Because he recognized that a cool job should not be mistaken for a career. His diver's job, even with a bachelor's degree, paid live-at-home-with-the-parents wages. He knew he needed to pursue an advanced degree to be more competitive for advanced positions. Grad school it would be.

He spent those three years as both a student and a teacher. To help pay for grad school, Chris taught biology for pre-med students at a local test prep agency and also served as an adjunct biology laboratory professor at a nearby community college. Deciding he wanted to study the ecological impact of a nonnative aquarium fish on south Florida waters, he met first with a scientist doing work at a government lab to help identify an appropriate species, one sparking both concern and funding opportunities to study the problem. Hence his thesis: "The Life History and Ecology of the Introduced African Jewel Cichlid *Hemichromis letourneauxi* in Dade County, Florida." In addition to dissecting numerous specimens to document what flies, plants, or fish they were consuming, Chris spent months bent over a microscope conducting the reproductive portion of his study. Length and width; length and width; length and width, he measured, fish egg by fish egg, until he'd done so for some fifteen thousand eggs. "It was incredibly tedious," he says, explaining that he looked forward to the once-a-month collection trips to Miami, fieldwork that helped balance the necessary but frequently mundane lab work.

"While I would have wanted to be in the field a little more, I also realized I didn't want a full-time field position," he says. "Fieldwork is tough. There's a lot of time prepping. It's intense—long, dirty, hard days—not as sexy as it looks on the Discovery Channel."

> "**F**ieldwork is tough. There's a lot of time prepping. It's intense—long, dirty, hard days—not as sexy as it looks on the Discovery Channel."

Nor could Chris see himself staying in academia. As much as he enjoyed teaching, he could not imagine continuing on for a Ph.D. and settling in somewhere as a marine biology professor. That research-driven life, he'd learned, requires a perpetual "searching for funds, writing proposal after proposal to stay afloat. I'd done one proposal," he said. "The thought of doing that over and over again wasn't appealing."

Chris frankly assessed the careers he came into close contact with during his graduate studies. Knowing himself, his likes and dislikes, he effectively closed certain career doors—and in so doing helped narrow his search.

After graduation he collapsed for a couple weeks to rest up. When he resurfaced, he turned to the Internet, surfing environmental career websites like Ecojobs.com for Florida leads and getting his resume in order. Needing to work while he looked for a job, Chris found a perfect interim solution that kept him busy and brought in some money, but was flexible enough to allow for days off to network or go for an interview. He signed up as a substitute public school teacher, and then settled in for a short time as a biology teacher in early spring.

Meanwhile, Chris continued to ask those he knew in marine biology for any promising job leads. The strategy worked. A professor at the UCF Biology Department knew the director of marine science education at Harbor Branch Oceanographic Institution, America's third-largest oceanographic research institute, after the Scripps Institute of Oceanography and the Woods Hole Oceanographic Institution. Harbor Branch, located on Florida's southeast coast, needed a marine science education program coordinator. Chris's marine biology background, now buttressed with a master's degree, and his varied teaching experiences, including his most recent substitute teaching stint, made him perfect for this job. He started in May 1999.

"It was a rich experience, a neat mix of marine science and business," he says, explaining that Harbor Branch is best known for its twin fleet of yellow submarines with a big, two-person observation bubble on the nose. About 60 percent of the time, Chris found himself teaching marine science, both in the classroom and in the field. The other 40 percent of his work involved various administrative tasks. He also helped develop content for the program's website and marketed the institution's marine science programs at marine science education conferences, where he set up booths and

Find interim opportunities that leave you the time and flexibility to pursue your ultimate goals.

displays. The variety of his job appealed to him. So did working in flip-flops and a bathing suit. One minute he might be sitting in a budget meeting; the next, taking a group of undergraduates out on a large research vessel to collect marine organisms or perform oceanographic research.

"Nothing beats seeing a group of elementary school kids wading into the water with nets and buckets for the first time to collect shrimp or crabs and see the excitement on their faces," says Chris. Yet as time went on, he found himself increasingly drawn to the administrative side of his job. "The business side really grew on me. I liked doing the marketing, liked overseeing the operations. We were a subsidized department, and there was constant pressure to watch the bottom line. We had to be conscious of spending and revenues, so my eyes were opened to the bottom line for the first time. As much as I loved going out with a group of undergrads on a research vessel, I was hungry to learn more about what went into the budget meetings."

A year and a half after he arrived, his department got wrapped into another division in a reorganization. The shake-up left Chris with a job, but concerned about the institute's continued educational mission and therefore his future. He started checking the postings at Ecojobs.com once again. Scanning job openings at various federal and state agencies, he saw a job that would not only give him a taste of city life, but also enable him to work in and learn about a new realm, the nonprofit world.

Chris interviewed for and won the job of regional conservation program coordinator with the National Fish and Wildlife Foundation. He was told he'd work for a year in the nation's capital, then relocate to Atlanta to oversee projects in the southeast.

Congress created the National Fish and Wildlife Foundation to raise and disperse money donated by the public and private sectors to various nonprofit organizations to help fund environmental programs. Chris helped screen proposals and then later managed the contracts of projects that received funding. At any given time, he and his staff of two might be managing as many as three hundred different projects, evaluating progress reports, signing off on funding requests, and making sure checks got issued. "I couldn't wait to hop on a plane and meet some of the people we were funding, or visit a marsh that was being restored, or a colony of birds that had been protected," he says, adding, "There were some people who were doing some really cool things out there."

"Out there": did those words bother him? "In some ways, I envied those people. In some ways no," he says. "I have very diverse interests, and some of those grantees have spent their entire lives focused on one mangrove colony of birds. That's too tight a focus for me."

His job at the National Fish and Wildlife Foundation, as he intended, broadened his perspective. "I learned about funding and contracts and how nonprofits operate and the various stakeholders. It was very valuable getting that forty-thousand-foot perspective on conservation and living at the crossroads of government and the nonprofit sector and the private sector."

Assessing where he'd been—in academia, at a research institution, and now at a nonprofit organization—and having broadened his perspective with his Washington job, Chris began sensing he needed to be elsewhere. "I knew I wanted and needed private sector experience. I'd been somewhat living in a bubble working at a marine lab and then at a nonprofit. I knew the private-sector was a big animal, and I wanted to explore it."

"**It's advantageous in the animal world to be opportunistic and adaptive. I think it's also beneficial in the hunt for the right job.**"

Being a biologist, Chris knew well the importance of adaptation in the survival of a species, which he likens to thriving in a career. It's advantageous in the animal world to be opportunistic and adaptive. I think it's also beneficial in the hunt for the right job."

Also influencing his decision was the matter of his expected transfer to Atlanta. As the time approached, his superiors decided on Tampa instead, and Chris did not relish relocating there at that time. So after a year and a half at the National Fish and Wildlife Foundation, he decided that as much as he liked and respected his colleagues, the foundation's mission, and many aspects of his job, it was time to move on. He had a vague sense of an emerging entrepreneurial streak, the early feeling that he might like to run his own business. But he had no idea what that might be and no illusions that he was ready to do so. He did know that he wanted his next job to be in the for-profit world.

Chris also knew, in updating his resume, that his job history appeared rather choppy: no longer than eighteen months at either of his jobs after graduate school. "I get that in interviews," he admits. "I'm very aware of the need to explain. And I've had ready answers. At Harbor Branch, they phased out my department. And at the National Fish and Wildlife Foundation, they wanted to place me in the Tampa area, and so lifestyle considerations entered in. It was not what I wanted to do, and I even recruited my replacement."

This time, too, he found his job in an online posting. Listed at CareerBuilder.com was an opening for an outreach specialist at an environmental consulting firm in the D.C. area. "I didn't call ahead, didn't do any advance networking, the kinds of things I know now can help. I just sent in my resume blind," he says.

Even so, Chris got a call. Why? Because his resume stood out. By now, he'd amassed a desirable collection of talents and experience. He had an advanced degree in science, and thanks to his work with various nonprofits and his teaching background, an ability to communicate complex scientific information to laypeople. That made him a perfect addition in the fall of 2001 to the eight thousand—plus employees at a Fairfax, Virginia, company called Tetra Tech.

The Tetra Tech group Chris went to work for performed mostly environmental assessments and environmental impact statements for federal clients,

Chris got a call. Why? Because his resume stood out.

including work for the Department of Defense on military bases. Chris was initially hired to help produce outreach materials on water resource issues for Native American tribes and an environmental impact statement for an Army base in Louisiana. He enjoyed the outreach education side of his job, attending public information sessions in school cafeterias and hotels, where background materials he'd help to write explained complex environmental laws and potential local impact.

"In our department there were archaeologists, water experts, noise experts, air quality experts, geologists, biologists, wetland experts—all these different people would come together on a project and analyze the potential impacts from all those areas," he says, explaining that he found it fascinating to see close-up how a single federal law, the National Environmental Policy Act (NEPA), "could spin off an entire contract consulting industry."

He did well in his job, earning a promotion after his first- and second-year anniversaries with the company. As he'd hoped, Chris continued to develop his business skills. "Project management, leading project teams, budgets, marketing and business development . . . I learned a tremendous amount in that job," he says. Also on the plus side, he noted several things about working for a consulting firm that he liked, such as the diversity of projects, working on several things at once, and that the projects had a beginning, a middle, and an end. Then he'd move on to another challenge.

By now, however, Chris knew it was time to take another job assessment, and he asked himself the key question, "Can I see myself doing this as a career?" Year after year of working in the NEPA trenches, he realized, would someday grow too routine for his liking.

What *did* he see downstream for himself? Chris wasn't sure. Perhaps he'd find a business to run that fit his talents. Maybe he'd return to the nonprofit world. Or he might settle somewhere else in the private sector. Regardless, he felt he'd identified his next rock in the river. No matter what he chose, he knew he'd be better prepared to succeed after getting an MBA. This was not, in fact, a new idea; as far back as his first job at Harbor Branch, he'd sensed the importance of a solid grounding in business.

"Business skills go hand in hand with any field," Chris says, noting, "having formal management training will help set you apart and prepare you—if you're working in a small urban nonprofit, working in a research laboratory, even teaching English in Southeast Asia. Having an understanding of budgets, operational efficiency, marketing, strategy, finance, economics, accounting, and organizational behavior will be valuable to you and your organization."

At Tetra Tech, Chris wasn't surrounded by MBAs, but he was rooming with one at the time. He saw in Russ, who had an MBA from the Darden School of Business at the University of Virginia, many of those skills he felt he'd be wise to learn. And he also saw that Russ's job as a management consultant paid significantly more than his own salary—something hard to ignore with his thirtieth birthday now in his rearview mirror and thoughts of achieving a bit more financial independence starting to pop up with increasing frequency, if not urgency. So he registered to take the GMATs in the spring of 2003 and studied hard for them. His score of 710 made him a viable candidate at the nation's top business schools.

"I felt like I had a ticket to an incredible career, a winning lottery ticket," he says, after deciding upon the Fuqua School of Business at Duke University, where he arrived in the fall of 2004. His first year, he acknowledged, stretched him. "Being a nontraditional business student, surrounded by people years younger, but many of them with an undergraduate degree in business and a much better grasp of number crunching inside a business, has been challenging,"

"**H**aving formal management training will help set you apart and prepare you— if you're working in a small urban nonprofit, working in a research laboratory, even teaching English in Southeast Asia."

he says. And rewarding: "I've probably grown more than anyone else in the program."

Contemplating his summer internship options provided Chris a good vantage point for reassessing his future plans. He'd written in his admissions essay that he wanted to get an MBA and then leverage his sharpened business skills by returning to the nonprofit or environmental field. "That's still somewhat of an interest of mine," he says. "But throughout [this first year of business school] I've been struggling with a philosophical decision: Do I go back to my past, my background, or do I use this shot, my MBA, to go a more rigorous, traditional route for a couple years—get that training and experience in the corporate world. I think it's easier to go back to a non-profit [later] than to first go to a nonprofit and then to the private sector."

His business school classes and the alluring array of summer internship opportunities have already broadened Chris's horizons. "Careers, companies, industries I didn't even know existed are now options," he says. He turned down an internship with a major IT firm in India that would have taken him to Asia to help facilitate a forum on disaster relief protocols to aid future disaster victims. Too weighted toward nonprofit experiences, he decided. He also passed up an internship job in the Philippines. This one, involving microeconomic work with the fish aquarium trade, fit him like a wet suit. "The position could have been written for me," he says, "but it felt like too much of my past, and I reminded myself I came to business school to stretch myself."

So turning down India and the Philippines, he decided to spend the summer of 2005 in Roanoke, Virginia. He'll report to the Egg Factory, which specializes in developing and commercializing intellectual property. Chris will serve as one of two MBA mentor/directors of a summer program that will teach about a dozen top undergraduate students how to develop and launch two actual businesses within the Egg Factory's corporate portfolio. While helping oversee the program, Chris expects he, too, will learn as much, if not more, from the Egg Factory staff as well as from visiting marketing and patent experts and venture capitalists who will lead various workshops, possibly making valuable contacts.

Noting that his father was an engineer and inventor, he's realizing more and more that he's got entrepreneurship in his genes, and says his summer internship will allow him to formally scratch this entrepreneurial itch while applying his MBA courses and leveraging his experience and passion for mentoring.

From where he stands now, on his business school rock, Chris has mental snapshots of how he imagines his future life. "Regardless of what I end up doing, I imagine that when I get there, I'll have traveled the world," he says. "I will be living near the water somewhere on the East Coast. I will hopefully have my closest friends and family nearby, and I will have a boat and be able to run it each night after work. Above all, I hope that I will have made a difference in the world. So I view my personal destination more as peace of mind, as opposed to a particular salary, job title, or organization.

"If you focus too much on the end, you will either miss opportunities or be unhappy when your plan falls through. Instead, I find myself more in the moment, more focused on what is around me, or at most one or two steps ahead, but typically no further."

Of this he is certain: That river of life he saw in his twenties now seems like a slow-flowing, quiet, shallow side stream. Business school has taken him to where that tributary empties into a much deeper, broader, more challenging flow. He's just starting to take the measure of this exciting, bigger river of opportunity, but already he's looking for his next career rock.

> **"I view my personal destination more as peace of mind, as opposed to a particular salary, job title, or organization."**

Chris's Smart Moves

- He not only pinpointed the graduate school biology program he wanted to get into, but arranged to meet with the professor he hoped to study with—gaining a champion in the process and identifying an important course that he still needed to take.

- While job hunting after earning his master's degree, he worked as a substitute teacher. By being on call when he chose, he had the scheduling freedom to do job searches and interviews.

- He didn't let especially attractive work environments prevent him from frankly answering the key question, can I see myself doing this as a career?

- He's ensured that his resume stands out from the crowd—coupling scuba diving with degrees in marine biology, adding nonprofit experience to marine institute work, moonlighting as a teacher and adjunct professor, and adding an MBA to private-sector consulting.

- **He's viewed his career as a series of evolving career moves,** adaptations in biological terms, that have made him better fit for career survival.
- **In every opportunity, he's reached beyond the job description** to broaden his skills, increase his value to the company, and strengthen his resume.

Balancing on the Career–Marriage High Wire

COLLEGE: University of Virginia, 1988

MAJOR: chemistry

PASSION: working to fund the development of technology and create high-performance businesses

EARLY EXPERIENCES OUTSIDE THE CLASSROOM: helped launch an on-campus clothing business called Peace Frogs

EARLY WORK EXPERIENCE: specialty resins sales rep for Monsanto

CURRENT PURSUIT: considering multiple options in Istanbul, Turkey, and elsewhere

Discovering and nurturing an upwardly arcing corporate career is hard enough as a solo high-wire act. Add an equally ambitious spouse, and all too often the wire starts to vibrate, as Judith Baker learned soon after making her first big career shift.

Deciding that she'd reached her limit after two years of a dual-career and dual-city marriage, she left a job she loved and a company she loved just as much—St. Louis–headquartered Monsanto—to join consulting giant Arthur D. Little in Boston. That's where her husband worked as a senior executive in the financial services industry. Only a few weeks after settling in at her new job, as if in an O. Henry tale, irony struck in the form of good news. Her husband was offered a highly lucrative, high-profile job-of-a-lifetime—in Manhattan. Twang went the wire on which they had just rebalanced their careers and marriage.

Although not quite at this level, Judith had been carefully thinking through important, career-affecting choices since high school, when she would have bet dollars to oats for her horse that she'd grow up to be a veterinarian. To this daughter of a much-traveled U.S. diplomat, riding horses represented a common denominator of a peripatetic childhood: born in Rio; then to Washington, D.C.; on to Bonn (grades K–five); back to Washington (sixth grade); next Rome (seventh and eighth grades); then back to the Washington area, where Judith attended high school in Falls Church, Virginia. It was there, after riding in Germany and Italy, that she owned her first horse and starting thinking about veterinary science.

Her interest stemmed from a vet she'd met in Rome. "Our dog was being treated by him, and I talked with him about his techniques—he used alternative techniques like acupuncture. I'd never seen an animal stuck full of needles before. Our dog had been half paralyzed, and it just blew my mind to see him walk again. The vet ran the clinic on the side, he told me. When I asked what he did full-time, he said he bought elite racing horses for the Saudi royal family. I thought, wow, that would be the most incredible job ever. I wanted to understand what the veterinary sciences were really about, which was why in high school I started working at a vet clinic in Great Falls, Virginia."

Judith had always been as talented in the sciences as she was interested in them. Nominated by her teachers for Governor's School the summer between her junior and senior years of high school, and encouraged by her father to follow her love of science, she studied astrophysics at the Virginia Polytechnic Institute and State University. The professor teaching that course asked if she'd be interested in coming to work at his lab the next summer, and until then, to undertake a special project on light diffraction during her senior year back at her high school. "That taught me to work independently and about scientific inquiry," she says. And it opened wide an elite career door, with the possibility of coming to Virginia Tech as a physics major and working with the professor in his lab.

"My parents were very excited," she says, recalling them saying, "That's fabulous, honey. And how do you feel about it?"

"My parents were very inquiry based, which sometimes drove me crazy, but in retrospect, I was deeply grateful that they asked questions that would guide my answers and encouraged me to take the quiet time to make an informed decision." Judith carefully considered the pros and cons of heading off to Virginia Tech. "To me, college was about learning how to learn in a multidisciplinary environment. The concept of the Renaissance person, which I was really steeped in when I lived in Italy, had stuck with me. I knew I wanted the sciences, but I felt that wasn't all of me, so when I came to look at college options, I was leaning toward a place where I could have high-quality science education and have exposure to a high-quality education in other areas as well."

> If you're a people person, the isolated environment of lab work, regardless of the research interest, may leave you socially and professionally unsatisfied.

> **"The concept of the Renaissance person had stuck with me. I knew I wanted the sciences, but I felt that wasn't all of me."**

She turned down Virginia Tech, selecting instead the University of Virginia, where she piled on the chemistry courses, fulfilling her major requirements by the end of her junior year. By then, she was working ten to twenty hours a week as a lab technician in a biochem lab running protein analysis assays. Her duties included taking blood samples from the refrigerator, spinning them down, taking off the serum, and putting it in teeny tubes in preparation for them to be radioactively tagged. Though it was repetitive, Judith did not find the work tedious.

"But I saw it as disconnected and lonely. I craved more of a connection with people." The Great Falls veterinary clinic had told her she'd be welcome to work there once she had finished veterinary school. "I really thought about it, because I liked working with them," she says. "But I also considered what my life would be like if I worked there the next twenty-five or thirty years, basically six days a week, sometimes seven, going to that building in Great Falls."

That image did not jibe, she realized, with her globe-trotting childhood or her desire to hopefully travel as part of her job. So Judith turned away from another open door, a second career that fit her talents and many of her interests, but one that in the final analysis did not excite her.

In fact, she treated college rather like a hallway offering a multitude of career doors to push open, if only to poke her head inside some for a quick peek. For example, one summer, she took an internship in a State Department annex building in Washington, D.C., as an intern in the Bureau of Oceans and International Environmental and Scientific Affairs. Thinking maybe the Foreign Service might be her passport to world travel, Judith was hedging her career bets with a minor in foreign affairs, and sought a view of government work with an exposure to scientific policy on a global level. Her task was to help put together a conference to address the issue of the emerging hole in the ozone layer. "I thought it was a fabulous idea that such a conference was funded," she says, explaining that her excitement soon turned to disappointment when she encountered the calcifying effect of bureaucratic inertia.

However, she had become involved with something outside her classes that *did* catch her fancy. Serving on a student government committee, she met a UVA student and budding entrepreneur named Catesby Jones, who enlisted her imagination and support in launching a clothing business on campus. The business, Peace Frogs, which has since evolved into a successful, environmentally oriented clothing company, was then breaking in with a line of colorful shorts bearing the images of various world flags.

> **S**he found being in on the organic start of a business exhilarating, and, in contrast to her work in the lab, she thrived on the personal interaction.

Following the company's first big promotion, a quarter-page ad in *Rolling Stone*, Judith helped man the phones when the orders started coming in. She found being in on the organic start of a business exhilarating, and, in contrast to her work in the lab, she thrived on the personal interaction with Jones and the other early Peace Frogs founders. This extracurricular experience, she says, made her "really curious about understanding more about business." Accordingly, she started taking courses at UVA's commerce school, especially senior year, after she'd already wrapped up her chemistry degree and was turning her attention to life after college.

She made the campus careers office her bridge to the future, first taking a number of self-assessment tests, then combing the lists of companies arriving for on-campus recruiting visits. The testing pretty much reaffirmed aspects of herself that she already knew. She was highly analytical, extroverted, and thoughtful. "But after all the experiences I'd had, it was like a validation, like a lens that helped me reclarify my thinking," Judith says.

She looked into many fields, interviewing with investment banks, pharmaceutical companies, oil companies, and chemical companies. The latter offered the most logical fit, considering her chemistry major, but what sealed her decision to accept Monsanto's offer was the immediate connection she felt with the interviewer, a UVA alumnus named Jim Trice. "He was a chemical engineer and a real Renaissance man—well-read, well-traveled," she says. "He talked about the team atmosphere and commitment to excellence at Monsanto. They flew me to St. Louis for an interview. I would have never imagined moving to the Midwest, being born in Brazil and having lived in Germany and Rome, but after [visiting the company and talking with employees and] seeing the genuine intelligence and warmth of the people, I said to myself, this is where I want to see what it's like to work in my first job. They designed in broad experiences across businesses. I really felt that at Monsanto I could create and have people help me cocreate my career."

Hired as a sales rep in the company's specialty resins group, Judith reported to St. Louis the summer of 1988 and began a rigorous four-month training period. By the time she began calling on customers in six states, Judith was well versed in her company's products and already appreciative of the essence of her job. "A scientific sale is not about selling," she says. "It's actually really about understanding the fit for the need, and a lot of that is discovering what performance is required for an application." Her starting salary of about thirty-two thousand dollars "felt like a million bucks," and she got a company car to help her cover her territory.

And cover it she did, successfully enough after her first year that she gained additional states, and by the end of her second year with Monsanto, she was calling on customers in thirteen states, as far west as Colorado and Texas and as far east as West Virginia, sometimes flying to meet with them.

Envisioning an MBA as a helpful and necessary springboard higher up the corporate ladder, Judith looked into business schools. She first considered an executive MBA program at Washington University that would allow her to get her degree over several years while still working at Monsanto. But impatient to sink her teeth into high-level business education, she applied to UVA's Colgate Darden Graduate School of Business Administration and notified her superiors of her intention.

That's when Judith learned an important career lesson. Many corporations, eager to keep valued employees in the fold, especially rising stars, will pay for their graduate education. "The company said to me: 'We don't want to lose you.' Nor did I want to lose them," she says, explaining that she was one of three employees who received a similar "unbelievable" offer at the time. "Monsanto offered full tuition and expenses. In exchange, we agreed we'd return to the company in an agreed-upon job and stay for the equivalent of how long we'd been gone—in my case, two years."

Judith happily returned to Monsanto in July 1992, much wiser about the ways of business and management, especially after two overseas experiences. The winter of her second year of graduate school, taking advantage of an exchange program, she studied at the Stockholm School of Economics and became part of a team that traveled to Brazil to examine the impact of technology on the country's transactions market. "At the time, Brazil was one of the largest check-writing countries in the world," she says.

But even more rewarding was her previous summer's internship in India. There, while assigned to the president of a polymer company to help design and execute a major corporate turnaround, her learning curve accelerated dramatically when the country's prime minister, Rajiv Gandhi, was assassinated. "It was like a stick of dynamite exploded the country's economy," she says, explaining that after the initial widespread shock, manufacturing oligopolies and state-set prices began to give way to a free-market economy, sparking competitive pressures to modernize, as did the liberalization of the rupee, which encouraged exporting.

Every day brought new lessons, including one fairly early in her stay, which Judith terms a "life nugget." Her first few weeks in this new setting, she'd buried her head in reports about the company she was charged with helping, turning down invitations to dinner, saying she was too busy. "I was plowing ahead but getting nowhere," she says. Only after having dinner with the plant manager and his family did she begin to make some headway at the company. "After dinner we sat in his car and talked, and he gave me the real scoop. But he wasn't ready to do that, nobody was, until they got to know me and felt they could trust me." Thereafter, she'd never forget that business, especially conducted in different cultures, requires people skills and situational sensitivity every bit as much as analytical and financial acumen.

> **Business, especially conducted in different cultures, requires people skills and situational sensitivity every bit as much as analytical and financial acumen.**

Back at Monsanto, Judith regained her former fast track, initially as market manager for two product groups, Modaflow and Scripset. The second required regular trips East, which is where she started dating the man she would marry in January 1994. Born of weekends together and workweeks apart, the marriage continued as a tale of two cities and two determined careerists, each working exceptionally long days. With Monsanto's blessing and support, Judith officially began splitting her time between St. Louis and Boston some nine months into her marriage. This followed a detailed analysis of travel and time costs that showed the merits of a "satellite office" in Boston, actually a well-outfitted area in the couple's apartment.

But that hectic lifestyle would soon seem tame. Returning from her wedding and honeymoon in Australia, Judith read a waiting email that invited her to be part of a new process and twelve-member development team reporting directly to Monsanto Chemical's president. Serving on this key corporate initiative was both an honor and much more work, even after dropping her management responsibilities for Modaflow. "Typically, I'd catch the 6 A.M. flight from Boston, which would get me to the office about 8:15," she says.

By 1995, with the design initiatives well under way, Judith was spending most of her week in St. Louis, living out of a suitcase. After nearly two years of seeing the marriage take a backseat to their jobs, Judith started asking, "How long can I continue to do this? It wasn't as much the physical wear and tear, but more just where was this going. I was being considered for a strategy job back in St. Louis and other product line jobs, and I knew that I didn't want to be that far away from my husband."

Now questioning the long-term viability of her two-city solution to her career-marriage conundrum, for the first time Judith took interest in a call from a corporate recruiter, this one with a job possibility at a General Electric divisional office in Pittsfield, Massachusetts. As it happened, while Judith looked into this job, another possibility arose.

Attending a three-day weekend self-improvement seminar in Boston, she bonded with another attendee, a woman who worked in Boston for Arthur D. Little. "I really think you should talk to the people in our company," the woman advised Judith. "I'd never considered consulting," Judith says, "but the way she explained her company... She said it focused on technology and management consulting. I love working with technology and thought . . . interesting. So I soon had lunch with one of her colleagues, the head of their chemicals practice. He said, 'Why don't I take you upstairs and let you meet a few of the folks in our practice.'"

What Judith had intended primarily as an informational interview was turning into something more. Judith never expected what happened next, discovering that "in the world of consulting the pace is faster, the proverbial New York minute." Within forty-eight hours she'd been offered a job for significantly more money than she was making at Monsanto.

She now needed to turn her analytical skills inward, for she faced a career decision of epic proportions. She loved Monsanto. It had proven every bit the perfect company for her, nurturing and incredibly accommodating, not only when she wanted to go to business school, but also in helping her structure her job to better fit her personal life. The job with GE would get her experience in another blue-chip company also known for grooming managers. But a jump to Arthur D. Little seemed her best course of action.

Judith took the job with Arthur D. Little because it offered her what most married couples take for granted: the opportunity to finally live with her husband and share more of their lives and thoughts and dreams together, instead of making do with a never-ending stream of good-bye and hello hugs. Judith started as a manager at Arthur D. Little in February 1996, and was thrown in almost immediately on an intense, leanly staffed project aimed at turning around three businesses of a major Fortune 500 chemical company. Only a few weeks later, her husband broke the news that he had received a job offer he'd recently told her might be in the wind. The job would mean a jump from executive director of his current Boston financial services firm to president of an asset management company in New York.

Twang went the high wire that Judith thought she had steadied with her career shift. Thinking rationally, purely analytically, she saw her husband's job offer for what it was. Perhaps the job of a lifetime, the kind of offer that might not come again. Big-time responsibility and big-time bucks. Of course he had to take it. But thinking emotionally, and unavoidably as the spouse who had just hopped off her own career track and shifted industries to live with her husband, she felt betrayed by fate. How could this happen? Not now.

They tried to make things work. She kept the Boston apartment; he got one in Manhattan. They slipped back into their old pattern of catch-as-catch-can visits. Judith occasionally arranged for project work that took her to New York. In fact, it was almost moot where they lived: the demands of their current jobs didn't allow them very much quality time anyway. "My first six months at ADL, I was working all the time, traveling a lot, leaving Monday at 6 A.M. and often not making it back until 10 P.M. or 11 P.M. on Friday." Her husband was routinely logging similar twelve-hour days, often stealing quiet time on the weekends to plan for the upcoming week.

They continued like this for months—and more months. As time went on, Judith realized that she liked Boston. She really wanted to continue to live there and not in New York. But more tellingly, she began to face up to career-induced cracks in the foundation of her marriage and a fundamental question: Considering their career aspirations, could they make enough time to create a home and family?

When her husband invoked the solar system, Judith felt a crack widen. "He said there has to be one sun and one earth in every relationship. His implication: 'I'm earning probably five times what you are, Sweetheart, so why don't you pack it up.' I'm like, wait a minute, my paradigm was one of partnership.

"As we basically grew and were road testing our relationship and making life decisions together, it was evident we had different sets of values. He had hit the big payday. Why wasn't I cooperating? I was just starting into this new career and I wanted to prove myself, not just drop it like a hot rock and run to New York and be a corporate wife," she says, explaining that they tugged back and forth on this career-marriage rope for a while, finally seeking help in counseling.

Neither, however, wanted to let go of their career. One reason for Judith's tightening grip was her broader perspective. "My generation of young women has been told the sky's the limit. Go for it. I had seen the world and been armed with tools and basically proven myself and was on my way up. Now I've started my way up another company, and I'm determined to climb. I'm about thirty at the time, and I know I do want to have a family, but I also know that I wanted enough of a core experience under my belt when I took a breather [to start a family]." It was a bittersweet moment, indeed, when Judith realized she could love someone profoundly but also recognize that "given what we wanted to do with our lives, we were not a fit." Judith and her husband were divorced in early 2000.

Judith moved steadily higher at Arthur D. Little: manager, senior manager, associate director and head of Arthur D. Little Capital, overseeing a diverse asset fund with over eighty-five holdings and venture funds. At the end of her six-year stay with the company, she was basically doing two jobs—associate director, bringing in new clients, and, in her "night job," head of the capital fund, helping the company's new CEO, Pam McNamara, value the assets and ultimately represent them to potential buyers in the company's spring 2002 bankruptcy proceedings. Judith had never had a female boss before, and she relished the opportunity to work closely with and for another woman. Just prior to the company's dissolution, Judith and several other ADL employees left for a much smaller Boston company called Strategic Decisions Group.

But before doing so, while in Washington to help her mother move to a retirement community, Judith met a man and started dating him, even while at first telling herself, "No way." Nicolas was a career diplomat. The daughter of a diplomat, Judith knew the drill—a couple years in one country, back to Washington, then off somewhere else. Nicolas's recent assignments included Helsinki and Rome, but after they met, he was stationed in New York at the United Nations. Judith knew this drill, too: a Logan to LaGuardia romance.

At her new company, Judith was charged with growing their biotech consulting business. As at Arthur D. Little, she spent much of her time cultivating new clients. "The way you [move up] in consulting is you become a kahuna, a rainmaker," she explains. "I realized at Strategic Decisions Group that I missed actually managing a business and being responsible for the bottom line of a business—realized that my skin was not in the game." Ironically, although she was continually promoted and told she was talented and could handle the responsibilities yet another rung higher on the corporate ladder, making ever more money, Judith had, in fact, risen beyond the point in her current field of consulting where her job provided the same satisfactions as before.

On the personal front, however, things were going much better. She married a second time, on July 4, 2004, again accepting the challenge of balancing careers, marriage, and family.

The couple settled in Princeton, New Jersey, temporarily, while Nicolas attended intensive Turkish language classes prior to his next diplomatic posting. Judith had by then left Strategic Decisions Group, accepting and enjoying a much more hands-on job as the chief operating officer of a small, New Hampshire–based company—one that offered her the flexibility to live where she wanted, which was in Princeton with her husband.

How did she find such a job? By broadening her experiences and contacts outside her primary working sphere. While working at Arthur D. Little, she'd accepted an offer to join the board of a Salem, New Hampshire, based company called Safety Net Solutions that provides software, security, and systems integration services to the government and commercial sector. She would receive a small compensation and expenses to attend the meetings—

in other words, no great financial reward. But accepting this extracurricular post proved an empowering career move.

"Some people have high expectations they'll get everything they need from their job," she said, "but I really advise people to seek a total experience that complements your job with nonprofit work and time on something like an advisory board. A lot of young companies and smaller companies are looking for experienced people who can bring their experience and expertise to the board. I was asked to join the Safety Net board to help transition between CEOs."

Before long, her board work led to an offer to step in as COO for Safety Net Solutions. Judith had effectively manufactured her own opportunity. The Safety Net offer seemed a good way to transition from the consulting industry.

She's enjoyed the experience of helping a dynamic small company through a key transition period, and now Judith is preparing for her own transition. To what, she isn't yet sure.

Job hunting in one's native land is hard enough, so how does one look for employment in a foreign country? By networking like there's no tomorrow. That's just what Judith did, working every connection she could think of, and arranging as many as twenty-two informational interviews during a two-week scouting visit. She pressed new contacts at Princeton University, where she and her husband were learning to speak Turkish (she less intensively); she queried classmates from graduate school; she even sought leads from old family friends dating back to her father's time in the diplomatic corps.

> # How does one look for employment in a foreign country? By networking like there's no tomorrow.

"Contacts, even incredible contacts, can come through a lot of different venues," she says, relating that she networked to one of her best contacts in Istanbul via the wife of a diplomat friend of her father's. "Had I not listened to her, I'd have missed [meeting with] a guy who's on the board of one of Turkey's largest banks—he connected me to five people, I think."

When we last spoke, Judith's future was uncertain, but full of opportunities in Turkey, Europe, and the United States. "If need be," she says, "we're willing to do the commute for two years. Worst-case scenario, flying to see each other every six weeks."

Judith speaks optimistically, based on their shared values and similar perspective, of solving the even dicier matter of adding children to a two-career marriage. Now several jobs into her career, Judith knows the kind of work she enjoys most—working to fund the development of technology and create high-performance businesses. She also cherishes the time she spends on boards of nonprofits, such as Women Entrepreneurs in Science and Technology, and advising small biotech companies.

"If the plane were going down, would I change anything? I have had such an amazing set of experiences and have worked with such amazing people, I wouldn't change a thing. I also feel there's a lot left to do and a lot I really want to sink my teeth into.

"At this point," Judith continues, "we're committed to looking for the best options and working through the best solution for us, and the process of getting there is what life is all about, particularly in relationships. We're co-creating our solution. It's exciting. It's terrifying. It's frustrating. It's enervating. Perfect solutions are rare. It's a roller coaster. It's life. And I love it."

> "We're co-creating our solution. It's exciting. It's terrifying. It's frustrating. It's enervating. Perfect solutions are rare."

Judith's Smart Moves

- She chose her college and thought of her career by looking beyond her much-praised, obvious talent for science, realizing that she had other interests also worth fulfilling.

- Thinking hard about her intended career path while in college, she envisioned not only the work, but also the life she'd be living doing

that job. Thus, she decided to abandon her childhood dream of becoming a veterinarian.

- **She discovered a previously unidentified interest by expanding her liberal arts education beyond the classroom.** Helping a college friend launch an on-campus clothing venture, she became enthralled by the challenges of starting and running a business.

- **Busy as she was in a taxing management job, she made time for extracurricular projects, like serving on three boards, including the advisory board of a small tech company**—a move that led to a job as the company's chief operating officer.

- **Seeking employment in a foreign country where she knew no one, she networked like crazy,** considering contacts from all directions—professional, educational, personal, even going back to childhood.

Benefiting from Many Coaches

COLLEGE: Hartwick College, 1999

MAJOR: psychology

POSTGRADUATE: MA in sports management, University of Massachusetts, 2001

PASSION: the power of sports

EARLY EXPERIENCES OUTSIDE THE CLASSROOM: job shadowing, event management internship

EARLY WORK EXPERIENCE: manager of marketing and corporate relations at the University of Connecticut

CURRENT JOB: marketing promotions associate for team sports at New Balance Athletic Shoe

Michael Bruny, who has repeatedly sought and benefited from the counsel of others, helped get his life back on track early in high school by heeding his own advice, words written in a still-trembling hand on the wall of his bedroom—his half of a divided room that he shared with his sister. His reminder to himself: The only way out is hard work.

Mike had just returned home to his apartment building in the Flatbush section of Brooklyn, a building filled with families of Haitian descent like his own, after being mugged on his way back from school. He'd gotten off a city bus and was walking the few blocks to his home when someone grabbed him from behind. "He put a choke hold on me," Mike recalls. "I felt something behind my head, if not a gun, something hard."

Mike told him he didn't have any money, which proved true when the mugger rifled through his wallet. So the mugger took the one thing of value

Mike did have, a Ralph Lauren down jacket, then told him to keep walking and not look back.

In a way, that's exactly what Mike did, by considering this frightening brush with the violent, underachieving side of city life to be a personal wake-up call. Writing a motivational mantra on his wall helped him change the course of his life and become the first in his immediate family to graduate from college.

The mugging forced him to realize how many corners he was cutting as a high school freshman, even while making a name for himself on the gridiron as a running back with the Brooklyn Skyhawks, a Pop Warner football team. In school Mike was hanging with the wrong crowd, skipping classes, barely studying, doing just enough schoolwork to get along. "Having immigrant parents who don't fully know the system," he says, "you think you can put things over on them." But one day, Mike's father let him know how wrong he was about that, too. He told his son bluntly that he was old enough to make his own decisions. "You can continue the way you're going," he said, "but don't talk to me when you come into this house."

That ultimatum stung "worse than any hand he could have laid on me," says Mike, who sought a new start at a different high school, raised his grades to high B's, and started on the football team as fullback and linebacker, before tearing a knee ligament his senior year. When he could play again, he switched to wide receiver and safety. Hartwick College, in the upstate New York town of Oneonta, recruited him, and that's where Mike decided to go to college.

He arrived at Hartwick ready to pull on his shoulder pads. He was less ready for the academic rigors of a demanding, small liberal arts college. Influenced by his experience rehabbing his injured knee, he thought he might want to be a physical therapist. That pointed to a biology major and postgraduate physical therapy training. Mike, however, didn't do especially well in his freshman biology class. "It seemed so abstract, learning about individual cells, so far away from anything I really wanted to do," he says, recalling that he got a C in the course. In truth, his struggles went beyond that one class.

"I didn't really know how to study," he says, "because I'd never really had to before." He learned basic study skills in a first-year seminar and

Adversity can hold you back or catapult you forward. Make it a motivational force.

credits his Hartwick professors and fellow students with helping him learn the kinds of transferable skills needed in virtually any career. Where did those transferable skills take him? To his current job as a marketing and promotions associate at New Balance, the athletic shoe company.

How did Mike end up in corporate America? Certainly not via anything resembling a straight path. He signed on with New Balance in August 2004, eight years, one job, one graduate degree, and three internships, not to mention several days of "career shadowing," after changing his mind about his Hartwick major.

When it came time to declare a major at the end of his sophomore year, Mike chose psychology. He'd enjoyed the psych classes he'd taken and wanted to dig deeper. Still guided by his interest and comfort level around sports, he'd started considering a career in sports psychology. Thanks to his college's careers office and the school's one-month winter J-term, he got to sample that and two other sports-related fields.

Hartwick's program, called Metrolink, provided students with daylong glimpses into several potential careers. Mike was one of a busload of students who traveled to Boston, New York, and Washington, D.C., for career-broadening and job shadowing experiences with various Hartwick alumni. In the New York metropolitan area, he stayed overnight with an alumnus in Greenwich, Connecticut, and spent the day at the elbow of another Hartwick graduate who worked for a sports marketing company in nearby Stamford. In Boston, he spent a day at Northeastern University's Center for the Study of Sport in Society. And in Washington, he met with a sports psychologist, one who had several professional athletes as clients. That day, though much less exciting, proved the most important of the three.

"That probably helped steer me away from sports pyschology as a possible career," Mike says. The more the sports psychologist talked about her job, the less he wanted to do it himself. "It didn't seem like much structure. It just didn't click." And so he crossed that profession off his list and kept his mind open to other possibilities.

Mike spent his senior year J-term as an intern at a New York City sports and media company called Interactive Sports. This, too, he arranged through the Hartwick careers office. Though he did mostly menial jobs, like transcribing interviews taped by others, the experience proved doubly valuable. "It was the first time I'd met an owner of a company who was a black man, and that was inspiring," says Mike, who has remained friends with the sports media company owner.

If there has been one constant in Mike's unscripted path to his present job, it's been his openness to seeking help and acting upon the good counsel and assistance of others who have taken a liking to him and aided his job or career search. His father, a hardworking automobile mechanic, was the first to really put him on what Mike calls "listen mode."

"Mike, I know you're getting tired of hearing the old man talk," he would say. But Mike never did tire, and he listened hardest when his father switched to a saying in Creole French, like "If the young knew and the old could." Even now, with big decisions to make or his calendar overly busy, Mike still hears his father's voice, slowing him down, helping him clear his thoughts. "Life is simple, Mike. People complicate it."

As a teenager, Mike came under the wing of a Jamaican shop owner named Horace Green, who owned a spice shop on a corner not far from Mike's apartment building. Mike helped after school and on weekends, packing spices, and he also lent a hand when it came time to rebuild the store. He learned the meaning of an honest day's work and more from the shopkeeper. "I can remember packing spices and Mr. Green saying to me, 'Mike, do what you love and people will pay you for it.'" At that age, Mike didn't yet know what he loved, but he held onto those words, and he credits his first mentor with helping him "follow his heart."

At Hartwick, Mike's mentors continued to pile up. Some he sought out. Others came to him, attracted by his willingness to work hard and his receptive, upbeat personality. Early on in college, still struggling to adjust to the workload, Mike approached a classmate for help. "He was an honor student, a white guy who's a lawyer now, and I felt comfortable enough to open up to him. 'Darren, man, how do you do such and such? And I'd ask him x, y, or z. He took me to the library and taught me how to write papers. I remember him telling me, 'You can contact your professors during the summer and ask them what books you're going to be reading in the fall and get a head start.'"

Mike has attracted and cultivated mentors for several reasons. Of crucial importance, he has been unafraid to admit what he doesn't know—not just to himself, but also to someone else. Consider, too, how he asks for help. Without coming across as obsequious or fawning, he poses his question in a flattering frame. He doesn't ask, "Can you tell me how to . . . ?" He's learned instead to ask, "How do *you* do . . . ?" Who doesn't want to help someone who implicitly compliments his or her abilities?

By the time he graduated, Mike had lined up an internship, starting that fall, in the athletic department at Syracuse University. There, he had such a good relationship with his boss, an assistant athletic director who took him under her wing, that he called her Mom. Mike worked in event management for the lower-profile sports, scheduling practice fields and, on game days, setting up ticket booths, hiring public address announcers, and supervising student workers. Sometimes he'd work seven days a week. "I was usually the first to arrive and the last to leave. There wasn't much glamour in it," he says, but he declares the yearlong experience a wise career move.

For one thing, the internship helped him sharpen many professional skills. He still has a copy of a letter he wrote to an executive of Victoria's Secret that helped elicit a five-hundred-dollar donation of fragrances to a silent auction fund-raiser at a Syracuse sports banquet. He'd walked up and down Main Street, talking to local merchants, including the Victoria's Secret boutique. There, he was told that approval for any such donation had to come from corporate headquarters. Rather than drop that ball, Mike called company headquarters, tracked down the person to whom he needed to make his request, and drafted the successful letter.

> **"I was usually the first to arrive and the last to leave. There wasn't much glamour in it."**

He keeps the letter in a scrapbook, along with other mementos from his past. "Anything that's flat," he jokes, like reminders of his J-terms at Hartwick, bylined articles he wrote for various Syracuse sports publications, concert ticket stubs from a vacation trip to Jamaica. "I think it's

Don't be afraid to admit what you don't know.

extremely important to have an accomplishment book," he says, "a place where you can go and say 'I've been through x, y, and z'"; in short, a confidence booster in times of need, a simple way of celebrating his wins.

His Syracuse internship also afforded him the opportunity to discover the inner workings of a big university athletic department—and see and inquire about the day-to-day responsibilities of various potential jobs in fund-raising, sports information, even the athletic director's job itself. "I learned that if I wanted to someday be an AD, I'd need an advanced degree," he says, explaining that he talked this over with "Mom," his Syracuse mentor, who counseled him that for sports management his best choices would be Ohio University or UMass.

> **"I think it's extremely important to have an accomplishment book—a place where you can go and say 'I've been through x, y, and z.'"**

Mike chose UMass and earned his one-year master's degree in sports management in May 2001. He applied for but did not get a job with the Big East Conference in Providence, Rhode Island. Although too late for this occasion, Mike remembers the words of a mentor at UMass.

"Mike, did you ask them who got the job?"

Puzzled, Mike asked why he should do that.

"Because there might be a position open where that person came from."

For the first time, Mike felt the sting of rejection, but instead of turning his back on the source of this disappointment, to his credit and eventual benefit, he shrewdly kept in touch with the person who interviewed him, a man named Tom McElroy. "As soon as you're done with an interview, write a thank-you note," Mike advises, explaining that he keeps on hand a ready stash of cards he bought at an office supply store. "And then stay in touch afterward, via email or phone calls. The pretense can be as simple as holiday wishes, or changes or updates in your status."

So lacking a job, and filling in with another internship after graduate school, Mike notified McElroy that he'd landed at a Stamford, Connecticut, company called Octagon Sports Marketing. McElroy soon alerted him to a fellowship opening at the Big East Conference. Mike applied for this, but again was turned down.

Finally, though, McElroy's helping hand paid off. By then, both he and Mike had moved on—Mike, back to Syracuse, where his former connections had landed him an interim position back in the athletic department while he continued his job search, and McElroy, Mike learned, to second in command in the athletic department at the University of Connecticut. Not only that, McElroy told Mike he was looking to hire a manager of athletic marketing and corporate relationships.

Not altogether certain what the job entailed, Mike asked McElroy to send him a job description. He took that to the person in charge of athletic marketing at Syracuse and asked for his help: "Can you give me a sense of what this job involves and whether it is a good fit for someone just getting started?" The response proved encouraging: "You can do that, you can do that, you'll learn that. I can teach you that before you go."

Mike got that marketing post at the University of Connecticut and enjoyed and learned much at his first real job. His second of two years there was especially exciting, for in 2004 both the men's and the women's basketball teams won the national championship. In fact, it was at the Final Four tournament in New Orleans that Mike ran into a friend he'd kept in touch with since grad school. The woman, who worked for the New Balance shoe company, pulled him aside in the lobby of the Marriott Hotel and told him the company was thinking of adding a new marketing and promotions position, a job revolving around team sports, which he might be interested in.

As with his current job, networking had tipped him off early to a job opening. And yes, he was interested. Though he enjoyed the work at the University of Connecticut, he knew something was missing. "There were certain things—the nitty-gritty of marketing, like getting to know your consumer, industry trends, things I didn't think I would learn staying at UConn," he says. He'd already been thinking about possibly getting an MBA. So given the chance to jump to a more numbers-driven job with a thriving corporation in his area of interest, athletics, Mike jumped. He

Through networking, you can often learn of job openings before they are advertised.

started work in August 2004, a month after marrying a woman who was two years behind him at Hartwick.

At New Balance, he's found the pace of work much faster, with one exception: "There's definitely more meetings. You could easily meet your day away," he says. In his new job, he's taken advantage of on-site seminars and classes on topics like improving professional effectiveness or proposal writing. "You get an email of what's offered in the next six months, and then ask for your manager's approval to sign up. It's really like getting a course catalog in college. The classes might be on three consecutive Wednesdays from eight-thirty to twelve-thirty."

> **"I don't want to be in a position where I'm just another cog in the wheel. I want my job description to be 'I make it happen.'"**

So, out of college and out of graduate school, Mike continues to sharpen his skills as he learns the ropes in his new job and an entirely different work environment. He admits he's still feeling his way into his career, keeping an open mind and staying in touch with those he's befriended in his previous educational and job settings. Hard work is still his mantra.

Does he have a career destination in mind? He thinks a moment, then answers, "No." Asked if his current lack of a destination bothers him, Mike replies, "Yes and no. Yes, because I would like to know, but at the same time, I have faith that I'm on the path." That said, he has pinpointed athletics as a field that suits him. And he's also arrived at a kind of litmus test for any new job. "I know what I want to do and what I don't want to do," he says. "I don't want to be in a position where I'm just another cog in the wheel. I want my job description to be 'I make it happen.'"

Mike's Smart Moves

- He admits what he doesn't know and seeks help from others, often by inquiring how they do what they do so well.

- He's kept a scrapbook of his accomplishments. Reliving one's successes can help restore or build confidence in the face of frustrations and disappointments.

- He writes thank-you notes after job interviews and stays in touch with a wide network of friends, former colleagues, and others.

- He attends company-sponsored classes and seminars to polish his professional skills.

Fashioning a New Career
Six Years Out

COLLEGE: University of Michigan, 1998

MAJOR: general studies

PASSION: art (broadly defined)

EARLY EXPERIENCES OUTSIDE THE CLASSROOM: internship in the corporate office of Ralph Lauren

EARLY WORK EXPERIENCE: recruited on campus for the assistant-buyer training program of a nationwide retailer

CURRENT JOB: accessories buyer for a national retailer, part-time journalist

In the bedroom of her Manhattan apartment, Sharon keeps a six-inch-by-six-inch, hand-carved wooden box that she brought back from a trip to India. She calls it her wish box. Tucked inside is a sheet of paper, updated or replaced from time to time, on which she writes down the more important things she wants to achieve in her life.

Whenever the box catches her eye, Sharon thinks of and visualizes her goals. These days, her primary wish shows her at a career crossroads. Six years out of college and six years into an upwardly arcing career in high-end retailing, not to mention a job that snugly fits an early childhood passion, she nevertheless is planning a major career shift.

She's doing more than simply wishing, of course. Sharon's replaying some of the same job-seeking, career-defining strategies that she employed back in college at the University of Michigan. And she's approaching her self-labeled, late twenties "midlife crisis" with aplomb, now a much savvier job and career seeker after gaining both confidence and workplace survival skills and climbing a good ways up the corporate ladder at a major American company.

Just as important, Sharon continues to follow the lead of her parents, who, she says, "always encouraged us growing up to find our passion and explore it." Her father was an oral surgeon with a practice in an adjacent town and a staff position at two Long Island hospitals. Her mother, an Israeli native, helped run his office.

"Where you gravitated, that was encouraged," she says. "I drew a lot and painted a lot, so my parents arranged for art lessons outside of school. I also liked to dance, so I took dance lessons as well." But what she took to most naturally of all was fashion design. Sharon still has notebooks filled with sketches of dresses she drew during class—in second grade. Not content with the wide array of clothes she could buy for her Barbie dolls, she fashioned her own out of fabric or tissue paper. She admits, "I played with Barbies to a really late age."

When applying to colleges, she sought schools with a strong art department as well as top liberal arts programs—schools far enough from home to stretch her independence. She said yes to Michigan because she felt an inspiring energy the minute she stepped on campus. Sharon matriculated in 1994 and took a lot of art classes her freshman and sophomore years.

But then Sharon changed direction. "I phased out of art," she says, explaining that she did so after, in effect, taking her career pulse. "It would have meant staying an extra year to get a BSA with a major, and I was so itchy to get out into the world. So I got a BA in general studies without a major. I couldn't wait to get into the workplace, to get my feet wet, kind of like conquer the world." She was already picturing herself with a job and an apartment in New York, riding the subway, shopping, meeting friends after work at bars and restaurants. "I couldn't wait to get started. I wanted to get ahead."

Sharon's way to get ahead, leapfrogging past the masses of other graduating college seniors? Internships.

"After my sophomore year at Michigan, I decided I needed to do internships, which put you a step ahead," she says. So instead of her customary summer lifeguarding job, which paid her about ten dollars an hour, she worked three days a week that summer for no money at all at the Nassau County Museum of Art and three days a week as a salesperson at an Abercrombie & Fitch store. In other words, she sacrificed money for experience in a field—art—which at the time held potential career opportunities.

Sharon's way to get ahead, leapfrogging past the masses of other graduating college seniors? Internships.

She essentially created her own internship. She called the museum, asked whom she could speak to about a possible intern position, sent her resume, and interviewed successfully for the spot. All that effort and guess what: Sharon discovered she didn't want to be in the museum business. She saw how much politics went on behind the scenes, how everything hinged on getting funding, and especially how slowly things moved. The pace of the nonprofit world didn't match her full-speed-ahead personality and ambitions.

That's the beauty of internships. These short-term experiences offer a great way of trying on potential careers, rather like so many blouses or sweaters, and seeing whether they fit, whether you feel comfortable in them, and whether they match your personality and style. Sometimes the most successful internship isn't one that provides a scintillating three months, but rather one that turns out to be stone-cold boring. Better to spend a couple months learning what you *don't* want to do and maybe change your major or switch to plan B than remain unenlightened on a career path that's not right for you.

Terming herself "very experience driven," Sharon decided she wanted a second internship and sought to couple it with a horizon-stretching study abroad program. When it turned out that the University of Michigan didn't offer quite what she wanted, Sharon shrewdly cast her net beyond her own school. A friend of hers had spoken glowingly of her work-study experiences in Paris through Boston University. After consulting with her advisor

Bad internships can be just as helpful in determining your career path as good internships.

at Michigan, Sharon made connections with the BU program and headed off to London spring term of her junior year. There, she followed a half day of classes with an internship at a London-based magazine. She'd had an interest in communications and magazines as far back as high school and thought this a good way to learn more about magazine journalism.

She learned one lesson very quickly. Namely, how quickly magazines come and go. Her magazine stopped publishing a couple weeks after she arrived. Another magazine position wasn't available on such short notice, but her overseas advisor landed her a spot with Gordana of London, a high-end designer of scarves stocked by the likes of Harrods. Sharon did all manner of jobs, everything from helping stylize their catalog to researching market openings elsewhere in Europe.

The summer between her junior and senior years, Sharon pursued yet another internship. This time, a personal connection paved the way. "A friend's mother was president of the factory outlet division of Ralph Lauren; she created an internship for me," says Sharon, recalling that her position, working with the head buyer and the head creative person in the company's New Jersey headquarters, was so stimulating that she hardly minded her daily commute, which was often two hours each way. She'd ride the Long Island Railroad into Manhattan, take the subway to the Port Authority Bus Terminal, then board a bus for the twenty-five-minute ride to Lindhurst, New Jersey. Many days, twelve hours would pass before she'd be back home to her parents' house on Long Island.

"It was tough, but I did it because I was so enthusiastic about getting such a great opportunity. I learned a lot about allocating (merchandise, moving it from store to store to help it sell faster), and I went to market with the buyers," she says. "I liked the pace of it. You're usually working on three different seasons at once: knowing what's happening right now and reacting; as a buyer, projecting what's going to be happening and what you're going to be buying in six months; and helping out the designers, looking much further out."

When campus recruiters descended on the University of Michigan the fall of 1997 at the start of Sharon's senior year, her resume shone brightly because of her internships. She received offers from four companies—

Young & Rubicam, the big advertising firm; department stores Macy's and Mervyn's; and a third nationwide retailer, which flew her to New York for a second round of interviews over two days.

"My resume was definitely up to par," she says. "My classmates' experience was mostly along the lines of working in retail stores. They didn't know the global market. I'd worked in London with a designer and at the headquarters of Ralph Lauren, in addition to working retail for two years on and off at Abercrombie & Fitch."

She started as one of twenty trainees at the New York–based luxury retailer in September 1998. Nowadays, this training program lasts a year. Back then, the training ended after six months. Sharon spent about 65 percent of her training time in class studying retail math and how to mark up and mark down goods, and she spent the remainder of her training shadowing a succession of different employees in far-ranging jobs—the buying office, the planning office, and, of course, time on the store floor watching everything play out, the marketplace at work.

Sharon lived with her parents during her first six months on the job, then moved into Manhattan and shared an apartment with two other girls after she finished her training and stepped up to the position of assistant buyer. A year or so later she moved to the apartment of a friend, subletting it while she was away. "*Sex and the City* it was not," she says, laughing, explaining that starting out she had nowhere near the disposable income of the character played by Sarah Jessica Parker on the popular TV series. No, she wasn't eating at five-star restaurants or going out six nights a week to the latest "in" spots, but she was experiencing her dream of living and working in New York City.

The work has had its pleasures, and Sharon advanced from an assistant buyer of contemporary collections and private-brand sleepwear to associate manager of knitwear and wovens. What she's liked most has been having a hand and a strong say in a new item that really catches fire. "I worked on a $130 rabbit fur scarf that feels like mink," she says. "At the last minute we decided to put in all these different colors—light green, beige, lilac, light blue, ivory, black. It just blew out the minute it hit." The back-and-forth collaboration with the designer, the camaraderie of creation, then seeing a finished product snapped up by eager consumers—that's what Sharon finds exciting about her job.

Trouble is, she feels this rush less and less, as corporate downsizing and other workplace realities settle in like an oppressive fog. She was the only employee to survive sweeping cuts in the accessories department a couple of years back. Her co-workers in her new area (she had no say in the re-assignment), eager to hold onto their jobs in times of continued firings, tend to have their heads down, self-consumed with their own jobs and job security. Sharon has nobody mentoring her, no one helping her grow, no one steering her to the new skills necessary for career advancement.

More telling, in dusting off basic career questions she first asked as a teenager—Who am I? What do I really want?—she wasn't sure that she wanted to continue up the corporate ladder at her luxury retailer. She looked at her boss and her boss's boss and realized that she did not aspire to their jobs. Nor did changing companies seem like much of an option, for the whole retailing industry was suffering.

"A lot of my friends are also unhappy in their jobs," Sharon says, joking that "it's nice to know you're not the only freak on the block." She observes, "The things you thought would make you happy when you're twenty-one or twenty-two aren't necessarily the things that are going to make you happy when you're twenty-seven or twenty-eight."

Talking to a close friend about the uncertainties and unfulfilling nature of her current job helped her start asking the important next questions: If not her retailing career, then what? What would she like to do? And how could she go about making the switch?

Sharon thought back to her aborted internship with the London maga-zine and her unexplored interest in journalism. "Listen to yourself," her friend told her. "If you've always wanted to do something, try it."

Sharon's first step was a small one, an exploratory feeler. She got a brochure of course offerings from New York University and signed up in the summer of 2003 for an evening journalism class on interviewing.

The NYU journalism class not only taught the basic skills and fine points of interviewing, but did so with the aid of guest speakers from numerous local media outlets. "The class gave me an amazing opportunity to meet all these editors," Sharon says, leading into a story about how important it is in seeking a job or career to make your own luck.

She was on the subway heading to class when she noticed that the woman next to her was wearing a Patagonia jacket with the logo of one of the city's four major newspapers. Sharon heard a little voice in her head say, "Talk to this person. She's smiling. She seems nice. If she works for *Newsday*, maybe she'll know of an opportunity there."

"Yes, I do work at *Newsday*," the woman said in response to her query.

Sharon pushed through the door she'd opened. "Oh, I'm on my way to journalism class. I'm really interested in getting into the field." When Sharon explained about her background in fashion, the *Newsday* editor became more than friendly. She got interested. And she announced, "We actually need help on our online fashion page." Business cards changed hands, an interview at *Newsday*'s offices followed, and that same summer Sharon started writing short items for the paper's online edition as a freelance intern. Yes, Sharon was fortunate to have sat down on that particular subway car going to class, but she refuses to characterize her career-boosting encounter as sheer luck.

"Luck," she says, "equals opportunity meeting preparation. I took the initiative. I put it out there. I didn't just sit at home saying, 'Hmm, I really want to do this.' I was taking a class. I was talking to people. I'm a big believer that you have to make things happen."

In her gig with *Newsday*, Sharon is paid by the hour and works about ten hours a week researching and writing fashion stories, perhaps a piece on the latest hats or what to wear to Thanksgiving dinner. Most importantly, she's doing this while still working at her full-time job in retailing. Now in her late twenties, enjoying a Gramercy Park apartment paid for by her accessories buyer's salary, Sharon is in no position to forgo her management job in retailing for the woeful wages of entry-level jobs in a notoriously poor-paying industry like journalism. Nor does it make sense to.

"You can't just jump into something. You have to learn about it, understand how it works, the components that go into it," she says, explaining that she reached back into her college bag of job-seeking strategies to overcome the catch-22 of breaking into a new career, namely, that to get a job you need to have experience, but how can you get experience if no one will give you a job? Once again, she took an intern position. But some things had changed. She notes, "You can't have ego issues about starting at the bottom at age twenty-seven."

She's come to enjoy the newsroom at *Newsday*, where she's found more of a team spirit and less hierarchy than with a nationwide upscale retailer. "At *Newsday*, you might be two seats away from your editor," she says. "It's a more equal playing field."

With her foot in the door, Sharon's already networking and leveraging her contacts into more reporting and writing opportunities in areas beyond her point of entry: fashion. Covering the high-profile event known as Fashion Week, she met *Newsday*'s entertainment columnist backstage; finding him a bit out of his element in the tight little world of high fashion, she offered to help him identify the players and suggest up-and-coming models to interview. "It's a whole other world, the fashion industry. Everyone's connected to everyone else, and this designer's married to this person. I know a lot of that and gave him an insider's perspective," she says, noting that the grateful columnist soon reciprocated by assigning her to go to parties and red-carpet events as a stringer. At these events, Sharon asks questions of the arriving designers and celebrities and passes on the quotes to the columnist to use in his column.

> To get a job you need to have experience, but how can you get experience if no one will give you a job?

In the summer of 2004, Sharon got to work the Republican National Convention—not the political doings at Madison Square Garden, but the evening parties, some of which didn't start until 10 P.M. She'd get back to her apartment by one o'clock or so and then write until maybe 3 A.M. and, if necessary, finish her piece the following morning. Because of the assignment's multiday nature and the sleep-sapping hours, she decided it best to take time off from her full-time job, meaning she sacrificed vacation days to further her part-time job.

The sacrifice has paid off—both in valuable experience and in an exciting new job opportunity. Networking at the Republican convention, she met an editorial contact at *People* magazine; by early 2005, Sharon had started stringing for them—interviewing celebrities at special events—something she finds exciting and challenging. "I like the pace of it. It's very quick. You have to be on your toes," she says. "You don't know what to expect, and it's all about reacting. Most of the time, celebrities don't want to talk. You have a limited time there on the red carpet. It's about finding a way to get them to talk—researching the person, being personable yourself."

Looking for other writing opportunities and experiences as she prepares for a possible leap to full-time journalism, Sharon has closely monitored the job postings at an Internet site called mediabistro.com. That's how she landed another client, an online publication called *DailyCandy*, which touts the latest hot products and trendy establishments. She contacted them even though the posting said they were looking for reporters in Chicago, where they were launching a new division. "You've got to think outside the box,"

> **"I don't know where all this is going to take me, but I know I really enjoy it."**

she says, explaining that she had hoped the person she contacted would like her fashion credentials and recent reporting experience enough to forward her name to *DailyCandy*'s New York office. That's exactly what happened.

"The New York editor called and said, 'I got your resume.' She explained they needed people by region in the city and needed someone on the Upper East Side," Sharon relates. Again, her foot was in the door. "Turns out nothing I've done for them has had to do with the Upper East Side." She's written more than a dozen stories for *DailyCandy*, one on a self-proclaimed (not to mention, expensive) petographer, who specializes in photographing pets—especially those of celebrities. These clips have helped swell her scrapbook of published articles. Sharon now takes the scrapbook to job interviews, like the successful one at *People* magazine.

"I never thought I could do half the things I'm doing now," she says. "I don't know where all this is going to take me, but I know I really enjoy it, the pace, the people I'm working with." Because she realizes most jobs in the media don't pay especially well (TV anchormen and editors-in-chief aside), Sharon is wondering whether she might initially need to supplement a full-time media job with some fashion industry or retail consulting work. "Everything's still very vague," she says, declaring, "I want to keep things open in the beginning stage. I don't want to limit myself."

She *can* point to a key highlight early on: her encounter with Donald Trump at a Victoria's Secret party during fashion week. "He doesn't speak to male reporters. His fiancée doesn't speak to female reporters," she says, explaining that the male entertainment columnist at *Newsday* wanted her to elicit something good from Trump. Sharon was getting nowhere until she remembered her editor's previous advice—to always ask at least one question tied to the event you're covering. So she piped up: "Would you ever consider an episode of *The Apprentice* about Fashion Week?"

Trump's face came alive. "Hey, that's a great idea," he said and told his fiancée to make a note of that. A few months later, an episode of *The Apprentice* aired on just that theme. And yes, Donald Trump recognized Sharon the next time he saw her.

Sharon's Smart Moves

- **She pursued internships,** creating her own when necessary, even after six years in the workforce.

- **When she felt the flame dying in her corporate career, she asked herself a key question:** Could she imagine being happy in her boss's job, or the job above that?

- **She's trying on a new career** with the safety net of not yet abandoning her current career.

- **She's networked relentlessly,** landing one position thanks to a conversation she struck up with a fellow subway rider.

- **She focuses her ambitions and career goals** with the help of her wish box.

3

A
Life
of
Service

Tales of a Government Junkie

COLLEGE: Harvard University, 1987

MAJOR: government

POSTGRADUATE: master's in public management, University of Maryland, 1992

PASSION: making government work better

EARLY EXPERIENCES OUTSIDE THE CLASSROOM: administrative assistant at the Harvard Business School

EARLY WORK EXPERIENCE: secretary at WGBH-TV, Boston's public television station

CURRENT JOB: director of the Rhode Island Department of Labor and Training

With some children, it's easy to foretell their future. At three they're playing show tunes on the piano. At twelve, they're hitting baseballs out of sight. Or at sixteen, they're banking ten thousand dollars a month from an Internet business they run from their bedroom. With others, like Adelita Orefice, you have to look a bit harder.

In Adelita's case, you need to flash back a number of years and follow her to the town library in Sallisaw, Oklahoma. She's a high school student with an unusual hobby. She attends city council meetings—finds them fascinating, in fact. "All these regular folks, farmers in overalls, the town banker," she's thinking. "Almost no one (except the council members themselves) comes. And they're making all these decisions." At first, when somebody asks her why she's there, Adelita says, "I'm just here to watch." But after a couple of incredulous looks, she spins a more plausible cover story.

"School project," she fibs, realizing how odd her attraction to the prosaic grind of local government must seem.

Odd, but prescient; for today, many government jobs later and now head of the Rhode Island Department of Labor and Training, Adelita answers to the title of Madam Director. Her unscripted journey to this high-profile cabinet-level post, a job that enables her to pursue her avowed passion for making government work better, is instructive for many reasons, not the least of which being that she's zigzagged to this career zenith despite finding herself the "trailing spouse" not once, but twice. That is to say, twice she's had to change jobs to help facilitate her husband's career. Along the way she's proved adaptable and flexible, traits probably instilled in her as a much-traveled military brat, the oldest of three children.

Ask her where she grew up and Adelita laughs. "Everywhere," she says, mentioning Governor's Island, just off Manhattan; Glen Burnie, Maryland; Cape Canaveral, Florida; Morro Bay, California; and Sallisaw, Oklahoma. Back then, her father was an engine mechanic, first in the Navy, then with the Coast Guard. "He's Italian American. My mom's Mexican American. They met at a USO dance in California when he was in the Navy and got married a month later," she says.

Adelita's the first on either side of her family to attend college. Her father graduated from a vocational high school in Buffalo and did two tours in Vietnam. Her mother, who grew up in Oakland, California, has a high school diploma, but Adelita considers her functionally illiterate, stuck at about a second-grade reading level, having received one "social promotion" after another. Money was always tight growing up. The Orefice children qualified for free and reduced-price lunches at school. Her father fixed cars on the side to earn money for such "extras" as restaurant meals and school clothes. Vacations? "You go visit Grandma," she says.

Adelita always did well in school, though her parents didn't pay much attention until she started to make a name for herself on her high school debate team. A 4.0 student in a school with no AP courses, she found preparing for debates a lot like independent study. "It was intellectually stimulating, not structured like other high school courses," she says. "You'd get to create your own cases, do your own research, and the topics were around current events, issues like nuclear proliferation. My dad was in the military, and I understood the issues."

Debate also seemed like her ticket to college, so when her debate coach took a job with another school a couple hours away, Adelita followed him there with her parents' blessing and assistance, rather like a star football player seeking a higher profile program. To accomplish this, her mother moved with her, staying six months in a rented apartment and working at a nearby Wal-Mart until Adelita moved in with a local family.

The move paid off. Adelita, as expected, anchored the debate team at her new school in Bristow, Oklahoma. She took top honors in the state her senior year for original oratory, a seven- to eight-minute speech that she used to compete all year long. She also did well in a category called extemporaneous speaking, not unlike a public speaking version of the Food Network's *Iron Chef* cooking competitions. With no advance notice, speakers are given a topic and then get thirty minutes to prepare a five- to seven-minute speech. "In my current job, that happens to me a lot," she says, referring to all the dinners and functions she attends as head of a big state program. "On a moment's notice, somebody will ask the director to say a few words. Or, as has happened a couple times in the last three months, I've been called to fill in for the governor at an event. And I don't have a speechwriter." Her debating experience, she stresses, taught her "how to think on my feet and taught me that I could speak in public."

There's little doubt that Adelita's debating triumphs also helped instill in her the self-confidence to make the very huge leap from her modest upbringing and rural Oklahoma high schools to the hallowed halls of Harvard University. Though she attended on a full academic scholarship, she still needed to take out loans to help cover other expenses, and she worked some twelve to fifteen hours a week from matriculation to graduation. At various times, she cleaned toilets with the dorm crew, typed papers for two dollars a page, worked as a research assistant for an English professor, and assisted in the development office at the Harvard Business School.

The yawning socioeconomic gap separating her from many of her classmates became achingly clear her second day at Harvard. She'd popped into the dorm room of a student who had just returned from a shopping spree in the commercial jumble of Harvard Square. Laid out on her bed were two sweaters, price tags still on them. Adelita gulped when she read them. She had worked all summer in a Wal-Mart menswear department back home in Oklahoma to save up for college. Two hundred dollars happened to be the same amount she'd just deposited in her new student account.

Debating had Adelita leaning toward becoming a lawyer. But there were other reasons for looking toward law. "Success in my family was defined in a number of ways," she says. "One was going to college. Another was driving a high-end car like a Mercedes. Another was owning a home," she says, something her peripatetic parents didn't accomplish until she was in high school. "And there were probably a handful of careers that made you successful—doctor, lawyer."

With such a limited career view, Adelita's choice of law was a default position. She selected government as her major, taking courses in political theory, international relations, and comparative government. But the classes she remembers most, and, indeed, the classes she did best in, spread across many academic departments. "A class on Shakespeare, Chinese history, architecture, music, medieval art. Never," she says, "would I have chosen these, had (such a broad interdisciplinary approach) not been required.

"What my liberal arts education gave me was the passport to the middle class or professional class, the language and signposts for what educated people talk about," says Adelita, noting that this broad educational base has aided her time and again in her professional career, for instance, in finding common ground with a member of a board she serves on or striking up a conversation with the person seated next to her at a government dinner.

> "What my liberal arts education gave me was the passport to the middle class."

As her senior year at Harvard wound to a close, Adelita stuck to her plan and applied to law school. She got wait-listed at Yale and accepted at Harvard, Boston University, and Columbia. Needing a break from classes and just as urgently some money in the bank to supplement the aid she'd been promised at Columbia, her first choice, she asked that her acceptance be deferred for a year.

In retrospect, she says, in looking for an interim job she should have done more networking with faculty members and her previous employer, the Harvard Business School. "But I didn't really understand networking then," she says, noting, "I tried the campus career center, but wasn't very successful." Feeling constrained by the fact that she only expected to be working for a year, she signed up with a temp agency and took secretarial jobs for a couple of months—until she answered an ad for an administrative assistant to a senior manager at WGBH, Boston's public television station.

There, Adelita did mostly secretarial chores and made a decent salary—about five thousand dollars more, she learned, than a couple of her Harvard classmates who were working as legal assistants at the station, interning before heading off to law school. As the months passed, her enthusiasm for law school dimmed. "In the back of my mind, I think I always knew I didn't really want to go to law school," she says, explaining that her original interest stemmed in part from what she'd seen on the popular TV show *L.A. Law.* But she could no longer see herself as a corporate attorney, certainly not one defending tobacco companies or criminals. And why go to law school and pile up a good bit of debt to work, say, for a public interest firm for thirty thousand dollars a year when she was already making that as a secretary? She wrote to Columbia that law school was not for her.

So now what? The public television station seemed a good place to work. Maybe she could get an entry-level production job on *This Old House* or another of the WGBH-produced shows. Any such job, she discovered, meant a cut in pay from her current secretarial post. "I don't really have a passion for that, so why take a cut in pay," she reasoned.

She was walking through the Harvard Business School campus on her lunch break one day when one of her former bosses at the business school waved to her. He said he'd been about to call her, knowing Adelita was still in the Cambridge/Boston area because she'd kept in touch with a couple of her former coworkers. He told her the school, which had just received a twenty-million-dollar gift to start an ethics in business program, needed to hire staff. Would she be interested?

When your gut is telling you not to go to law school, don't go!

Adelita didn't need her Harvard diploma to instantly recognize the value of networking (inadvertent though hers had been), which provided an inside track and helped her land a job with the new business school program as a curriculum development analyst. As such, she coauthored a case study used in some of the classes and helped track down and modify existing case studies to spotlight various corporate ethical dilemmas. As part of her job, she sat in on some of the classes. Doing so helped Adelita learn more about herself and her likes and dislikes. She recognized that, while she could never see herself working eighty-hour weeks marketing toothpaste or working to build shareholder value, several aspects of business appealed to her. "The leadership stuff. How you manage an organization," she says, "and business and government."

> She recognized that, while she could never see herself working eighty-hour weeks marketing toothpaste, several aspects of business appealed to her.

Screening case studies involving the overlap of business and government and sitting in on some meetings at the university's Kennedy School of Government, Adelita found herself jazzed by catching various glimpses of "the systems and mechanics of policy making, which sounds really wonky, I know." In essence, she'd drifted back toward her forgotten pastime of attending city council meetings and her fascination with democracy at work.

By now Adelita was married. Her husband, Jack, eight years older than she, worked as an admissions officer at Brandeis University. They hadn't yet celebrated their first wedding anniversary when Jack was offered a job as associate director of admissions at the University of Maryland, a good career move for him. Adelita hadn't yet identified a career, and leaving her Harvard Business School job posed no great sacrifice. She would, however, have to look for a new job once they moved to College Park, Maryland, just outside Washington, D.C.

The first few months passed uneasily for Adelita, as her initial job search went nowhere, hung up on the issue of money. She figured that she should make at least the same salary as at the job she'd left at the Harvard Business

School, but what she didn't yet appreciate was that her remuneration there far outstripped her skill level. To expect anything comparable in the nation's capital, she began to realize, she'd need a graduate degree. Still jobless, she applied to the schools of public management at the University of Maryland, Georgetown University, and George Washington University.

Adelita wasn't used to sitting around at home. She got a dog for company and ate too much and started feeling sorry for herself. Fortunately, she soon realized that instead of looking at her trailing spouse–induced unemployment as a glass half empty, she could view it as half full, as an opportunity to do anything she wanted in the remaining six months until she expected to start grad school.

Why not try something she'd often wondered about, like teaching? She managed to land a long-term substitute job, filling in at a nearby public elementary school. She enjoyed teaching the combined second- and third-grade class, and over dinner with her husband found herself reviewing her day's work. Jack had taught at a prep school for four years after graduating from Brown, before moving into admissions work. To some extent they compared notes. More importantly, Adelita began to appreciate the value of a new practice, which she's continued to this day: engaging in periodic career conversations, be they with her husband or close friends.

"Saying what I felt out loud was enormously helpful," she notes, after articulating what she liked in a job. What she liked most about teaching, she realized, was managing her own class and making decisions, responsibilities that hadn't been part of her previous low-on-the-totem-pole jobs. She had started to identify some of the signposts that would steer her to her path in life.

But first came graduate school. As at Harvard, Adelita worked while she pursued a double major in social policy and public sector financial management at the University of Maryland. The summer after her first year, she interned with the congressional oversight agency then called the General Accounting Office. Though she performed well and got a job offer to work there after graduation, Adelita turned the offer down because she'd gotten an inside view of the work atmosphere during her brief stint at the GAO and found the agency a "super bureaucracy" with

Share your thoughts and dreams with trusted friends and ask for honest feedback.

countless layers of review. Becoming a small cog in a wheel that turned slowly didn't suit her.

So her senior year she applied for the prestigious Presidential Management Intern program (see KC's story for a second example of a PMI experience), which offers fast-track government jobs to the cream of interested master's degree recipients from America's top universities. Adelita made it through the rigorous PMI admissions process and was considering posts at the Health Care Financing Administration, the Department of Education, and the Office of Management and Budget. But an interview at another federal government agency also appeared.

That year's graduation speaker at the University of Maryland was U.S. Secretary of Labor Lynn Martin, who told the dean that her agency would be happy to offer interviews to two top students. Thanks to her 4.0 GPA, Adelita was one of those students. Her visit to the huge Department of Labor building, home to a workforce of five thousand, landed her in the office of the assistant secretary for administration and management. There, she met a Dartmouth graduate named Tom Komarek, someone she now refers to as "the mentor of all mentors."

The interview went well, but Adelita expressed a concern before leaving. She wasn't clear what her job might be, and because the interview had been set up outside the PMI framework, she asked whether she'd be rotated through a succession of different jobs, as in a PMI internship, to help round out her training. Komarek said he'd get back to her.

That night, talking with her husband, Adelita said, "I don't know anything about labor, but I really like this guy. I think I can learn from him, and I didn't get that strong a feeling from my other interviews." The next day she received a fax from Komarek. Overnight, he'd created a PMI spot for her and mapped out a two-year plan for her rotation through the agency.

Adelita leaped at the offer. In doing so, she turned down a more glamorous post at another government agency, basing her decision mostly on the good vibes she had about the person she'd report to. Her title, which didn't exist until the day she reported was special assistant to the assistant secretary for administration and management. Thus began Adelita's multi-job, two-city stint with the federal Department of Labor.

Choose your boss, and your job will be a lot easier.

"Tom was good about grooming people for the future. He would put me in situations, then we'd go to lunch and talk about what I'd learned," she says.

Not long after Adelita's two-year PMI stint came to a close, her boss retired, an event, on the order of an occupational hazard, that impacted her as well. The incoming assistant secretary wanted her own people around her; Adelita wasn't one of those people. She had begun making alternative career plans, applying for an assistant to the provost position at the University of Maryland, when her "mentor of mentors" called to see how she was doing. Deeming her departure a loss for the department, Komarek contacted a few old friends at the agency, and, even in retirement, helped her switch to a high-profile position at the Labor Department as chief of staff to the assistant secretary for policy and budget.

"That job was a stepping-stone for every job I've had thereafter," she says. But Adelita would never have taken the job had she not been goal oriented rather than salary oriented and flexible enough not to get hung up on GS levels, the government's pecking order.

"The lesson for me, and I've told others who've come to me for career advice: Don't worry about the pay when you have a lifetime opportunity to do something," she says, declaring the experience "is worth some dollar value." That position came with a high level of responsibility and exposure and helped her continue to grow as an administrator.

A year or so later, another choice loomed. Adelita's new boss was headed to another post at Labor and wanted her to come with him, again, in a high-visibility, similarly demanding type of role. Now, however, she had to weigh a brand-new consideration. She was five months pregnant.

> "Don't worry about the pay when you have a lifetime opportunity."

After a brief maternity leave, Adelita wanted to return to work. The thought of dropping out of the workforce for a few years did not appeal to her. "Being a mom is the best thing, but I know enough about myself to know I'm not a stay-at-home mom," she says. "Career is important to me." Accordingly, Adelita talked with two female friends in high-level jobs, both mothers; one, in fact, a single mother, who ascribed to the notion that women can have it all. Adelita doesn't disagree, but she's refined that sentiment. "The real truth," she counsels, "You *can* have it all—just not all at once."

The Department of Labor, appropriately enough, had a terrific on-site day care center, which greatly facilitated her return to work. She opted now for a much lower profile position, one with a forty- to forty-five-hour workweek that would allow her to slow down and enjoy her newborn son and the pleasures of motherhood. She felt she could do so because she was no longer struggling to establish a reputation at the department.

Adelita reached this key career decision by stepping back, taking a longer, less immediate view of her life. "I realized I needed to pace myself over what would probably be as much as a forty-six-year period. I can slow down for now," she told herself. "I don't need to be some big thing by the time I'm forty." She started viewing her career in terms of bigger blocks of time, in four-decade segments. She saw herself as still being in that first working decade, having laid a solid foundation for her ongoing working career. She'd learned how government works, what kinds of experiences she likes to have, the kinds of bosses she likes to work for.

Working fewer hours in a less challenging job, Adelita discovered that she had the time and the desire to get involved in government at the most local level. She started attending meetings of her neighborhood association, the North College Park Citizens Association, and soon became secretary and then president. "My new job at Labor was pretty much nine-to-five and out of the limelight and the hot issues," she says. "And I loved this local stuff— trash and snow removal issues." Her ability to cut through governmental bureaucracy and get things done made her a logical choice for association president; in her year leading the neighborhood association, she helped get a fitness trail and a playground built.

Then it was time to move again. Brown University, in Providence, Rhode Island, wanted her husband to come work as a development officer. Jack's parents had retired to Cape Cod. Adelita and Jack had talked of moving back to New England, where they'd first met. Jack took the job in August 1997.

This time Adelita wanted to do things differently—not to have to look for a job in the confusion of adjusting to a new community. She wanted to arrive in Rhode Island with a job in hand. The U.S. Labor Department, not wanting to lose a valued employee, one groomed for possible high-level posts, worked to help Adelita find a potential position. Three turned up, offering various pluses and minuses.

The job she selected was as a pensions investigator. She'd have to downgrade to a GS-11, take a twenty-thousand-dollar pay cut, and commute an hour and a half each way on the train to Boston. However, with flex hours, she could take a 5:30 A.M. train from Providence and be at her desk at 7 A.M. Leaving work at 3:30 P.M. she could be back home in time to pick up her son at day care.

She enjoyed the work. Pensions and health care were emerging as hot public issues, and she thought a future career option might be to market her skills outside government. After about a year and a half, however, Adelita found herself in another career conversation with her husband.

It was time for her to seek something else, return to a job that more closely fit her true passion. When Jack asked her what she wanted to do now, *really* wanted to do, Adelita answered, "I want to run something, a small nonprofit, an office, a business. I want to be a boss." Plus, having burned herself out with her long commute, she wanted something local, in Providence, the state capital.

Adelita transitioned from federal to state government after answering an ad in the paper and interviewing and landing the job of director of finance for the Rhode Island Department of Education. Responsible for a staff of twenty and an annual budget that grew from $750 million to nearly $1 billion by the time she left, three and a half years later, Adelita satisfied her aching career desire. The buck stopped with her. She was the boss.

Soon, she also addressed her long-standing avocational interest—community involvement—by becoming a volunteer board member of a century-old social services agency in Providence called Federal Hill House, which provided local day care programs and senior assistance. A blast from the past had alerted her to the board opening. Her first mentor, Tom Komarek, had called to tell her a college friend of his was looking to fill a board vacancy he thought would interest her.

Anyone looking for an example of the value of networking need only remember this extracurricular position that Adelita accepted. Not only was she tipped off to the post and championed by a former boss, her very service on such a prominent local board connected her with other prominent local movers and shakers. It was, in fact, a conversation with one of those board members in January 2003 that led her to her current dream job.

Gene Gasbarro, a board member and her mentor Tom Komarek's friend, asked Adelita how things were going at the Department of Education. She confided that she was thinking it might soon be time to move on to something else. She mentioned that she'd already applied for the doctorate program in political science at Brown.

"Really," he replied, then shared that through a far-flung networking grapevine, he knew the person in charge of recruiting for the incoming governor, Donald Carcieri. Gasbarro offered to pass on her resume.

So it happened, via something akin to six degrees of networking separation, that Adelita found herself in the new governor's office. Listening to him describe his political aims and two cabinet-level openings, director of

As she worked to rebuild lagging partnerships and attended countless "rubber chicken dinners," she gained experience, political savvy, and confidence.

Elderly Affairs and director of the Department of Labor and Training, she liked him immediately.

By the time she got home, a message awaited her on her answering machine: the governor wanted to offer her the top job at the Department of Elderly Affairs. Adelita now oversaw fifty employees and a forty-five-million-dollar budget. At thirty-eight, she was the youngest cabinet member. As she worked to rebuild lagging partnerships with other state agencies and various community-based organizations and attended countless "rubber chicken dinners," she gained experience, political savvy, and confidence. She successfully handled a couple of controversies and the inevitable media interviews, and she'd been a guest on a couple of local Sunday morning TV talk shows.

So, when about a year later, Governor Carcieri offered her the still-unfilled cabinet post of director of Labor and Training, Adelita felt up to the challenge of the bigger, much higher profile job. Her domain now encompasses some five hundred employees and a $430 million budget. There's more travel in this job. She's quoted more often in the media. Her picture is prominently displayed on the department's website. (That, especially, proved to her parents that she's a success.) She's making more money. When business takes her to the general assembly, like all cabinet heads, she's directed to a seat of honor in the front.

One could, she stresses, get a bit of an ego from such trappings, which include use of a state car, a Crown Victoria. Adelita turned it down. Granted, at just a tad over five feet tall, she could barely see over the steering wheel. But such a flashy car just isn't her style. She's not about flash. It's the nitty-gritty that interests her. Her favorite part of her job is systems change. "In government, we have these systems, whether for seniors or workforce development," Adelita says. "The problem is, government generally doesn't do a good job of revisiting them and making sure they're keeping up with the times. Some were designed as much as twenty years ago and still work like they're twenty years in the past. They're not dynamic. To do good government work, you have to do systems change and also manage the culture change that follows."

> **"If I won the lottery I would not quit my job."**

Her current job, she says, enables her to now and then achieve what she's finally pinpointed as her passion in life, namely, making government work better. How might she then finish off the second chapter of her career story?

She might pursue that Ph.D. she's often contemplated or teach as an adjunct professor. She could also see herself as the director of a nonprofit organization. But for now she couldn't be happier. No longer is she the trailing spouse. In fact, her husband recently relinquished a couple of job possibilities, deferring to her current position and effectively repaying Adelita's previous career sacrifices on his behalf.

Not long ago, hashing out some archly complicated issue, Governor Carcieri jokingly asked Adelita, "So, how do you like it now? She looked at him and laughed. "I've got to tell you, honestly, for the first time in my life, if I won the lottery I would not quit my job. I'd take a dollar salary," she said, "and still come in to work."

Adelita's Smart Moves

- **When making job decisions, she has learned to look beyond salary considerations,** also valuing job experience, contacts, and skills to be gained in a new position.

- **She has periodic career conversations with her husband and close friends,** having learned that it helps to say out loud what she likes and doesn't like about her current job.

- **She doesn't try to script her future,** thus leaving the door open to opportunities she might not otherwise have considered.

- **She thinks of her career as unfolding decade by decade,** and she has accordingly better managed it for the long haul.

- **She has made time for volunteer jobs outside her work responsibilities,** expanding her knowledge and skill base and making valuable personal connections.

Writing the Score for the Symphony of His Life

COLLEGE: Wake Forest University, 1992

MAJOR: English

PASSION: the arts, especially symphony orchestras

EARLY EXPERIENCES OUTSIDE THE CLASSROOM: internship in the North Carolina Symphony's public relations office

EARLY WORK EXPERIENCE: overseeing conductor-training programs as artistic service coordinator at the American Symphony Orchestra League

CURRENT JOB: senior director, Points of Light Foundation and Volunteer Center National Network

Many college students, if they visit their campus careers office at all, do so as graduation nears and job uncertainty throbs like a toothache. Not David Styers. As a freshman at Wake Forest University, he pushed open the door to an office then called Career Planning and Placement.

"I knew as an English major that my career path was not all that set. My friends who were accounting majors or pre-med or pre-law, they knew what they were going to be doing after graduation," David says. "I knew I needed help and guidance and couldn't wait till second semester senior year to figure out what I was going to do after graduation."

David sat down with a career counselor named Susan Brooks, beginning a mentorship that helped him discover not only his passion in life, but also a way to find a job aligned with that passion. Her early advice centered on helping David make the most of his summer vacations, first helping him explore an interest in journalism by steering him to a newspaper job. David had, in fact, arrived on campus dreaming of a career in broadcast journalism. "I wanted to be the next Dan Rather or Charles Kuralt," he says, not by chance citing CBS news anchors.

CBS offered the best reception of the few stations that the Styers's home in the western North Carolina town of Hickory received. Many nights the TV came on primarily for the news. Evenings were for reading the newspaper, doing homework, and practicing the piano. Like his two older brothers, David took piano lessons and sang in the youth choir at the First Baptist Church in Hickory.

"Music was a major fixture in our house, and church was our main extracurricular activity," he says. "Wednesday nights we attended prayer meetings. Most of Sunday was spent at church—Sunday school and worship in the mornings, youth choir in the afternoon, evening worship. If we weren't at home, we were at church—or visiting family or on vacation."

Education received equal attention in the Styers household, for both of David's parents were educators. Initially a high school science teacher, his father became an assistant principal, a principal, then moved to the superintendent's staff to become director of vocational education and dropout prevention for the local school system. His mother taught English and history to middle schoolers before taking a thirteen-year hiatus from paid work to stay at home raising her children.

A ninth-grade English teacher opened up the world of literature to David, sparking a lifelong love of reading. "Out of college I'd be reading Charles Dickens and people would say, 'You're not in school anymore, you don't have to be reading Dickens.' I'm like, that's the point, I'm out of school, so now I have more time to read. I feel almost withdrawal symptoms if I don't have a great work of fiction in my briefcase for the commute and business trips."

The summer after his junior year in high school, David studied American literature and modern theater with other gifted North Carolina students at Governor's School. He was news editor of the school paper his senior year and wrote a weekly column about the high school for the local Hickory paper. He graduated as valedictorian of his class of more than three hundred.

His parents had met at Wake Forest. So, too, had an aunt and uncle. His oldest brother had also graduated from there. "Although it was not decreed that I go to Wake Forest, it wasn't discouraged," David says. He arrived on campus eyeing a career in broadcast journalism, already knowing that he'd major in English because Wake Forest didn't offer a journalism major.

David's aspirations would, in fact, change, though certainly not fall term, when, working for the school newspaper, he brushed elbows with several of his broadcast idols. The first presidential debate of the 1988 election brought Michael Dukakis and George H. W. Bush to the Wake Forest campus—along with the national news media. "I got to actually meet Dan Rather on the sidewalk and watch Tom Brokaw conducting interviews. I thought, this is exactly what I want to be doing."

> "**I** got to actually meet Dan Rather on the sidewalk and watch Tom Brokaw conducting interviews. I thought, this is exactly what I want to be doing."

After his sophomore summer, he thought differently. Following the advice of his champion in the careers office, David landed a part-time reporting job with a small town newspaper, the *Weekly Independent*, in Rural Hall, North Carolina. He covered town meetings and wrote features about interesting local folks. "I'd drive out into the country, interview the person, spend the evening writing the story, and get it to the copy editor the next day," he says. However, he felt the flame on his journalism pilot light dimming, not because he didn't enjoy the writing, but because the work life of a reporter didn't suit him.

"My father's career in education meant he enjoyed a fairly controlled schedule, working regular school hours Monday through Friday, though some days he stayed on to supervise after-school activities. I think that that lifestyle suited me more than the sporadic days of a working journalist," he says. "I enjoyed the work but realized then that it was never going to be my calling."

As it happened, just as David was closing one career door, another one swung ajar, thanks to a second part-time job that summer. This time it wasn't the job, answering telephones and tending to recording logs, that caught his fancy, but the atmosphere of the office where he worked—the public radio station on the Wake Forest campus.

"Sitting there listening to classical music hour after hour, I fell madly in love with it," he says. He had a new passion to consider and to discuss with Susan Brooks in the careers office his junior year.

But first, in the fall, David headed to London to study British theater and British art. He enjoyed living in London, and his studies. "I think if I could relive my college career, I would have majored in art history—and scared my parents even more." He came alive with the exhilarating rush of life in a big city, something he'd experienced only in brief metropolitan visits, and he mentally added city life to his still-inchoate career leanings.

Back on campus for spring term, David began entertaining thoughts of going into teaching, like his parents, and he started looking into whether he still had time to take the necessary courses to graduate with a teaching certificate. It wouldn't be easy, but he could do it. "But both my parents discouraged me," he says. "They didn't want me to follow in their footsteps into education. They both felt that since they'd entered it, the profession had declined—life in the classroom, salary. It wasn't what they envisioned or hoped for me."

> Work environment is very important. Long hours are more tolerable when you like the people.

Still looking to connect his English major with a career, David followed yet another careers office lead and applied for a state-sponsored summer internship offered through the University of North Carolina at Chapel Hill. Of the two dozen or so internships available in various state government offices, one appealed to him immediately. "The internship was with the director of public affairs at the North Carolina Symphony. I thought, that's something I could do with an English major," he says, adding that the previous summer, in stitching together enough part-time jobs to stay on campus, he'd written a few press releases for Wake Forest's public affairs department. Moreover, this internship would return him to the realm of classical music.

Return him it did, providing an insider's view of a symphony orchestra that enabled him to glimpse an exciting career option. David helped write press releases and ad copy, but because he was the only intern assigned to the symphony, he was also "loaned out" to other departments. Over the course of the ten-week internship, he got a good feel for the overall management of a symphony orchestra. "You go to the symphony and see a conductor and dozens of musicians on stage, and you have no concept that behind that stage are dozens of administrative and backstage staff members to make that concert a reality," he says. "That was a revelation to me, to realize there could be an administrative or management role for me, because I knew I'd never be an orchestral musician."

As if a wondrous clear chord had sounded in his head, David now knew what career music he wanted to make. "I finally figured it out. I decided I wanted to go into nonprofit orchestra management," he says. "And I had my senior year in college to figure out how to make that a reality."

First stop: the careers office, naturally. Wake Forest's Babcock Graduate School of Management didn't offer classes in nonprofit business management. But Brooks suggested an alternative: Salem College, a small women's college across town, which did offer such courses. David took one course that fall at Salem (the lone male in a class of ten) and another in the spring, often stopping in at the Wake Forest careers office to comb through a book that Brooks recommended: *Jobs in Arts and Media Management.*

That resource provided David his two best leads in a very bad job market. He applied for a summer internship at the Kennedy Center and a year-long fellowship in orchestra management with the American Symphony Orchestra League, a congressionally chartered nonprofit organization that serves nearly one thousand member symphony, chamber, youth, and collegiate orchestras nationwide. Either position would take him to Washington, D.C., as would his backup plan—graduate study in arts administration at American University. In short, he'd done his homework and fashioned a solid plan. Based on what he'd discovered in two internships (a love of orchestral music and potential jobs in orchestra management) and a term abroad (a desire to live in a big city), David had come up with three potential scores for the next movement of his life's symphony.

In his interviews with the American Symphony Orchestra League, he was one of the final twelve candidates, but he was not one of the ultimate six who received fellowships. He received better news from both the Kennedy Center and American University. So his immediate future seemed clear: a summer internship at the Kennedy Center, doing fund-raising work and database management, and grad school in the fall. Arriving in Washington, David began his Kennedy Center internship and stopped by his intended campus, meeting with some of his prospective professors and lining up a full-time campus job to provide tuition remission for his master's program.

Then he caught a huge break in the form of an invitation. Not only did it turn out that as a fellowship finalist for the American Symphony Orchestra League he got free registration to the League's annual conference, but that year's conference happened to be in Washington. "My colleagues at the Kennedy Center were jealous I got to go," he says, explaining that he welcomed the opportunity to reconnect with some of the organization's national staff members who had interviewed him.

At the end of July his phone rang. It was the human resources director at the American Symphony Orchestra League. The woman told him, "We have your resume. We know you were a finalist for the fellowship program and you're living here in D.C. We have some positions open. Would you like to come interview for any of them?"

While still on the line, David considered his commitment to American University. He respectfully turned down the HR director's offer. Immediately, David had second thoughts. After about a half hour he grabbed the phone, got the HR director on the line, and announced, "I've changed my mind."

Rethinking his spur-of-the-moment decision, he realized that American University would understand if he needed to withdraw, and moreover, he recalled his initial reason for applying to grad school—as a backup in case he couldn't find a job. When he did receive an offer from the American Symphony Orchestra League, David started in the post of artistic services coordinator overseeing the league's conductor training program.

With a bit of luck, and plenty of foresight and planning, he landed a dream job right on target with his passion. The job fit him like a glove.

Rarely did his workday need to vary from his preferred nine-to-five schedule. About once a month, leading conducting workshops, he traveled to cities like New York, Chicago, San Francisco, Salt Lake City, and San Antonio. He loved the travel and the opportunity to get to know many of his musical idols. "I'd get to meet all the great conductors of the day, though I was two years too late to meet Leonard Bernstein," he says. "And you always knew that you'd attend an orchestra concert at least one night per trip."

Then there was the league's box at the Kennedy Center. One of David's responsibilities was overseeing who got to use the organization's tickets, and, should there be no takers, guess who went? David says, "I spent many a Thursday night at the Kennedy Center concert hall listening to the National Symphony."

Before long his role increased beyond coordinating programs for orchestra conductors to overseeing services for orchestra managers. By 1998, after two promotions, he was also charged with overseeing the Orchestra Management Fellowship Program—the very program that had indirectly opened the door for his employment at the league. Those promotions, combined, boosted his salary by less than fourteen thousand dollars, not a great amount. "People aren't working there for the money," he says, explaining that he and others serve at nonprofits like the American Symphony Orchestra League because such mission-based organizations offer a reason to go to work beyond just earning a paycheck.

"I also liked the idea that you were encouraged to have a life outside the office," he says, noting that the league's top executives modeled that behavior. Accordingly, David felt comfortable devoting time to sing in the Grammy award–winning Washington Chorus.

David might still be at the American Symphony Orchestra League had it not moved to Manhattan in 1999. Although he liked New York as a place to visit, David didn't welcome working and living there. He'd bought a home in northern Virginia with his roommate, whose job was also in D.C. Accordingly, David chose not to make the move and left the league after seven wonderful years.

Could he find another dream job? He began networking, and among the people he contacted was Catherine French, the former executive director of the American Symphony Orchestra League, who had started an executive search firm to supply symphony orchestras with managers. French, who

> Deciding what criteria are important to you is critical. Don't compromise on your top priorities.

was working solo out of her apartment, said, "Why don't you come work for me?"

And so he did, helping her establish her database and filing system and then helping her move her business out of her home. Within a few months, David realized the work, as a contractor with no benefits, would best serve as a bridge to his next job. As summer turned into fall, he also determined some aspects of a job that he'd come to enjoy—and would want in his next workplace. "I missed having a real office environment, colleagues and a water cooler, happy hours and birthday parties," he says.

But he knew that replicating that kind of workplace in the realm of classical music would not be easy. "Although I had spent seven years in the field of orchestra management, I had never worked for a symphony orchestra," he says, explaining that he knew enough about the demands on a typical orchestra manager to know that job probably wasn't for him. "Nine-to-five hours, travel once a month—that's not the life of a typical orchestra manager, who doesn't have an office job per se, and has concerts at night, not to mention weekends."

Looking to stay in the nonprofit world and in Washington, D.C., David began with arts organizations and quickly expanded his search to include many of the national associations headquartered in the nation's capital. The Internet provided many of his leads, including a job posting at the Points of Light Foundation. Here, he had a contact. The former director of conferences and meetings at the American Symphony Orchestra League, who had also chosen not to relocate with the league to New York, had taken a job at the Points of Light Foundation. David called her and asked her how she liked her new workplace. "It's crazy and insane, but I think you'd fit in well here," she told him. "Let me set up an interview for you."

Thus David began the next movement of his career symphony. He accepted a job in late 1999 as manager of what became known as Join Hands Day, the debut of a nationwide day of volunteer service projects scheduled for June 2000. As such, he engaged the Volunteer Center affiliates of the Points of Light Foundation, the nonprofit founded in 1990 after President George H. W. Bush's famous speech comparing volunteers addressing serious social problems to a thousand points of light.

Know what's important to you in a job. Working alone may not be right for you.

He was far from what he knew and loved, classical music and symphony orchestras, but a lot of the skills David had learned in his former job were transferable to this one—project management, meeting logistics, marketing, and copyediting. Not long after he began his new job, he saw an internal posting for a job he thought he would like even more: director of technical assistance and capacity building for the organization's Volunteer Centers.

"What interested me about this position was it seemed so similar to a lot of the work I'd done with symphony orchestras, providing technical assistance, overseeing education training programs," he says, "only now for Volunteer Centers. And as a director position, it would allow me for the first time to supervise staff."

David got that director's job and has been at the Points of Light Foundation ever since. "It's given me the opportunity to really grow outside my comfort level, to learn about so many new things, issues of community, social needs, problem solving, organizational development, capacity building, and training," he says. "The concentrated focus on Volunteer Center development has been as fulfilling as my time in the arts.

"My passion and love will always be symphony orchestras. It's like a childhood sweetheart. You might marry someone else, but your first love is always special," he says, happily acknowledging an advantage of his particular passion: he can enjoy it outside of work and thus separate it from professional pursuits.

"Part of my success has been due to my willingness to take on extra work," he says. The first occasion came when he sought out extra responsibilities by applying for the director's job. Later, immediately after September 11, 2001, he volunteered to do what many at the organization found they could not do right then—fly internationally on Points of Light business. "Many were afraid to fly the first three months after September 11. I took three international trips

Most liberal arts graduates seek a challenge in their work. Learning new skills outside your comfort zone provides that challenge.

A lot of the skills David had learned in his former job were transferable to this one—project management, meeting logistics, marketing, and copyediting.

120

and really caught the travel bug," David says, recalling with pleasure traveling by overnight train from Bucharest through the Transylvanian Alps to Cluj-Napoca, Romania.

In November 2001, he represented the Points of Light Foundation at an international conference in Geneva, speaking on volunteerism in America, his words translated into French and Spanish. He made valuable contacts at that conference, including connections with Australian attendees, who invited him to speak at a conference on volunteering in Melbourne in 2003. "I've become a national expert on the whole concept of volunteering. Last year I spoke at three or four national conferences, on things like volunteer management, volunteer program development, asset development, and outcome measurement."

Speaking at a conference in Charlotte a couple of years ago, David arranged to have dinner with his career-launching counselor, Susan Brooks, who'd left Wake Forest to pursue a career change of her own. She'd become an ordained minister and had entered a different kind of counseling. When David caught up with her, she was working as a hospital grief counselor. He says that calling and writing her through the years helped to reinforce the importance of maintaining long-term relationships. "It's helped me realize that the person who helped me today may also be invaluable fifteen years down the road."

In fact, David spoke with Brooks in 2004 and 2005, when cutbacks at the Points of Light Foundation and subsequent staff reorganizations led to a decline in morale, his included, and he considered the calls from headhunters and organizations seeking to hire him away. Ultimately, David decided to remain where he was, negotiating for increased responsibility and a promise of certain organizational changes and staffing increases.

"Just this morning I was asked by someone I was interviewing how I learned to be a trainer," he says. "It was not because of any course I took in college. I didn't know I could be a trainer, but when given the opportunity I just figured out how to start doing it, and I found I enjoyed it immensely."

Talking about achieving career satisfaction, he continues, "I think a lot of it is self-discovery, not necessarily relying on other people to figure out what box you should be in."

Going above and beyond can never hurt your career.

David is very cognizant of where he's ended up, which, in broad occupational terms, has returned him full circle to one of his earliest career leanings, one squelched by his parents. He may not stand in front of a blackboard regaling high school students with the finer points of Dickens, but in the nonprofit world where he's made his career, there's no mistaking his current calling. He's an educator.

Don't be afraid to use your mentors as sounding boards.

Only you know what will truly satisfy you in a career.

David's Smart Moves

- **He visited his college careers office long before senior year,** thus getting early help in identifying what turned out to be career-defining internships and in preparing for the career passion that he discovered.

- **He pursued three postgraduation options simultaneously,** providing himself with backup plans.

- **He was able to change career gears quickly when a better opportunity eclipsed his intended and expected option.**

- **He paid close attention to office work hours and work environments,** choosing careers and accepting jobs that met his desire for mostly nine-to-five workdays and frequent travel opportunities.

- **He has created opportunities for himself** by looking beyond his own job, being willing to take on extra work, and volunteering for assignments that can broaden his skills and exposure.

Still on the Road Not Taken

COLLEGE: North Carolina State University, 1996

MAJOR: political science

POSTGRADUATE: law degree, Campbell University, 2000

PASSION: public service, politics, possibly running for governor

EARLY EXPERIENCES OUTSIDE THE CLASSROOM: paid internship at the North Carolina House of Representatives

EARLY WORK EXPERIENCE: manager of a steak house restaurant

CURRENT JOB: attorney in private practice

"Down here, high school football is the biggest thing in the world," says Jonathan Breeden, whose love of the game illuminated an appealing career path for him at a very young age—not on the field, but off the field.

As early as ninth grade, Jonathan started doing stats for WEWO, a small radio station in his hometown of Laurinburg, an industrial town of twenty thousand in southeastern North Carolina. By the end of the season, he'd worked his way up to doing color commentary on the broadcasts. The next year he volunteered his services at another local radio station, serving as their statistician while keeping the stats for his high school football team.

Life on the sidelines was good. He enjoyed how the excitement ramped up before game day and being part of the must-hear, two-hour *Saturday Morning Quarterback* broadcasts, for which he contributed a three-minute taped spot previewing and predicting the results of the upcoming local college football games. He loved flashing his press pass and being close to the action. Little wonder, then, that Jonathan began dreaming of a career as a sportscaster. A decade later, he's still in TV broadcasting, though not professionally. He's happily charting another professional path, one that he decided suited him much better.

Football wasn't the only tug on Jonathan's personal compass growing up. A voice in his head echoed his parents' frequent admonishment: "We don't care what you become, but you need to have a license that will allow you to be in business for yourself." Then a CPA in private practice, Jonathan's father had lost his job years earlier when the company he worked for as an accountant went out of business. "CPA, doctor, even a haircutting license," they stressed, instilling in him the importance of having a hold on one's career reins.

Meanwhile, Jonathan entertained other dreams, imagining himself in front of a TV camera, living the life of a famous sportscaster. He sent for an application to Syracuse University, clued in to its celebrated communications program. But he decided that upstate New York was much too far from home and that "it snowed way too much for this Southern boy." With his parents dead set against a career in broadcasting, he ended up at nearby North Carolina State University. He did not, however, slam the door on something he loved.

"I decided I needed to get into a TV station and see the business," Jonathan recalls, explaining that his unpaid radio experience helped him land a similar unpaid position at WRAL, the CBS television affiliate in Raleigh. "I'll do anything you need me to do," he told Bob Holliday, the station's sports director. "I'll carry scripts, get scores." Experience, enthusiasm, and a willingness to do everything—the three Es—sealed the deal.

Holliday connected him with Tom Suiter, on-air host of the *Football Friday* show, a program so popular it knocked David Letterman off the local airwaves. Suiter had been Jonathan's idol growing up. Now Jonathan was working for Suiter, going to games, taking notes, learning the ins and outs of TV production in the trenches. But his wide-eyed joy soon faded.

"It didn't take six months for me to see it wasn't for me," says Jonathan, who credits his idol and mentor for taking him aside and explaining the realities of the business. "I had no idea," Jonathan says. "I knew the talent

> Once you've proven you have the qualifications, enthusiasm is one of the key ingredients in getting the job.

went on TV at 6 and 11 P.M., but I didn't know they worked the two-to-midnight second shift. Suiter said to me, 'Look, if you want to do this business, fine, but there are a few things you need to know. One, you will work weekends for the first ten years. Two, you will not make very much money for the first ten years. Three, you will most likely move more than three times in the first ten years. Four, you may be fired at least once for no other reason than they don't like the color of your eyes. And if you do make it—and it's a big if—you'll work second shift for the rest of your life.'"

That frank, unsugarcoated preview of a sportscaster's life hit Jonathan like a blitzing, 250-pound linebacker. In considering a potential career, he now realized, you have to look beyond the glamour of the job and take into consideration the lifestyle demanded by the job. Jonathan wasn't married yet. But he wanted a wife and children someday. The thought of not being home at night to tuck his kids in bed

> **You have to go beyond the glamour of the job and take into consideration the lifestyle demanded by the job.**

and the prospect of working weekends helped make broadcasting a road not taken—at least professionally.

Even now, just past his thirtieth birthday, Jonathan continues to work at the TV station, still unpaid—but essentially on his terms—seven to ten on Friday nights each fall. "I roll in about six; the show's over about midnight. I have a blast. I still get to meet the coaches and players. I love it."

As for the road that Jonathan *did* take professionally, he's just as happy as an attorney in private practice with his eye out for a possible move into politics. Being a lawyer, he realized while still in high school, would satisfy both his parents' hopes for him and his desire for public service. Lawyer also happened to be one of the good fits identified for him (another was hotel management) by a personality test he took in high school.

"What would be the best major for me?" he pragmatically asked a few lawyers in town before heading off to North Carolina State. Political science, they answered, counseling it would improve his ability to read and write. So it was that Jonathan took advantage of another internship his junior year in college. Seeing a posting on a bulletin board outside the poli-sci office, he applied for and was then selected for a work-study position with the North Carolina legislature. While working as an intern in the state house, making a couple hundred dollars a week, Jonathan also attended two seminars on local government and politics, earning six hours of college credit. The experience was eye-opening.

"When I got there in 1995, it was an historic time. Running on the Newt Gingrich Contract with America campaign, the Republicans took the house and had enough votes to do things," he says. "You could work on a bill, watch what happened, then it would pass, and you could see how things changed. I saw that [as a politician] you can really help people." Besides a big tax-cut bill and another to reestablish the Pledge of Allegiance in school classrooms, Jonathan points to the passage of a bill that rewrote sex education in the schools, "where it had to be abstinence based, which remains in effect to this day, and the Democrats are still mad about it. But according to everything I've read, the teen pregnancy rate is down since the bill passed."

Swept up in the Republican wave of change, Jonathan even ran for office himself his senior year at NC State, turning twenty-one midway through his bid for a seat in the state house of representatives. He attended classes in the morning, campaigned in the afternoon, and not only managed to raise fifteen thousand dollars to fund his effort, but got 42 percent of the vote against a Democratic incumbent in a district where Democrats outnumbered Republicans four to one. Though he didn't win, he confirmed both his political interests and abilities before heading off to law school at Campbell University in Buies Creek, North Carolina.

Jonathan chose Campbell because of its reputation for turning out skilled trial lawyers. Not wanting to work for a large firm and imagining himself starting out on his own, he wanted both courtroom training and classes that would help prepare him for private practice. Once again, Jonathan pursued an internship to broaden his skills. The summer of 1999, the year before he graduated and passed the bar, he worked in the district attorney's office back in his hometown. In fact, he worked for no paycheck, even while staring at a seventy-two-thousand-dollar loan he'd need to repay for law school.

"I did that for free, in return for getting answers to all the questions I asked," he says, calling his district court baptism a great learning experience. "It got me into a courtroom every day, where I saw that so much of what happens at that level, misdemeanors and traffic violations, is procedure, not law. I knew that until I built up a reputation in the community, it was going to be a long time before I got to superior court defending felony cases, that these would be the kinds of cases I would get when I started my own practice."

That day arrived on October 1, 2000, marked by a fresh stack of business cards announcing, Jonathan Breeden, Attorney-at-Law. Of course, he didn't have a single client.

Jonathan didn't just sit at his desk waiting for the phone to ring. Grabbing the business plan he'd written the month before, he started visiting banks in Garner and Clayton, towns nearest to where he'd rented office space in an unincorporated part of western Johnson County hard by Interstate 40. He needed a line of credit to tide him over until he could build up his practice to a level where he could sustain himself.

The third bank granted him a five-thousand-dollar unsecured line of credit—which he tapped that first fall and hasn't had to call upon since. Jonathan greatly increased his odds of success by continuing to do what had served him well in the past: he did not step blindly into something new.

He'd chosen the location for his office not just for its inexpensive rent, but also according to where it stood on the map. Namely, at a soon-to-boom exit off I-40. "I did my homework," he says. "I got projected growth studies from the county, learned the number of local lawyers from the state bar, asked the Department of Transportation what they had planned as far as roads, and got copies of local newspapers and read what was going on in Garner and Clayton, the next towns over."

Even before he finished law school and moved to the area, he joined the local chamber of commerce, heeding a law school professor who advised those going into private practice to become part of the community. "I got to ask local councilmen and businessmen what they thought of the area," he says. And he started making the kind of personal connections that would later lead to business referrals.

> Always know what you're getting yourself into. Do your due diligence.

Jonathan kept his business overhead to a minimum. He bought used office furniture and found a computer at an estate sale. He made do without a secretary by having calls to his office number automatically forwarded to his cell phone when he was in the courthouse. Initially, he went there even before he had clients. He realized he needed to learn the ways of the local judges and the prosecuting attorneys. He got put on the court-appointed list for assigned cases, and by hanging around the courthouse all day and making his presence known he started getting such cases—defendants too poor to hire their own attorneys. The pay then was eighty to one hundred dollars an hour. (A change in state policy has lowered that amount to sixty-five dollars.) About a month or so after starting his practice, he served his first paying client, a woman he represented in a divorce case involving child custody. He figures he made about $35,000 in 2001, his first full year as a lawyer.

His work isn't glamorous. He still does a lot of traffic violation, child abuse, and divorce cases. "Ninety percent of the people have drug or alcohol problems. Many are at the lowest point in their lives," he says, explaining this is what drew him to a career in law—the ability to help people in need. "If I work real hard, I can usually get them a much better outcome. I've become very knowledgeable about treatment programs."

At any given time, he's usually managing fifty cases nowadays with the help of a part-time secretary. His income these days? "I'm actually doing better than most of my law school classmates who took jobs with big law firms," he says. In his only previous paying jobs, as a host at an Applebee's restaurant and as a manager of a steak house restaurant while in college, Jonathan bristled when he saw employees dogging it. "If I've got a job to do, I go at it 110 percent," he says, declaring that being his own boss and working as a solo practitioner suits his personality much better. Besides, he gets to set his own hours.

Jonathan generally works from 9 A.M. to 7 or 8 P.M. Monday through Thursday, with an hour and a half break at midday—courthouse lunch hours. Most Fridays, he's out golfing, and he doesn't hesitate to call a former law school buddy or two at their big city law firm or corporate job and announce, say, from the thirteenth green, that he just sunk a twenty-foot putt. "I'm convinced that the way I practice law is the happiest way of doing it," he says. "The only people I know who are really happy practicing law are either in really small firms or they work for themselves."

As he's becoming better known locally, Jonathan finds himself mulling a second run for elected office. He explains that another factor in establishing his law office where he did was the conservative nature of local politics. A heavily Republican county, he knew, would greatly aid any future political ambitions he might have. "I might run for county commissioner," he says, with a primary goal at the moment of building his practice. "I want to establish myself as someone respected in the business community and build goodwill, so that if the time comes [to run for office], people will be there to back me."

How far might his political aspirations go? "Who knows," he says, "maybe governor."

Jonathan's Smart Moves

- He made informed career decisions after three very different volunteer and internship experiences.

- After learning that one of his passions would not make a suitable career, he stuck with it—but only as an avocation.

- He's chosen a profession and a niche within that profession that fit his personality and personal goals.

- He joined the local chamber of commerce to help sink his roots into his new community and expand his contacts.

A Six-Job Career Roller Coaster

COLLEGE: Mount Holyoke College, 1984

MAJOR: American studies and history

POSTGRADUATE: MBA in finance, American University, 1990

PASSION: organizational problem solving, being the go-to person

EARLY EXPERIENCES OUTSIDE THE CLASSROOM: director of development for a residential program for emotionally disturbed youths

EARLY WORK EXPERIENCE: NASA shuttle program analyst

CURRENT JOB: CFO of the Andy Warhol Foundation for the Visual Arts

Can a single college course help define a life? Absolutely. In fact, in KC Maurer's case, it was a course outside her major that helped her glimpse an untapped aptitude and passion and crack open a career door that has led her, finally, in the sixth job on her roller-coaster resume, to a dream post as chief financial officer of the Andy Warhol Foundation for the Visual Arts.

KC's office in the East Village in New York is a long way, even more so culturally than geographically, from her childhood home of Oil City, Pennsylvania, in the foothills of the Allegheny Mountains about one hundred miles north of Pittsburgh. Oil City isn't far from the town of Titusville, where oil was first discovered in America, and when KC was growing up, Oil City still boasted the headquarters of Quaker State Oil. Her family stood out in the provincial, blue-collar town. Her father was an industrial arts teacher and guidance counselor in the local school system. KC's mom was a psychiatrist and president of the school board. "Our family was different," she says, explaining that not only did they host a Swiss exchange student, but she herself studied abroad in South Africa the summer before her senior year in high school.

KC, the middle of three children, considered her mother a role model. "I grew up in a neighborhood with a lot of stay-at-home moms. And then there was my mom, who was not a stay-at-home mom," she says. "As a young child I always assumed I would be a doctor like my mother."

That, indeed, was what she told her advisor soon after arriving at Mount Holyoke College in South Hadley, Massachusetts. Of her high school graduating class of some three hundred, KC was one of but a handful of college-bound grads and one of only two females to cross the state line when heading off to college. Chomping at the bit to expand her horizons and challenge herself academically (her high school did not offer AP classes), she planned an ambitious dual major: chemistry, to anchor her pre-med track, and French, which she'd really enjoyed in high school.

"My first semester I took baby bio, baby chem, French, history, and baby philosophy," she says, explaining that before the term was over she found herself disavowing her I-want-to-be-a-doctor-speech to a new advisor. KC had had a change of heart. Three-hour science labs, she discovered, didn't really excite her. Nor did writing up lab reports. Not to mention that she felt in way over her head.

Her new advisor didn't bat an eye: "That's what college is for. You should take as many interesting courses as possible while you're here."

"Besides, I saw the full range of things that others were taking—sculpture classes, music theory, Italian—all kinds of interesting things," she says, noting that she approached her new advisor a bit anxiously, worried that she'd have to defend her decision to switch majors. Her new advisor didn't bat an eye: "That's what college is for. You should take as many interesting courses as possible while you're here." KC soon concentrated on American studies and history, though her father often joked that she really majored in campus affairs at Mount Holyoke.

Indeed, as in high school, she quickly gravitated to student government, becoming one of only two sophomores selected as student advisors. She served as a hall president for two years, and, come senior year, she was elected president of her class. Accordingly, she spent a lot of time with college administrators, including the school's president. Sophomore year she served on a planning committee that effectively recharted her life.

The committee planned various social events and academic offerings for the interim January term. In the course of those meetings, some informal lunch gatherings, KC became friends with a popular Mount Holyoke math professor named Harriet Pollatsek—someone she probably would not have otherwise gotten to know because KC had sworn off math courses back in high school. After a good algebra teacher in junior high, she'd had a couple of poor math teachers in high school and decided not to take calculus because the teacher, an assistant football coach, "had very little time for young ladies."

One day, inquiring about what courses she was taking at Mount Holyoke, Professor Pollatsek asked KC whether she'd considered taking any math courses. KC hedged, saying she didn't think math was something she was very good at. Professor Pollatsek proceeded to tell her a bit about her calculus course. "I can't promise you it won't be hard, but I think you'll find it interesting," she said.

Venture outside your comfort zone!

"Because I knew her outside the classroom and knew her to be very smart and very engaged in the business of teaching—she really wanted students to get it, feel her fire for math—I decided to take her up on her challenge," says KC, who can only shake her head, wondering how differently her life might have played out had she not ventured outside her comfort zone. That class, she explains, served her as a career beacon.

"I think it reawakened in me the idea that numbers could be fascinating," she says, "that analytical thinking related to numbers could be really interesting, and that a lot of concepts in the world are based on math. I had a good friend who was a math major. Suddenly, it became clear to me what Naomi was talking about, why she was so excited about math."

Looking back, KC puts her finger on a key element in this pivotal point in her life: the fact that her decision to take that calculus course came about because she'd established a relationship with the professor outside the classroom. "I got to see another side of her, got to know her as a person," she says. Likewise, the math professor got to know KC, and she obviously saw something in KC's personality and intellectual makeup that suggested she'd enjoy the math class. KC stayed with her American studies and history major, but the seeds of her ultimate career direction were sewn in that calculus class. Meanwhile, meeting various deans, the college secretary, and the college president, she caught glimpses of jobs that seemed interesting and challenging, occupations that had been beyond her frame of reference back in Oil City. Babysitting for the woman who was director of annual giving exposed KC to yet another college job, and it sparked another mentoring friendship that would later help jump-start her idling postcollege job search.

KC wandered over to the career services office her senior year. "I did the standard, knee-jerk thing—went to look at who was interviewing on campus," she says. "In 1984 it was mostly insurance companies and investment banks. I thought, why not?" Some of the companies were in New York, and she thought it would be fun to live in the Big Apple. She scored a couple of follow-up interviews in Manhattan, but in the end, no job offers. In hindsight, she's pretty sure why. "Probably it became clear that I didn't have any sort of a clue what investment banking was or what an account executive at an insurance company did. And I think I would have been horrible at either."

After graduation, clueless about her future, she took off for a month's travel in England, returning for a classmate's wedding. She'd barely landed back in the States when her mother passed on a phone message about a job opening in Springfield, Massachusetts, not far from Mount Holyoke. KC's network of Mount Holyoke contacts had paid off with a job lead. The woman in alumnae giving for whom she'd babysat had asked for and passed on a copy of KC's resume to a residential home for emotionally disturbed youths. The nonprofit Children's Study Home needed a director of development and public relations.

She joined the staff that August. Her salary wasn't much, fifteen thousand dollars, but without student loans to pay off, she managed fine. She found an affordable one-bedroom apartment in Springfield and "didn't have to eat ramen noodles every day."

KC was smart enough to move on after a year, recognizing this "first job" for the stepping-stone that it was—helpful in teaching her some valuable lessons, such as working with a board of directors and negotiating with a penny-pinching boss, but ultimately not a place where she wanted to stay. "Raising money for emotionally disturbed kids is very, very difficult," she says. "It's not a particularly sexy subject."

Especially compared to the arts. So when a friend tipped her off that the University of Massachusetts Fine Arts Center in nearby Amherst, Massachusetts, was looking for an assistant director of development, KC leaped at the opportunity. The UMass job, which paid a bit more and included state health and retirement benefits, offered a very different backdrop: paintings on the walls and a steady parade of performing artists. "It was a very vibrant place to work. I could attend various performances as many as six nights a week—Broadway musicals, chamber music, rock concerts, interesting lectures. I took jazz piano lessons," she recalls. The work was also more fun. "The performing and visual arts are much easier to sell. There are lots of opportunities for corporate sponsorships." The breadth of her liberal arts education stood her in good stead, for she'd taken a number of art history courses at Mount Holyoke.

KC thrived in her job and after a year found herself promoted when her boss retired. Two more years at the UMass Fine Arts Center taught her more and more about the inner workings of nonprofit organizations, not to mention a gap in her skills—one she'd do well to plug if she might want to someday head a nonprofit. KC had learned that many foundering nonprofits suffer from one-dimensional directors, programmatically strong CEOs who are short on business savvy. "I was responsible for putting together a budget and determining what spend rates were possible from the small endowment we'd developed—how many seats we needed to fill to cover our expenses for a particular program," she says. "I was doing a lot of it by seat-of-the-pants calculations, and I felt a bit overmatched."

A master's in business, KC realized, made perfect sense. She chose American University in Washington, D.C., because it offered her a full ride and because it had a strong nonprofit component. The wisdom of her career move showed in her GPA—3.95, much higher than her undergraduate grades—and her growing passion for what she terms the art, more than the science, of solving many financial management problems, like determining an organization's internal rate of return. "Oddly enough, I even found I loved accounting, something I wouldn't have ever thought I'd be remotely interested in," she says.

> "**O**ddly enough, I even found I loved accounting, something I wouldn't have ever thought I'd be remotely interested in."

As in her undergrad days, KC developed a close relationship with an administrator at the university, a bit of networking that led to her next job. Her second year at American University, she worked for an associate dean, helping him gather data and write reports necessary for the business school's reaccreditation. Talking with her informally, the dean advised that she apply to an elite postgraduate federal opportunity known as a Presidential Management Internship (PMI).

The program offers some of the nation's top grad school graduates a fast track in various government agencies. Competition is keen for these highly coveted midlevel government jobs. Besides one's graduate school grades, there's a rigorous application process that involves a written component, a series of interviews, and various group exercises. Once selected, a Presidential Management Intern then looks for a good match among hundreds of posted openings. KC interviewed at the Treasury Department, the Justice Department, and NASA.

Still lacking a clear career path, she considered a government job not too far removed from working at a nonprofit organization. The PMI program seemed interesting. It would be an eye-catcher on her resume. And, she learned, the program would unite her with scores of bright, young high achievers like herself at two annual conferences. "You allegedly attend seminars, but it's mostly an excuse to get together and party," she laughs.

Of the agencies she interviewed with, she found the best fit at NASA's D.C. headquarters, discerning an immediate rapport with the man who'd be her boss. But a job at NASA working on the Space Shuttle budget? Never in her wildest dreams had KC imagined she might someday have a hand, albeit a small one, like thousands of others, in a program that rocketed human beings into Earth's orbit. Did this make sense? Was this a good career move?

As she'd often done growing up, she called her maternal grandmother. KC remembers being startled one day by the sight of an open calculus book on her ninety-five-year-old grandmother's coffee table. It turned out she had been reading something about physics in *U.S. News & World Report* and had sought further enlightenment. Little wonder that KC valued her grandmother's opinions or that she huddled with her about the NASA job.

Her grandmother responded with words that KC has come to consider a kind of decision-making litmus test. "You don't have to be 100 percent sure," she advised. "You just need to be sure enough."

So once again, KC ventured outside her comfort zone, this time into a challenging new work environment. The PMI program called for a two-year commit-

> **"You don't have to be 100 percent sure. You just need to be sure enough."**

ment. KC stayed at NASA for six years, enjoying her time there as a budget analyst for the Space Shuttle program. "I was twenty-eight when I started at NASA. It was pretty heady stuff to sit in a room and develop congressional testimony and the next week be watching C-SPAN and see the administrator of the Office of Space Flight sitting in front of a congressional committee and suddenly hear your words come out of his mouth," she says. "My budget line was $525 million. I used to tell people we'd round to the nearest one hundred thousand dollars—and it was true."

She got to go to two shuttle launches and a landing. "There's nothing like it. It's energizing. It makes you contemplate the bounds of your own humanity," she says.

She found the work extremely interesting and did well, earning four promotions. But in the winter of 1996, budget cuts loomed for all federal agencies. NASA employees with less than fifteen years' tenure could expect pink slips. So with the handwriting on the wall, KC started looking for other opportunities—first within NASA. "But I couldn't find a good fit at head-quarters, which is what I wanted." Her search within NASA did land her two job offers—one in Houston and the other in Florida, at the Kennedy Space Center—but both had lifestyle strikes against them.

Then her phone rang, and she suddenly had another option. A friend, who didn't even know that KC was job hunting, called to say that she'd heard of a financial management position at a subsidiary of a big New York public relations agency. The friend had been an admissions officer at Mount Holyoke when KC was an undergraduate. They'd stayed in touch and KC had visited her several times in New York. The woman knew that KC liked the city—hence the job tip.

KC liked the people she interviewed with, especially Marc, the man she'd report to. The financial planning manager's job, which paid well, was soon offered. Since college, KC had always wanted to live in New York.

KC took the job and moved north. In this case, however, her job choice proved most unfortunate. Her boss, with whom she'd had an instant rapport, quickly showed a very different side. A friend of KC's, clued in to his office tirades, took to calling him "the mean bald man." The tirades stopped, when, implicated in a corporate scandal, her boss got fired. Stressed-out by all the turmoil, KC left after only nine months at the company.

Unfortunately, she jumped, if not from the frying pan to the fire, then unwittingly to another very hot frying pan. Her same friend—and yes, she's still a friend, laughs KC—tipped her off to another job that proved equally disastrous. This involved working as CFO for two small New York companies, both in the executive search business. However, the owner abused and belittled employees. Not out of character, one day she called KC at 6 A.M., screaming into the phone from Kennedy Airport, complaining that no limo was there to meet her—no matter that KC hadn't been the one to arrange for the pickup.

After a year of this unhappy work environment, and admittedly sinking into depression, KC addressed her untenable situation and the bottoming out of her formerly high-flying career path. How did she battle back? "One word," she says, "'therapy.' My mother's a shrink. I come by this naturally. I'm a firm believer in being therapized on an infrequent basis." She laughs

Geography is important. If you know you want to be in a particular place, find a way to make it happen.

as she outlines how her therapist helped her get her life and her career back on track. "My therapist told me I needed to find my hook, the ladder that was going to pull me out of this.

"I needed to find something that was going to get me out of bed in the morning. I was thirty-five years old and felt stale, depressed, forlorn, lost, out of balance, floundering." Her therapist's questions about what things made her happy soon swung over to what would make her happy professionally. KC asked herself some questions she'd have done well to have posed years earlier (though, admittedly, her various job experiences now provided more helpful answers)—questions she believes all job seekers and career definers should ask themselves periodically: Do you want to dress up for work every day? Are you more comfortable in a smaller pond? Or do you prefer a large organization? Do you care more about the product or the work? Do you want to work in a team or individually? For a profit or non-profit organization? In the city or country? In a domestic or international situation?

As she contemplated such questions, KC realized how much she wanted to return to her earlier nonprofit focus. "I wanted to do something that would make the world a better place, something that would either involve children or some aspect of the arts," she says. She called upon her alma mater's extensive alumnae association career development network. "You can search geographically, by decade, by types of businesses, including nonprofits and the arts."

KC sought to "beg, borrow, or steal any alum" she could find. In other words, she engaged in serious networking—making contacts, getting more contacts from those contacts—and in a few weeks, she developed a pretty good sense of the nonprofit world in New York City, where she still wanted to live and work. Not surprisingly, it was one of those contacts who helped land KC in her current job.

Visiting a Mount Holyoke alumna, the CFO of a nonprofit social services organization, on a warm summer day on the roof deck of her apartment, KC got the name and entrée to one of the partners in an executive search firm that specialized in nonprofit organizations. And, upon calling on her, KC got good news and bad news. The good news: The Andy Warhol

Don't underestimate the value of alumni connections.

Foundation for the Visual Arts needed a CFO. The bad news: The agency had three candidates under late-stage review. "But apply anyway," KC was advised. "You never know."

And, indeed, she got the job. "I'm convinced," she says, "because of my NASA experience. The chairman of the board said to me, 'Anyone who can work on the space station project can do this job.'"

Seven years later, she remains extremely happy as the CFO and second-in-command at the twenty-two-employee Warhol Foundation. "I'm in the right place," KC says. It's easy to understand why. She's paid well, gets thirty-five vacation days a year, can wear jeans to work most days, and arrives at 10 A.M. and leaves by 7 or 7:30 P.M. most nights. She never works weekends. In the summer, everybody heads home at 1 P.M. on Fridays. She's got a fifteen-minute commute by subway to her seventh-floor office in a late nineteenth-century Louis Sullivan–designed art deco building. She works in a veritable art gallery. The foundation's offices, including hers, are filled with various Warhol pieces. She's invited to gallery openings but only need attend the ones she wants to.

More important, she's fulfilled her goal of working for an organization that's supporting the arts, for the Warhol Foundation is noted for its timely, carefully targeted grants. "We're a very nimble organization," she says, explaining that after the collapse of the World Trade Towers, which she used to be able to see from the roof deck of her Brooklyn apartment, the Warhol Foundation quickly stepped in and provided emergency funding to a number of struggling visual and performing arts organizations in the deserted Manhattan neighborhoods below Fourteenth Street. The organization has also stepped in to plug some of the funding void created by the National Endowment for the Arts's reduced grants to individual artists.

She credits her liberal arts education with teaching her to think analytically.

> Just because an organization has almost completed its hiring process doesn't mean it's too late to apply.

KC estimates that she spends about 10 to 15 percent of her day number crunching in strict CFO mode. The rest of her time, she's involved in most aspects of the foundation's mission and mechanics. "I spend a lot of time on the phone and face-to-face with vendors, lawyers, accountants, board members, employees," she says, dubbing herself the foundation's go-to person, a kind of untitled chief operating officer. She's happiest, she says, when she's solving problems, financial or organizational, and she credits her liberal arts education with teaching her to think analytically.

Ultimately, she'd like to one day head the Warhol Foundation. "At NASA I was a tiny cog in a very big wheel," she says. "Here, I'm much more responsible for the overall health and well-being of the organization."

It's also possible to pinpoint a similar big upturn in her own health and well-being and identify the reason: her passion for her job.

Consider the issue of fit. You may wish to be a bigger cog in a smaller wheel.

KC's Smart Moves

- In college and graduate school, she got to know professors and school administrators outside the classroom and benefited greatly from those deeper, extracurricular relationships.

- She has continually challenged herself by moving outside her comfort zone.

- When she found herself in a career-induced depression, she sought professional help.

- She asked herself a comprehensive list of career-specific questions and was thus better able to fine-tune a very successful job search.

Listening to Her Inner Voice

COLLEGE: Dartmouth College, 1997

MAJOR: religion

PASSION: creating capital in low-income communities

EARLY EXPERIENCES OUTSIDE THE CLASSROOM: law firm internships

EARLY WORK EXPERIENCE: research positions at two Washington, D.C., organizations

CURRENT JOB: founder and executive director of Harbinger Partners

"I have found something that makes my heart sing."

So wrote Theresa Ellis in her journal soon after founding a company in 2001 to upgrade backward technology systems at needy nonprofit organizations in the Boston area. The entry glows with passion and pride. "It feels so wonderful and so hard-won," she added. "My life feels full and complete and whole in a way that it hasn't before. And that feels good and gives me quite a sense of peace."

By then, at the ripe age of twenty-four, Theresa had already explored and aborted her intended career path, held two jobs in the nation's capital, served as the board chairman of a nonprofit organization, and briefly worked as a self-employed consultant. At last check, five years after founding her company, her budget has expanded more than tenfold and her efforts are making a difference, Theresa remains confident that her continually reconsidered, constantly corrected career path now has her pointed in just the right direction—if not the one she or her parents foresaw for her.

"I grew up in the Midwest, writ large," she says, explaining that she lived first in Toledo, then moved to Wheaton, Illinois, for her middle school and high school years. Theresa's an only child. Her father worked for General Mills in sales and marketing. Her mother was a stay-at-home mom, as were many mothers in the conservative commuter suburb of Chicago, home to the fundamentalist Christian Wheaton College, Billy Graham's alma mater.

"My childhood," she says, with a pause, "was not especially happy. There were very specific gender roles in my high school. It wasn't okay for girls to be smart or ambitious." Theresa was both, serving as class valedictorian and student government president. She didn't share the old-school "rah-rah spirit" of Friday night football games and homecoming queens. But she did find a kindred spirit and inspiration when she visited her grandfather, the second-generation head of a family printing business, in Minneapolis many summers. He would take her to the office and tell her stories about his business. From him she learned a good bit about the seriousness and satisfaction of running a business. "Although I couldn't have told you ten years ago, he very much influenced the way I look at the world," she says.

Theresa wanted out of the Midwest, and Dartmouth College, in Hanover, New Hampshire, provided a perfect escape. She'd fallen in love with the school when she first saw the campus as a fourth-grader. Dartmouth served her well, especially after she heeded the advice of an upperclassman. "Don't so much pick your courses by the content, pick them by the professor," the student had counseled. In other words, seek out the best minds, the best teachers at the school, which was how Theresa wound up in Professor Ron Green's religion and ethics class winter term of her freshman year. "I'd had four years in high school not really being pushed," she recalls. "It was amazing to sit with a piece of literature for hours trying to get to the heart of it." She especially loved reading Kierkegaard and told her professor that she'd like do research

> "Don't so much pick your courses by the content, pick them by the professor."

on the Danish philosopher. "If you're really serious," he said, "spend the summer studying Danish; we can talk in the fall."

Theresa arranged for a busy summer. Staying with her grandfather in Minneapolis, she took Danish classes in the evening after working days as an intern at a small law firm, a job she found through the Dartmouth alumni lawyers association. Like many in search of a career, Theresa looked to capitalize on what she saw as her academic strengths. "My parents always knew that I really liked to read and that I was a good writer," she says. "Being a lawyer was something a good reader and writer would do, and it was also a prestigious career. That seemed fine. I had no aversion to it, but it was uninformed." A job in a law firm, she figured, would offer a window on this potential career.

That summer she did mostly menial tasks, especially a lot of filing. So she arranged for a second legal internship the spring term of her sophomore year. This time she worked for a big New York City law firm in its Paris office, and she experienced much more of the legal process, including case preparation and court arguments. She found it interesting and stimulating. "It was very much like a big mental puzzle, but I found I didn't particularly like the atmosphere in a law firm," she says, having felt uncomfortable with the hierarchical, classlike organizational structure. "Maybe what I'd rather do," she considered, "was work on the other side of the equation."

So taking her junior winter off campus, Theresa lived at home and worked in the office of a Chicago public defender. "She was a fabulous attorney, very committed to her work and very smart—a wonderful mentor," Theresa recalls. The experience proved invaluable, for it opened Theresa's eyes further to the workings of the law. "Law is a lot of process: File this motion, then lots of waiting for the next step. It felt very bogged down. There wasn't much movement." Theresa was discovering how much the context of a job meant to her, how much importance she placed on day-to-day details, thereby realizing that law didn't seem right for her. So she scratched it off her career plans.

Meanwhile, in the on-campus portion of her Dartmouth experience, Theresa was taking all the classes she could from two esteemed education professors and researching and writing her thesis on Kierkegaard with Professor Green. "I didn't quite believe him at the time," she recalls, "but Ron said it would give me the sense that I could produce things that were bigger than myself." She laughs unself-consciously now at her thesis title, "A Kiss Which Was Something More Than a Peck: A Study of Søren Kierkegaard's Philosophy of Romantic Love," but not at the importance of producing it, explaining that the diligent process of researching and writing a 150 page document would later help give her the confidence to write a business plan and start her own company.

> **"I became a much better writer, a much better thinker; I learned to ask better questions, and I learned I could do something of that magnitude."**

"Who would have ever thought that a religion major would be good for anything," she says, admitting that the content of her major hasn't necessarily aided her in her current job or her previous ones. "But the process [of writing that senior thesis] taught me so much. I became a much better writer, a much better thinker; I learned to ask better questions, and I learned I could do something of that magnitude."

With law out of the picture, Theresa was again career shopping, again looking at the world of possibilities through the prism of what she enjoyed. She liked the challenges and discoveries of research, and all her education courses had piqued her interest in education policy issues. So she looked to fill the summer between her junior and senior year with an internship on Capitol Hill. She applied for a volunteer job with the House Committee on Education and the Workforce. On spring break, she followed up on her letter of introduction with an in-person visit. "I don't think I'd have gotten the internship had I not shown up in person," she says, stressing the value of persistence.

As she finished her thesis, Theresa still had no idea what she wanted to do after graduating. She considered teaching, even applying for teaching positions at one hundred private schools. (Those letters resulted in one interview and no offers.) She also sought help from Dartmouth's careers office.

Sometimes an internship can help validate a career leaning. Other times, it can teach you what you don't enjoy.

Looking through books on nontraditional jobs, she found an organization in Washington, D.C., that seemed a good fit for her interests, a company called Policy Studies Associates that did policy research on education. "Like every kid graduating from college, I certainly didn't want to leave without a job," she says, explaining that she flew down to Washington, interviewed for the position of research assistant, and got the job. "I walked back to my hotel that night thinking I was the luckiest girl in the world."

Theresa lasted there just over a year. She learned from some talented bosses, notably how to write in a simpler, nonacademic style, but one day, on a research trip to a rural Louisiana bayou community, she again sensed what she terms a "job disconnect." She saw outdated textbooks, no working bathrooms—a world of difference from the schools she had attended. Her job was to go back to D.C. and write a report, when what she longed to do was roll up her sleeves and do something about these troubling school conditions. "I missed the doing. I wanted to actually help implement changes," she says. Around this time, Theresa wrote in her journal, "I'm beginning to think that corporate philanthropy would be a great fit for me. I'm enjoying the work with the foundations much more than the work with the government. It just strikes me that the system is more nimble and able to create change more quickly."

Soon promoted to director of research at a D.C. nonprofit organization called Community Anti-Drug Coalitions of America, her next job, she hoped to spark and see more tangible results after studying community coalitions from Nome, Alaska, to Miami, Florida. When her initial research project came to an end, Theresa left the nonprofit after a year and half, though friends counseled her to stay on. "You've been there less than two years, and you were only at your first job a year. You'll have a hard time getting another job if you keep that up," they argued.

"But I knew I wasn't happy," she says, after taking the time to reflect on her situation and what she wanted to do with her life. Writing in her journal helped clarify her thinking. She also honed in on her passions in letters. "My best friend and I exchanged letters, and I photocopied the letters because they were also a great chronology of my thoughts," she says. "It was like I was talking to someone, and in the writing process I got my thoughts out."

145

One of the subjects she wrote about was her volunteer work with the D.C. chapter of an organization called Literacy Volunteers of America. In school, Theresa had always stayed busy with extracurricular pursuits. At Dartmouth, she had served as an intern to the college president and worked on the campus campaign for Bob Dole's presidential bid. Fresh out of college, after making connections at a political function, she had been asked to join the board of a D.C. nonprofit that taught adults to read. Now, at twenty-two, she was the youngest of fifteen board members. Soon after she signed on, the organization nearly imploded. More than half of the board members quit. Bankruptcy loomed. Amazingly, Theresa was asked to become board chairman. She accepted.

"I had energy, and I really wanted to sink my teeth into something," she says. She read books about running nonprofit organizations, soaking up information like a sponge. Devoting twenty hours a week to her volunteer board work, in addition to her regular job, she recruited a new executive director for the organization and helped steer it clear of bankruptcy—learning all the while about budgets and strategic planning, and feeling, as in her college days, energized, "being up late because you love what you're doing." Theresa calls her service on that board "the reason I'm doing what I'm doing right now." In other words, her volunteer work, more so than her two paying jobs, provided the stepping stone—the experience and confidence—for her to start her own venture.

> **H**er volunteer work, more so than her two paying jobs, provided the stepping stone—the experience and confidence—for her to start her own venture.

Theresa had always thought being creative meant writing a novel or being a musician. But she came to realize that entrepreneurs who give birth to companies are creative too. Thanks to her experience with nonprofit organizations, she'd spotted a need that she felt she could address. The new millennium had dawned, but many small nonprofits suffered with late-of-the-art, not state-of-the-art technology. Many groups, Theresa discovered, limped along inefficiently with out-of-date hardware and software: computers still running MS-DOS and dot-matrix printers producing pin-fed pages whose edges needed to be hand torn. Many groups still did handwritten accounting in ledger books instead of using automated spreadsheets. She conceived of Harbinger Partners to come to the aid of these nonprofit groups by tapping the IT resources of local companies.

Her parents were aghast at her intentions, this speculative career path. "My mom cried when I called her on the phone. 'What are you thinking?' was the gist of it," recalls Theresa. Her father bristled: "We didn't send you to Dartmouth to ruin it." It, she says, alluded to the expense of an Ivy League education.

Her parents' reaction gave her pause. "I'm pretty close to my parents. That was a big, kind of "huh" moment for me," she admits. "But I also had mentors from college, an education professor and a government professor, who were saying to me, 'Go try it. See what happens. If it doesn't work out, you can always get a job.'"

Though her parents initially didn't agree with her choice (both have come around and are proud of her), Theresa stresses that they—and her grandfather—always made her feel she could do whatever she wanted to do.

> **"I** can remember my dad telling me I could be president if I wanted to—that sense of limitless possibilities."

"I can remember my dad telling me I could be president if I wanted to—that sense of limitless possibilities."

At first, the challenges of starting a nonprofit organization from scratch seemed limitless. But she'd raised money before. And though she'd never written a business plan—and had to first learn all it involved—she recalled writing her thesis. Surely she could do this, too. Theresa tapped into the Dartmouth alumni network, sending a copy of her business plan to a Dartmouth grad who heads a venture capital fund in Cambridge, Massachusetts, and asking to meet with him. "He didn't return my phone calls," she says. "I think I called him thirty-one times before he actually picked up the phone, and when he finally did I think he was skeptical. 'I want you to go segment your market, and when you've done that come back to me and maybe we can talk about how I can be helpful.'"

"I had no idea what it meant to segment a market. I went home, opened some books, and figured out how to do that. I went back to him about a month later and said, 'Okay, here's what I've done.' I think he was so shocked I actually had done it that he spent time with me."

> **"I had no idea what it meant to segment a market. I went home, opened some books, and figured out how to do that."**

Her new mentor provided more than business advice. For three years, he provided Theresa's fledgling firm about one thousand square feet of office space. In early 2005, Theresa moved her company to larger quarters in Harvard Square. She recently hired her sixth employee, and, with a fiscal 2006 budget of $550,000, she has plans to assist twenty-eight metropolitan Boston nonprofit organizations. That's up from six clients served the first year, and it brings the total number of clients to eighty-five. Harbinger Partners conducts on-site needs assessments, and then, acting as a matchmaker, brings in tech-savvy volunteers from corporations like Cisco Systems or Fidelity Investments to help the recipient nonprofits upgrade their technology systems. Theresa's company doesn't provide new computers or other hardware, but it stands ready with referrals of others who can help.

"Four out of five days, my job entails meeting with donors, meeting with prospective or current company partners, and meeting with large nonprofits that we're trying to partner with," she says. "The fifth day is staff management. So I don't order supplies any more. I still do some financial modeling, but less than I used to. My job has really evolved into being the public face of the company."

No matter how busy she is, Theresa makes time for something her mother taught her to do when she was a young girl. She pens as many as five handwritten notes a day, thanking people for things they've done for her or following up after meeting someone for the first time. "I can't tell

---

In a world increasingly driven by email, you can stand out from the pack by taking the extra effort to send handwritten thank-you notes and letters.

you how often I get phone calls from people commenting, 'It was so nice to get your letter.'"

"How long are my days? Uh, now, about twelve hours. But in the beginning, often fourteen to fifteen hours. There were nights I slept at the office.

"The satisfaction of building something like this from scratch is unlike anything else in the world," Theresa says. "The only thing close is being in love with someone." She shares that her husband sometimes jokes that he thinks she loves her company more than she loves him. "Which isn't true," Theresa says with a laugh.

Theresa's Smart Moves

- She tried on her intended career through off-campus internships, learning long before she graduated that she didn't want to be a lawyer after all.

- She succeeded on several occasions thanks to sheer persistence.

- She expanded her opportunities and knowledge base by networking.

- She's kept a journal of her thoughts and observations, especially as they apply to her career, and photocopies of letters to friends—becoming better able to listen to her own voice when making key decisions.

- She writes as many as five handwritten thank-you notes a day—a practice that makes her stand out from others, makes her memorable.

4

Fulfilling Creative Passions

Directing Her Dream

COLLEGE: Wake Forest University, 1986

MAJOR: theater arts and English

POSTGRADUATE: master's of fine arts in directing, University of Virginia, 1989

PASSION: writing for the stage

EARLY EXPERIENCES OUTSIDE THE CLASSROOM: taught drama at the American School in Lugano, Switzerland

EARLY WORK EXPERIENCE: fund-raising and public relations work for a small Washington, D.C., theater

CURRENT JOB: self-employed playwright and actress and professor of theater arts

Allyson Currin's career ambitions seemed crystal clear to her as a Wake Forest University freshman. In fact, they appear frozen in that year's college yearbook as part of a write-up on her as the female lead in the fall play, *The Time of Your Life.* "I want to be living in a city, acting and directing," she announced. "And I want to be teaching at the college level."

Flash forward to the present. Ally is doing all of the above. She's living in Washington, D.C. She's acting in plays, television commercials, and television dramas, and landing occasional walk-on movie roles. She's also directing plays and teaching acting and theater classes at George Washington University. Accurate as it was, her youthful career prediction missed what's now her true passion: writing for the stage. Like acting, it was writ large all over her childhood.

About as early as she can remember, Ally was putting on shows in the basement of her Winston-Salem, North Carolina, home, sometimes with friends, sometimes performing and dancing alone. "To this day," she says, "I think I could conduct the entire score of *West Side Story*. I think I still know it note for note." Her parents encouraged her creativity, incorporating her elementary school poems into the family's annual Christmas card. Ally wrote prose, too, notably a seventy-page novel in fourth grade that spawned two sequels. This writing, however, she did for her own pleasure and kept mostly to herself. She'd create her characters and spin her tales on weekends and at night, typing away, first on an old manual typewriter, then an electric. "I'd drive my brother nuts," she says. "But then it got so he couldn't sleep without the noise."

She played Paul Revere's horse—the play's narrator—and, even then, sensed she'd found her calling on stage.

Around the same time, she won the lead role in a school play about Paul Revere's ride, dressing all in brown and sporting a brown yarn tail. She played Paul Revere's horse—the play's narrator—and, even then, sensed she'd found her calling on stage. "It was, okay, red light. Complete recognition. This is it. The this-is-where-I-belong feeling that a lot of actors talk about," Ally says, noting, "I think I was hardwired to be an actor."

She certainly acted the part at Salem Academy, a small, all-girl private high school in Winston-Salem, where she performed in most of the school's theatrical performances—two plays and a musical or operetta each year. The summer between her junior and senior years, Ally enjoyed an intensive six-week immersion in the theater thanks to her home state's Governor's School program for gifted students pursuing various disciplines. "We had a philosophy class and an ethics and morality class, but most of the day you spent in your particular discipline," she says. "We put on two full-length musicals in those six weeks. It was very labor-intensive—making costumes, building sets, dawn to dusk. You fall into bed at night exhausted and stay up late talking with your roommate. It was great."

As if she needed it, that summer reaffirmed her desire to pursue acting and also helped with her choice of college. Ally wanted a good liberal arts school, and she chose Wake Forest over Emory because the former had a theater department. Unlike many of her classmates, she arrived on campus knowing exactly what she wanted to major in—theater and English.

Wake Forest's theater students put on four main shows a year, plus student workshop shows and smaller experimental plays. Ally performed in many of them, often in leading roles. "I acted my tuchas off," she says. And she became totally immersed in the life of the theater. "If the lights aren't hung, you stay up until 3 A.M. to do it. I love that about the theater. A deadline is a deadline. You're usually gritting your teeth, but somehow it all comes together. Not just academic theater, but professional theater, too. More than most people realize.

"**"If the lights aren't hung, you stay up until 3 A.M. to do it. I love that about the theater."**

"I played some wonderful character roles, comic roles, straight stuff. I got a broad range of roles and worked all the time," Ally says, explaining that as she plumbed the depths of her acting and singing talents and her creative yearnings, she came to two important conclusions. First, though she was a good actor, she didn't consider herself a great actor. And second, although she enjoyed acting, it didn't satisfy her deeper, creative hunger. "I realized that acting was not enough for me," she says. "I wanted a greater degree of control, control over the vision of the play as a whole."

Her father pointed to one path. "Why aren't you writing plays? You love theater. You love writing. Why don't you marry the two?"

"But he also thought for a while I should be a theater critic," Ally says, laughing. "Anything to keep me from waiting tables in New York, I think."

Ally wasn't ready for playwriting, which she deemed a most difficult literary form, one generally requiring the inner life of a character to be depicted solely through dialogue and action. Accordingly, she looked to the other theatrical path offering more creative control and made directing her focus while pursuing a master's in fine arts at the University of Virginia.

As a grad student, Ally taught introductory-level acting classes while taking intensive courses on all aspects of theater arts, from makeup to stage lighting. "If you have a black top hat sitting on a red tablecloth with a white doily, how do you light that? And what is each angle of light—violet, amber—that hits it going to be? The physics of that," she says, explaining the need for directors to have "the tools" to speak with lighting directors and costume directors. For her graduate thesis production, she directed a Soviet musical called *Strider*. Perhaps even more consequentially in hindsight, Ally also squeezed in a playwriting class.

She credits the professor, Doug Grissom, with "ripping the veil of secrecy from playwriting, making it seem less inaccessible, maybe even 'doable.' His message was, 'Just write it. You can fix it later.' That's something I say to my students today."

The first reading of her first play, entitled *Last Call*, wasn't easy on the ego. At Professor Grissom's urging, Ally and some of her fellow actor friends gathered in her living room and read the play. One of her best friends pulled no punches. "Ally, this is terrible. I don't believe any of the characters. I don't like any of the characters."

Afterward, her professor provided more constructive comments, asking, "What are you going for here? Let's talk about this section. Why did you write that?"

Ally's play was not particularly good. Nobody's first play is. "It's your mistake in the kitchen, your first attempt at a soufflé," she says, echoing her professor's advice: "Ally, if you read my first play . . . Yecch. Just keep writing. Just keep doing it."

Grad school, she says, "was like a three-year root canal. It's so much work, rigorous academic work and scene work and production work. So many all-nighters. But I emerged at age twenty-five with an MFA, and I needed those three letters behind my name if I wanted to teach."

Her father, apparently still intent on helping her avoid waiting tables in New York while pursuing an acting career, helped Ally land her first job out of grad school. And quite a job it was. By then, Ally's father, a Baptist minister when she was a young girl, had settled into his fifth career as head of the careers office at Wake Forest. That's how he knew about an opening for a drama teacher in a dream location, at the American School in Lugano, Switzerland.

Set in Switzerland's stunning lakes district, the school looked out on alpine meadows and snowcapped mountains. "It was ridiculously beautiful," Ally says, "and fifteen minutes by train to Italy." Ally taught middle school and high school students Greek tragedy, Shakespeare, and Restoration comedy, and she directed three plays that year. She had dorm duty one weekend out of three, leaving her free to travel the other two. Before the year was out, she had visited Italy, France, Greece, Germany, and Liechtenstein. In her remaining free time, she wrote another play. This one, titled *Dancing with Ourselves*, she knew was much better than her first.

After the school year ended, Ally spent most of the summer exploring more of Europe, returned to Winston-Salem for a short stay, and then, without a job or a place to live, headed to Washington, D.C., to attempt to live her dream and fashion a career in one of the most difficult of all professions, the world of theater. She had friends from school in Washington, and initially stayed a week here, a week there, while she looked for work. Like all actors seeking their first professional stage role, Ally had a head shot taken, polished her resume, and readied a couple of audition pieces. Her plan was to network her Washington contacts and market herself as an actor and a director. She hungered both to be on stage and to direct others.

> "My thinking was, get to know people in the theater community from the inside. That way, I won't have to be just another kid knocking on doors."

Ally's first job in Washington satisfied neither of those hungers, and she basically hated it, but it proved to be a brilliant career move. Through a grad school classmate who'd landed a job as assistant to the artistic director at Source Theater, Ally learned that the small nonprofit company needed to hire a fund-raiser. She knew nothing about fund-raising. Still, she interviewed for the job, which paid all of eleven thousand dollars a year, and when offered the position, Ally shrewdly took it.

The fund-raising job got her in the theater door. "My thinking was, get to know people in the theater community from the inside. That way, I won't have to be just another kid knocking on doors," she says. "It was invaluable to learn the nuts and bolts of a small not-for-profit theater, but also important to get to know the critics in town, all the artistic directors, and the power players. It made it a lot easier when I went to audition or asked an artistic director to read a script, because everyone already knew me."

Even just being there made a difference. Should someone call in sick for an evening reading, Ally might be asked to fill in on stage, script in hand, taking a role in an early test-drive of an in-development play in front of an audience.

She shared a four-bedroom house in nearby Silver Spring, Maryland. She taught an occasional evening acting class at Source Theater and also made a little extra money teaching acting classes for children at the Bethesda Academy of Performing Arts. Still, money was tight. At one point, she had to borrow a thousand dollars from a friend.

After about a year, Ally landed her first professional role at the now-defunct Goosebump Theater in Arlington, Virginia. She played the "beauty queen type" in a two-act ensemble play about a women's exhibition basketball team in the 1950s. The play ran five or six weeks, typical for small-theater productions. Ally received about two hundred and fifty dollars—not per week, for the entire run of the play. She couldn't have been happier. She'd made her professional debut and added a line to her resume.

Then her career started coming together. "The artistic director of my theater saw me perform in that play and was willing to take a chance on me in a wonderful part in a wonderful play called *Lloyd's Prayer*," Ally says, explaining that that role led to another, and another. Soon she was acting in three shows a year, while still working days at Source Theater, where, in addition to fund-raising, she'd taken on public relations work. She would arrive for her desk job around 10 A.M., get off work in time for rehearsals from 6:30 to 11 P.M., go out afterward with her fellow cast members, and make it to bed by 2 A.M. "A great life," she says, "when you're young."

Ally directed her first play, a comedy about gender and racism, in Source Theater's summer festival in 1991. In advance of the following year's festival, she told the festival director about the play she'd written the year she'd taught at the American School in Switzerland. That summer, part of her play *Dancing with Ourselves* was performed in the festival.

At the 1993 summer festival, Ally not only directed a one-act play, but she had the gut-wrenching experience of sitting in the audience on opening night when *Dancing with Ourselves* debuted in Washington in its entirety. Earlier, she'd vomited in the bathroom. "I've gotten better," she says, "but the most nerve-racking part of my theater life is opening night of a play you've written." Ally need not have worried. The audience and the critics loved her play, and her career as a playwright was launched. Not that writing plays paid any better than acting in them. She thinks she received two hundred dollars for that short festival run of her work.

"Yes, the pay is horrible. I tell my students, 'Don't consider the theater as a career unless you absolutely *have* to do it. If there are other options, if you can make yourself happy in community theater and have a job doing something else, that's what you should be doing,'" she says, adding that those who do make it professionally in the theater "are people who have a very strong sense of themselves and have an incredibly realistic view of their limitations and their weaknesses as well as their strengths.

"**"Y**es, the pay is horrible. I tell my students, 'Don't consider the theater as a career unless you absolutely *have* to do it.'"

"You have to take your knocks. I call it the 'smile and nod.' Someone's telling you you're too old for a part or too young or they want somebody prettier. I auditioned for a role in *The West Wing*—and they decided to go with an Asian look. You smile and nod. You don't let [the disappointment] seep in. It's like a callus. It hurts at first; then you get the callus and you can withstand it."

The other big event of 1993 was Ally's marriage to an international trade lawyer. Her husband's income, which provided a financial safety net, made it easier for her to leave her fund-raising and public relations job at Source Theater the following year. By then, the job had served its purpose. She was also burning out—the summer festivals, especially, ramped up the workload. Moreover, she wanted to concentrate more on teaching while she continued to act and write more plays.

Ally started teaching an English composition course and a literature course at Prince George's Community College, which she viewed as a stepping-stone to other teaching positions. "It was a community college, but it was pushing me toward a more serious teaching goal," she says, explaining that her classroom equivalent of summer stock prepared her for the leap to more prestigious colleges and universities. The chair of the theater department at St. Mary's College, an established Washington, D.C., actor, was sufficiently impressed with Ally's work to offer her a visiting professorship to teach playwriting for a semester. Then Goucher College made a similar offer. In the late 1990s, she began teaching acting at George Washington University, and she has also taught a variety of courses (playwriting, play analysis, theater history) ever since.

Meanwhile, Ally has continued to act—on stage, in various Washington theaters, and in other venues as well. Until her twin girls were born in 1997, she worked fairly regularly in television commercials, which can pay handsomely after you work enough to qualify for Screen Actors Guild membership. "I remember doing a commercial for Time Life Music," Ally says. "Driving to Baltimore on a Saturday and filming for a couple hours and getting paid $250. My husband, Chris, who travels all over the world on business, has seen that commercial all hours of the night and day in Hong Kong, Tokyo, Brussels, and Rio.

"I was SAG early, about two years into my professional work, and I joined Actors Equity five years ago (after meeting those qualifying standards)," she says, explaining that she's aligned with two casting agencies, one in Washington and one in Baltimore, which bring her acting opportunities. A role on the CBS Saturday night drama *The District* brought a flood of emails from friends she hadn't heard from in years. She's also appeared on *Homicide* and *America's Most Wanted*, which film in the Baltimore/Washington area. To date, the Hollywood portion of her resume stops most notably at *Random Hearts*, with Harrison Ford and Kristin Scott Thomas.

"If something good, something high profile that pays well, comes along, like an audition for Jason Alexander's wife in his new TV show, I'll do it," she says, explaining that she's backed off from the cattle call for lesser roles. "It used to be I'd get a call every couple weeks, but it's so time-consuming to pursue it, and it's boring and just not fun." Not to mention that, as the mother of two young girls, she has the added challenge of taking her daughters with her to auditions should her babysitter cancel at the last minute.

While she still enjoys portraying characters on stage, Ally has come to realize she is happiest writing for the stage. "Acting is lovely and important to me. I hope I'll always do it. There's a kind of freedom in acting; you're responsible for your performance and your connection to the other actors on stage. It's like being a kid in a way. Whereas being a director is like being a parent. There's something about watching the audience's enjoyment of a play you've written that made me realize, this was why I was put on this planet."

> **"There's something about watching the audience's enjoyment of a play you've written that made me realize, this was why I was put on this planet."**

Various local awards—for individual plays and the growing body of her work—have validated this feeling and kept her striving and aspiring to write a breakthrough work. "Even when you're Laurence Olivier and seventy-eight years old, you have to keep aspiring," she says.

Ally's life is a juggling act with four balls in the air: acting, teaching, writing, and family. She's found it a rich and fulfilling, if sometimes dizzying, blend. "When I'm not in a show or writing, the teaching keeps me creative," she explains. "I really enjoy exposing my students to the little hole-in-the-wall, black-box theaters in the rough neighborhoods, taking them not to Arena Stage or the Kennedy Center, but to the small professional theaters, where the really good cutting-edge stuff is going on."

Ally has come to view success in this highly competitive, very difficult career as hanging on three hinges. The first is talent, of course. The second is confidence. "I think confidence comes first from your family, then it's self-generated," she says. "When you don't get a role, you don't let it get you down. Or when you get a horrible review, and I've gotten them, and you don't want to get out of bed, you say, 'Oh, well.'" The third hinge is ongoing preparation.

"You have to be prepared. I tell my students this," Ally says. "You have to have worked and worked and worked, and made your life your workshop, so that when you get that brilliant idea or role, you've got the skill and the technique to pull it off. Or when you get a phenomenal offer of a role, one you've been craving for all your life, you've mastered your voice, your body, your creativity, your imagination, in order to give it the kind of life it deserves. You have to be a finely honed instrument.

"What I love most—and it happened around the time I got married when I had two shows running simultaneously, and at various other times—is when there's this glut of work, a variety of work. You're sprinting from a performance to a talk-back after a show you've written, and you're teaching a full course load, and you're flying to Vermont to speak at a writer's retreat, then you're flying back to make another performance. Life in the popcorn popper, I call it. That's fun. That's magical.

"As long as I'm getting productions, I'm pretty happy. I've won a lot of nice awards. I'm sitting here looking at one of them. Everybody's forgotten about it, and it's collecting dust. What matters is that I've got these great commissions lined up and people want to work with me. That's the cool thing."

Passion for the work, even when it requires long hours and demanding schedules, can be energizing.

Ally's Smart Moves

- She immersed herself in her chosen field in college and graduate school, plumbing her talents and interests.

- She took a foot-in-the-door office job that got her known in the local theater community and helped pave the way for her first on-stage roles.

- For many years, she privately pursued her passion for writing, honing her skills and building her confidence for the day she'd be ready to step out publicly as a playwright.

- She's learned how to deal with rejection and criticism.

Marketing by Storm

COLLEGE: University of Pennsylvania, 1989

MAJOR: psychology

PASSION: creative expression—her own and helping audiences to see and appreciate the creative expression of others

EARLY EXPERIENCES OUTSIDE THE CLASSROOM: DJ and station manager at her university radio station

EARLY WORK EXPERIENCE: promotions department intern at WBCN radio in Boston, assistant promotions manager at Boston Top 40 station KISS-108, director of special events at Isabella Stewart Gardner Museum in Boston

CURRENT JOB: founder and principal of Marketing by Storm

Cara Storm, who had changed jobs three times while moving up in the radio industry, could feel another, even bigger move coming on. As marketing and promotions director at radio station WKLB in Boston, one of her tasks was securing tickets for various on-air giveaways, typically to local concerts. But lately, branching out more and more, she found herself looking to the arts for ticket giveaways and calling the marketing directors of local museums, theaters, the symphony orchestra, and the ballet.

Cara, who speaks of happiness using phrases like "my soul was singing," found herself responding to the emerging notes of a compelling and familiar melody. "I started realizing the phone calls weren't just about, 'Hey, could we give away tickets to your show?' There was often a second part to the conversations," she says. "Part two became 'Tell me what it's like being the marketing director of the Museum of Fine Arts' or 'Tell me what it's like handling advertising at the Boston Ballet.'" When calling her counterparts at various arts organizations, Cara found herself initiating informational interviews, eager to learn more about their jobs as she began contemplating a major career change, a move to a new industry that was a familiar, warm part of her past, a return to a resonating cache of childhood memories.

Cara grew up the middle of three girls in an Orthodox Jewish household in the Boston suburb of Newton Centre. Her father, an internist, commuted an hour west to his job as medical director of a company that manufactured airplane parts. In those days, her mother ran Around the Corner Antiques, and she later ran an antique consignment shop, both in Newton. The Storm girls grew up with an expectation to work hard and achieve. Cara attended a Jewish day school from sixth through ninth grades where they took the word "day" seriously. Her classes stretched from 8:30 A.M. to 5:30 P.M. Then came homework.

Weekends, the family often made a beeline into Boston, typically bound for such cultural destinations as the Museum of Fine Arts or Shakespeare in the Park along the Charles River, and they regularly attended plays at Brandeis University's Spingold Theater. At first, Cara balked at going to the theater on Sunday nights, complaining she had too much homework to do. "My parents said, 'Fine, bring a book. You can read during intermission.' But after a while, I didn't bring a book anymore because I was enjoying it so much," she says. At home, voices sang along with soundtracks from musicals like *Hair, Tommy*, and *Joseph and the Amazing Technicolor Dreamcoat*. Thanks to her parents, she became a lover of the creative arts. Cara participated in school productions, though she stayed backstage, helping with makeup and sets, not herself a performer or accomplished musician (she quit piano lessons because of her heavy school workload).

In this context, her earliest career notion makes sense. "I wanted to be an architect. I didn't even know what that meant, but I do remember a vision of a sun-drenched office with a drafting table. Maybe I was thinking of Mike Brady on *The Brady Bunch*," she says, laughing. "But it was the idea of sitting at a drafting table and drawing, creating something for the public."

An A student both in private school and at the public high school she attended, Cara earned admission to the University of Pennsylvania, where she became a psychology major.

Cara especially enjoyed such seminar classes as behavioral psychology and clinical psychology. "With only ten to twenty students in the classes, you use your brain differently. You're not just sitting in a big lecture hall taking notes; you're discussing the material and getting your hands dirty. It's the difference between being taught and learning," she says, adding, "Marketing is certainly related to psychology. I'm not saying that I refer on a regular basis to my psychology textbooks, but in marketing you have to consider how people process things, how they think, how they gravitate to things. I think being a psychology major has made me a better marketer because it's made me a better communicator. Effective marketing is all about understanding your audience and communicating a message to them in a way that will resonate. But it wasn't psychology that led me to marketing. It was radio.

And it was her college station, a small, student-run operation, that helped propel her into radio. She signed on for a DJ shift at WQHS after accompanying a friend to her air shift there and because Cara, too, was big into alternative music. Junior year, Cara moved up to program director; senior year, she became the first female station manager in the station's history. She most enjoyed getting to listen to newly released records before everybody else, giving airtime to talented new bands not yet on anybody's radar and deciding which cuts to play.

Summers she worked in an ice cream store—for the money, the intellectual downtime, and the ice cream. She did not line up any off-campus internships to learn about potential careers and jobs. "I think I saw my time at WQHS as being a radio internship," she says. She even made her first industry contact there, a previous station manager named Eric, with whom she stayed in touch. Eric had gone on to intern at WBCN, a big rock station in Boston. When Cara decided in her senior year at Penn that she wanted to seek a career in radio, she sought his help.

"People told me, 'You're not going to be able to get a job in a major market right off the bat. You have to put in your time at a small station in a small city and work your way up in the industry.' But I didn't want to do it that way," Cara says. "I grew up in Boston. That's where I wanted to work. I told myself, I'm going to Boston. If that means I'll intern for free until I can prove myself, then that's what I'll do." But in a city like Boston, awash in college students, radio internship positions are nearly as scarce as Red Sox World Series championships.

"I do think a lot of getting started is about who you know," she says. "Having somebody like Eric, who'd been at the station, who could vouch for me—as being smart, focused, a good writer, and a music lover—really helped."

Cara interviewed at WBCN and immediately followed up with a thank-you note. Her take on the after-interview note: "It isn't just about thanking the person for meeting with you. The thank-you note is an opportunity to drive home a point. Maybe you clicked with your interviewer in some way and you want to reinforce that, or you want to use it as an opportunity to mention something that is going to make you really stand out."

Dubbing herself "a music head" and longing to work on the music side of a commercial radio station, Cara naturally hoped for an internship in programming or music. However, there was an immediate opening in promotions. She could start there sooner. Sensing the importance of getting her foot in the door, Cara accepted the nonpaying job in the station's promotions department—and in so doing, effectively changed the course of her life by pointing herself down a totally unanticipated career path.

> **"If you're changing careers and trying to go from for-profit into the arts, volunteer where you want to work."**

Little wonder that these days, when asked for career advice on breaking into her field—arts marketing—she stresses the first big lesson of her own career. "I tell people, if you're changing careers and trying to go from for-profit into the arts, volunteer where you want to work, volunteer at an event. It's all about getting in the door and impressing people with what you can do, with your talent, your energy, your smarts. Get in the door and let that lead you to the next thing."

At her first commercial radio job, Cara shared a desk two days a week with other part-time interns in what had previously been a storage closet, mostly answering phones and mailing out prizes to contest winners. She got by living with her mother (her parents had divorced) and earning a bit of money the rest of the week tutoring students in Hebrew and doing database work at a stock photo agency. During her hours at WBCN, she looked for openings and opportunities to expand her duties and get some exposure in other areas of the station.

"Because I liked to write and not everyone sitting in the promotions department did, I volunteered to write press releases, which meant also working with the creative director," Cara says. "That gave me a chance to learn a bit about the kinds of publicity the station was trying to get, not just via their own airwaves, but in other ways throughout the city."

Later, promotions director Cha-Chi Loprete praised her, albeit in a somewhat backhanded way: "You were such a pain. You kept coming to me saying, 'Give me something to do. Show me how you're doing what you're doing. Teach me how to schedule promos. Teach me how to write on-air copy or coordinate a backstage meet and greet.'" Contained in how he framed that praise, Cara notes an important lesson for all interns: There's a time and place to try to leverage an internship position. She stresses, "You have to know when it's okay to ask someone to take the time to train you and when you need to leave them alone so they can do their job."

By increasing her sphere of activity at the station, Cara essentially made her own first break. When it came time for the station's promotions director to go on vacation, he tapped Cara to fill in for him while he was gone. "It was like a dream come true. I'd been noticed. I wasn't just an intern passing the summer working in the promotions closet putting bumper stickers on things," she says. That memorable week, she handled all backstage aspects of a station-sponsored concert. She'd been backstage before, but this was different.

"Now I was orchestrating everything: calling the contest winners and telling them how to pick up their tickets; meeting with the band's manager to arrange the meet and greet; and making sure the station's banner hung prominently on a backstage wall, so when the contest winners had their pictures taken with the band, the station was prominently promoted in the background.

"I was very aware that I was very young to be doing all this. But it's funny. If you carry a clipboard around and act like you know what you're doing, people really think you know what you're doing. It's all in the attitude. And I realized how fun it was. I was backstage with a band whose music I really liked and had the opportunity to hang out with them. That felt pretty cool."

> "**If** you carry a clipboard around and act like you know what you're doing, people really think you know what you're doing."

It felt so cool, in fact, that Cara was compelled to ask WBCN's creative director an administrative question. She knew that filling in that week, she would be getting her first paycheck from the station. "I know I'm getting paid for my hours working at the station sitting in the promotions director's chair," she asked, "but do I also get paid for getting to meet Squeeze backstage at the Orpheum?"

"Any time you have to be at a certain place at a certain time on behalf of the station, that's work," he said.

"This rocks," Cara thought, confirming her desire to continue to explore a career in radio, when her boss returned from vacation and she went back to being an intern. As the year was ending and with no jobs open at the station, Cara started sending her resume to other Boston stations. Thanks to her internship, her resume now bore the call letters of a major local radio station.

She landed a job at a mixed-format station known as Mix 98.5, as marketing coordinator and research director, earning a midtwenties salary—therefore, still living with her mother. She liked her boss, who taught her about creative promotions and helped hone her writing skills. But just short of a year on the job, Cara got laid off in a station-wide downsizing. The good news: She now had another Boston radio station on her resume and a great letter of recommendation from her boss.

She had no trouble landing a job as an assistant promotions manager at KISS-108, a Top 40 station. She stayed two years, leaving to take a better job at another Boston station, WKLB. In the media industry, often the best way of climbing one rung higher toward one's dream job is to leap to another

If you're enjoying work so much you forget it's work, it's a good sign.

ladder. That's precisely what Cara did. Instead of reporting to the head of the promotions department, at WKLB Cara now headed the department as marketing and promotions director. Not only that, she'd almost doubled her salary. That was the good news. The downside? WKLB was a country music station, a far cry from her preferred genre of alternative music.

"I was less excited about the music and the format, but I was still in the medium that I wanted to work in and, in my midtwenties, promotion director of a major metropolitan station," she says. Cara had proved all those early naysayers wrong. She had not had to start at some small station far from the city and work her way back to Boston. She had done it her way. Four years out of college, she was managing a staff of four or five and sitting in executive meetings at the station "in a room with the big boys—the station manager, the general sales manager, the program director—setting goals for the station" and coordinating major promotional events.

WKLB, then trying to turn Beantown on to slide guitars and songs about cheatin' spouses, started sponsoring a big stadium show at the Foxboro home of the New England Patriots, featuring such artists as Clint Black, Wynonna Judd, and Faith Hill. Promoting such a major event as much as eight months in advance with direct mail and TV spots expanded Cara's marketing and advertising horizons. She also learned how to juggle all the details of actually staging a major event.

She learned event coordinating from a real pro, one of the biggest names in concert promotion. "The station wanted the best, so they hired Al Dotoli, who had worked for Sinatra, Elvis, and Arrowsmith, to name a few. I was told I'd know if I passed muster if I got an 'atta boy' from Uncle Al," says Cara. "So here I am in my twenties, working alongside this guy who worked with Elvis. When

> "**S**o here I am in my twenties, working alongside this guy who worked with Elvis."

the event was over, and it was a huge success, Al gave me a framed pair of original tickets to an Elvis concert, the concert Elvis would have performed had he not died immediately before. On the mat inside the frame Al wrote, 'You get the atta boy.' It was a very proud moment for me."

Experiences like that helped Cara realize not only that she was good at marketing and promotion, but that she was really happy doing event coordination. Her mother observed that she wasn't surprised at all by her daughter's success as an event coordinator. She reminded Cara how much she had enjoyed putting together antique wooden jigsaw puzzles as a young girl. Her mother bought the puzzles at estate sales and garage sales and enlisted Cara's help to learn whether any pieces were missing.

"I loved doing those puzzles as a little girl," Cara recalls. "I like seeing how something that's all scattered in pieces comes together. Usually those puzzles would have no picture on the box. The concerts were a lot like those puzzles. There's an end result. Everything comes together, but much like the puzzles, I would sort of imagine my way to what I thought would be the end and work my way toward it."

Soon she would turn a similar eye to her own career. Nearing three years at her fourth spot on the Boston radio dial, Cara found herself assessing not only her career progress and growing skills, but also more fundamental aspects of her current job. She loved her work, but not the country music niche into which she had drifted.

Moreover, Cara recognized that increased conglomerate ownership of radio stations was pushing the industry toward more formulaic programming. "I felt like I was drifting farther and farther away from the original reason I got into radio," she says. "I didn't necessarily feel like my soul was singing anymore in radio." So when she found herself seeking promotional tickets from marketing directors at various Boston theaters and museums—institutions she'd loved going to as a young girl—it was almost by instinct that she started asking about their jobs and began looking to make an even bigger leap—not just to another radio station, but off the airwaves, to a cultural institution.

While still in radio, Cara called Joan Norris, the marketing director at Boston's Isabella Stewart Gardner Museum, a small gem of an institution. Cara set up an informational interview to discuss how to switch industries. Afterward, Cara followed up with a thank-you note, and some weeks later, a holiday card—an implicit reminder that she was still around should a job open up at the Gardner.

Several months later, after leaving the country music station, she interviewed for a publicist's position at Boston's prestigious Museum of Fine Arts with the museum's director of public relations, Dawn Griffin. Cara did not get the job. But she benefited from the interview nonetheless.

As in many industries, in the arts, everybody tends to know everybody else. It so happened that soon after Cara missed out on the job at the Museum of Fine Arts, Joan Norris, from the Gardner, told Dawn Griffin she was looking to promote some upcoming museum concerts and was considering radio as a means for advertising, but didn't know much about radio buys. In their conversation, Cara's name came up.

As she had done in radio, Cara broke into museum work with a foot-in-the-door position. She gladly accepted Norris's offer of a contract work position a couple days per week. Beginning with radio buys and ticket giveaways, her bread and butter in her previous career, she quickly impressed her new boss—enough that when the museum's director of special events left for maternity leave, Cara was asked to coordinate that year's holiday galas. The door to her new career had opened a bit wider.

The Gardner, with its art-filled galleries and stunning interior courtyard, offered a pinch-me-I-must-be-dreaming kind of workplace as Cara continued in special events work for the museum. Though working in a separate building, she stayed in touch with Norris, her initial mentor. "I would cross the courtyard to see her, as a colleague, and sometimes we would have lunch," Cara says. Little did she fully appreciate the career impact of maintaining this friendship. Or how soon she would feel that impact, for when the director of special events returned from maternity leave, Cara needed to find work.

Through the industry grapevine, Norris learned of an opening for a director of marketing and communications at the DeCordova Museum and Sculpture Park in the Boston suburb of Lincoln. Her glowing letter of recommendation helped Cara get the job. As director of marketing and communications, Cara was back to calling the shots, moreover, in what she deemed her preferred line of work.

"I could have stayed at the Gardner in the direction of special events and maybe turned that into my museum career. But I really felt I was a

"**M**arketing was something I was absolutely in love with." The job, she says, "felt like being in a good relationship. Everything was clicking. It just felt right."

marketer—and still do," she says.

"In radio, you're trying to get people to not only listen to the station but to come to the station's events and feel a connection to it, feel it's their station," she says. "With a museum, I want you to take your Saturday or Sunday afternoon and see the value of spend-ing it in a museum, and feel connected to it, so much so that ultimately you'll become a member of the museum."

"At the DeCordova I felt really lucky. It felt like a very good fit. I was utilizing the skills that I had developed. I was a marketer—and marketing was something I was absolutely in love with." The job, she says, "felt like being in a good relationship. Everything was clicking. It just felt right."

So why did she leave after nine months?

"Life and whimsy and lark came into play," she answers.

But let's not forget a good dose of courage and an approaching milestone, her thirtieth birthday. Everything changed in the spring of 1997 when Cara flew to San Francisco for a long weekend to see friends and, for the first time, visit one of America's most beautiful cities. Her "picture-perfect postcard weekend" included a visit to the San Francisco Museum of Modern Art, which had recently moved into a beautiful new building.

She had hardly returned to Boston when one of her San Francisco friends emailed her with an intriguing possibility. He'd gone on the SFMOMA website and seen a marketing job posted. "You could move out here," he wrote. "There's a job doing what you do at the number one museum in the city."

Thinking about turning thirty soon and wondering, "Am I going to live in Boston all my life?" Cara flew back to San Francisco and interviewed for the job. "I was ready for an adventure, a new city, a new chapter in my life. And I think I was curious to find out whether I could get the job, to see how I measured up at a bigger museum."

She measured up just fine. The job of marketing manager was hers, announced SFMOMA's director of marketing and communications, Jay Finney, her boss to be. So Cara took a three-thousand-mile leap of faith and accepted the job.

Although she didn't know it starting out, Cara had been preparing, job by job, for this career-defining step up. The step offered greater challenges and visibility, a leading role on a much bigger stage. The San Francisco Museum of Modern Art, with more than two hundred employees, was the city's premier museum. As such, it hosted prominent touring exhibitions by Keith Haring, Alexander Calder, and the René Magritte show in 1999.

As she'd been promised, Cara had a real budget, as opposed to a go-make-miracles happen shoestring. "With Magritte, I didn't necessarily bank on the fact that everybody knows his name, but I did think that a lot of people would be familiar with his images," she says, referring to Magritte's iconic painting of a man wearing a dark suit and bowler hat, his face obscured by a green apple. She designed a multimedia campaign to make the exhibition as compelling to as wide an audience as possible—not just those who appreciate art, but also first-timers, those who'd yet to set foot in SFMOMA. She placed print, radio, and TV ads, put up billboards, and advertised the show on the sides of buses. But her biggest coup proved to be the guerrilla advertising idea she came up with while focusing on Magritte's unforgettable green apple. In her supermarket, Cara had seen stickers on produce advertising other store items. Why not advertise the Magritte exhibition with stickers on Granny Smith apples, she thought?

She had to work through all the details of this nontraditional advertising, like tracking down produce-safe stickers and figuring out whom to deal with at the upscale markets she sought as partners. And she told the produce managers that she didn't want to pay to have the stickers put on or to hang a Magritte poster near the Granny Smith apples. She could provide a few free passes to the show, and she suggested the upscale markets would benefit in the eyes of their customers by virtue of this partnership with the arts.

The buzz started in the stores and spread from there. Other stores caught wind of the promotion and asked if they, too, could get some Magritte stickers for their green apples. The museum's board members encountered

Achieving a career goal is often preceeded by many smart moves.

the clever campaign while shopping; they were very pleased.

Cara glowed. After much career and job maneuvering, she held a job that perfectly matched her talents, her upbringing in the arts, even her personality. It was true that, as time drew near for a big show, work hours could stretch till 8 or 9 P.M. But rarely did Cara need to come in on Saturdays or Sundays. "In the arts, management and boards tend to recognize the need for work-life balance and tend to discourage weekend work," she says, explaining that the project nature of the job, especially, appealed to her. "I get bored easily. I need to feel the job is changing, which was what was so great about working at SFMOMA. Shows would come and go. There'd be certain constants, like running newspaper ads and hanging outdoor street banners, but each of the more than three dozen annual shows would be different, and there was always the challenge of choosing the lead image, deciding which image is going to sell this show the best, and coming up with the big 'Magritte apple idea' for each show."

By 2003 Cara had advanced to marketing director and was well into planning for the July to November Chagall exhibition. As soon as she'd heard the museum would be hosting the Chagall show, she'd told senior management, "We need to have meetings on this as soon as possible. This is going to be huge."

The show was arriving straight from Paris. SFMOMA, in fact, was the only U.S. venue. "There hadn't been a Chagall show on the West Coast in maybe fifteen or twenty years," she says. "It was a complete retrospective, a painting show—which is the most popular medium—approachable, narrative, storytelling kind of art, and a big, recognizable name, the kind where you don't have to say, you know, the one who . . ."

Cara pulled out all the stops for the Chagall show. She worked with the city's tourism department and local hotels to arrange hotel and museum packages, which she advertised coast-to-coast, including ads in the national edition of the *New York Times.* Her out-of-the-box move this time was capitalizing on Chagall's Russian and Jewish heritage, reaching out to the Bay Area's large Russian community with special Russian-language group tours and arranging customized tours for Bay Area synagogues and other Jewish organizations.

The show did better than well. It became the most successful exhibition in the museum's history, setting records across the board: highest attendance, highest admissions revenue, highest sales in the museum store, most catalog sales, most audio tour rentals, and most new museum memberships. The show's high visibility kept Cara's phone ringing long after the Chagall banners came down. Other arts marketers called, asking how she'd orchestrated some of the details, like the hotel packages or various promotional efforts. Other organizations sought her out as well, seeking her advice on marketing their upcoming programs.

Cara was flattered, but after a few calls it dawned on her that she was giving away a lot of free advice. "Hmm," she realized, "I think I might have a business here."

Calls from headhunters pointed one way—to a larger market. In fact, Cara did interview for a job in New York.

Cara began exploring a simmering option: starting her own arts marketing business. She had previously done a bit of consulting work on the side, a small, ten- to twenty-hour project for a smaller museum in the city, which she had cleared with her SFMOMA superiors. Now, she looked into a bigger consulting project, working with the Asian Art Museum, which had recently opened a new building and was planning a summer 2004 geisha exhibition. "That's going to be huge," she told them, receiving the same "Do you really think so?" response as when she predicted great things for the Chagall show at SFMOMA.

With a job offer in New York looking more and more likely, Cara found herself nearing another major fork in her career road. She thought about how much she'd grown to love San Francisco, and how much self-confidence she'd built up in the last seven years after leaving Boston. "It's empowering to pick up and start your life over," she says. Cara chose the much less familiar path. Withdrawing her candidacy at the Manhattan museum, Cara left SFMOMA to go out on her own. "It was something new, exciting and scary at the same time," she says. "And I think it's good to try things you're afraid of."

She named her home-based business Marketing by Storm and began with a tailwind of work, having already lined up three clients in her last weeks at SFMOMA. In addition to consulting on the marketing efforts

Keep evaluating what you do. You may discover potential new directions.

for Geisha: Beyond the Painted Smile, for the Asian Art Museum, Cara would be promoting the San Francisco Jewish Film Festival and had also arranged a two-day-per-week gig at the city's Contemporary Jewish Museum. This would provide unanticipated benefits beyond an initial financial cushion. Having always worked in an office setting, buoyed by daily interaction with coworkers, Cara had never known the much more isolated life of the sole practitioner sitting at a desk in a spare bedroom. Fortuitously, then, her two-day arrangement at the Contemporary Jewish Museum (since ended) offered regular watercooler chat sessions, a helpful transition to her new career of flying solo as an arts marketing consultant.

And flying she was, quickly adding work for the San Francisco Public Library, the San Francisco International Arts Festival, and several of the city's dance and film festivals, as well as additional consulting work for SFMOMA. By the end of her first year as a consultant, Cara's business had grown to include a dozen clients, and revenues shot right past her former salary at SFMOMA.

Her boyfriend, who has his own advertising business, gave her this bit of advice when she started Marketing by Storm: "You'll feel like you're always working and like you're never working." She has, indeed, found that to be true. "You feel like the work never stops, especially when you have a home office. Your computer's right there, so you can be working on a strategic plan at 10 P.M. on a Friday night and doing invoices on Sunday afternoon. On the other hand, if I manage my time right, I can take off on a sunny day and go for a run in Golden Gate Park at 2 P.M. or start preparing for a gourmet dinner in the middle of the day."

Cara admits she's still perfecting the art of juggling multiple client projects, and, except for a few days after Christmas, she hasn't taken a formal vacation. "There isn't a system of someone in HR telling you how many days you've accrued, or," she continues, "co-workers urging you to take a vacation because you're stressed-out."

Because she didn't need a bank loan or investors to start her business, Cara wrote no business plan before she hung up her shingle. Nor has she given much thought to a five-year plan. Asked to look down the road a bit,

> Sometimes your career can only move if you're prepared to take risks.

175

she says, "I think I'll keep doing this. It feels like a natural progression for my career. Maybe I'll find others doing similar things [to partner with]. I've been specializing in arts marketing, but there's also a real need for arts PR and communication specialists, so maybe I'll join forces with somebody else in that arena. But at this time, I don't desire to grow this into a huge company with a large staff and downtown offices.

The first check Cara received from one of her clients included a thank-you note. "That was so lovely," she says. "It made me feel good. My clients are referring me to other organizations. And that makes me feel good, too."

How does she see the future? "Working with new clients as well as repeat clients. Seeing my art education—and life education—continuing to grow. Finding more of a balance between work and life. Continuing to serve on the board of directors of Creativity Explored, a San Francisco art center for adults with developmental disabilities. I want to continue to enjoy my friends and family and hope that family is in my future also," she says. "I do think that having my own business, being able to have flexibility in the number of projects I take on, is complementary to all of this.

"At some point, will I get a job offer from a client and be intrigued enough to consider going back part-time or full-time to a place? Possibly. I don't want to rule that out. But I don't have a desire to do it right now. I've created Marketing by Storm; it's successful on many levels, and that's very fulfilling."

> Job satisfaction can come in a variety of ways, even from making clients happy.

Cara's Smart Moves

- She's broken into difficult industries and hard-to-crack companies and organizations by accepting unglamorous, foot-in-the-door jobs—moving up after demonstrating her energy and talents.

- She's changed jobs often, but always with a purpose—seeking more skill-building responsibilities in a more senior post or a bigger stage on which to showcase and develop her talents.

- She's twice braved big, "scary" leaps—first, moving coast-to-coast, leaving behind family and all of her business contacts; later, departing a prestigious, high-profile job and a steady paycheck to start her own business.

- She started her own business with three clients already in the fold, thus hitting the ground running with focus and momentum.

Making Music Pay

COLLEGE: Illinois Wesleyan University, 1993

MAJOR: music

POSTGRADUATE: master's in music, University of Southern California, 1995

PASSION: musical entrepreneurship

EARLY EXPERIENCES OUTSIDE THE CLASSROOM: created two campus jobs for himself

EARLY WORK EXPERIENCE: cellist with the Los Angeles Opera

CURRENT JOB: founder and CEO of several small businesses and a professional cellist

If blessed is the person who successfully pursues his or her passion in life, then Todd French is doubly blessed. Thanks to his energy and deep-seated entrepreneurial bent, he's found a way to continue his boyhood love of music and also pursue another talent he discovered: turning ideas into thriving businesses. A professional cellist with the Los Angeles Opera, Todd is also the founder and president of an innovative small business called StringWorks.

Todd would make a perfect poster boy for multitasking. Not only has he pursued two very different but complementary careers, he's done so simultaneously—sometimes overlapping them in real time. "I've come up with a lot of my marketing or strategic ideas or ideas for new instruments while I'm actually playing," he says. And

> Todd would make a perfect poster boy for multitasking.

he also taps away on a Palm Pilot or cell phone keyboard during long rehearsal rests for the string section, enabling him to check his email and thus stay in touch with his office even while seated with the orchestra.

Todd was born in the central Wisconsin town of Appleton in 1971, the second child of working-class parents. His childhood provides hints of his eventual success, recurring melodies that were originally drowned out by a din of underachievement. "I was always the class clown," he says, "the kid cited for excessive talking. Nowadays, I probably would have been diagnosed with ADD. If I wasn't challenged, I didn't apply myself."

He rarely did homework or studied for tests. He did just enough schoolwork to maintain a 3.0 average. But Todd was no couch potato. At age twelve he had a weekday afternoon and weekend morning paper route, no cushy job in subzero Wisconsin winters, to which three frostbitten toes attest. In high school he trained for and competed in so-called paperweight triathlons, scaled-down versions of the well-known ironman competitions that required *only* a quarter-mile swim, a fifteen-mile bike ride, and then a three-mile run.

By then he was also the youngest member of a local symphony orchestra, demonstrating musical talents that first surfaced at age five, soon after he attended his older sister's violin recital. Told by his parents that he couldn't take up the cello, the instrument that struck his fancy at the recital, Todd effectively forced their hand with a stunning display of his innate musical ability. He went into his sister's room, picked up her violin, and proceeded to play by ear the song he'd heard her practicing.

Music lessons started immediately, and Todd starred in local youth symphonies. But he derived more pleasure, he recalls, from his improving times in the triathlons. Music came easy to him. He didn't have to work at it to be good. "I don't think you have a true sense of accomplishment if you're not really applying yourself," he says.

Early in high school, when the subject of possible careers came up, he considered sports medicine or chiropractic medicine because of his triathlon experiences. "Music didn't seem glamorous, and it didn't seem like what I wanted to do professionally," he recalls.

Nonetheless, Todd realized his musical talents could qualify him for a college scholarship, and when he visited Illinois Wesleyan University in Bloomington, Illinois, as a high school junior, he immediately sensed a good fit. There, as a full-scholarship student, he found himself surrounded by top-notch professors and classmates passionate about music. He blossomed.

"It was a community serious about academia. I had to apply myself to keep up—and actually wanted to," he says. "When I started taking some of the music theory classes, I realized how little I knew. Here's this superstar cellist who plays incredibly well but who doesn't really read music. I knew what the notes were, but if you showed me the key signature, I couldn't tell you if it was B minor or F-sharp major."

His cello teacher told Todd he had a lot of talent—then leveled an ultimatum: "If you want me to work with you, you have to be serious about this and really commit to it."

He did. "I went from being forced to practice forty-five minutes a day in high school to willfully and happily practicing four to five hours every day," he says, adding that the more he excelled in music festivals, playing alongside talented cellists from Yale and the Julliard School of Music, the more he thought about pursuing a master's degree and making music his life's work.

Meanwhile, Todd scratched another itch. Wanting a car his junior year, he knew the only way he'd get one would be to earn the money for it himself. Instead of looking into a campus job in the library or dining hall or applying for a job in a downtown retail store, Todd created his own job. Talking to prospective music majors visiting the campus, he'd recognized that he was much better able to answer many of their specific questions than the folks in admissions. So he proposed a new position at the school of music—student recruiter—and, of course, offered himself for the job.

"What I'm good at is convincing people to do something," he says. "But I can't say I'm necessarily a good salesman. I'm not comfortable selling unless I'm passionate about something." He was passionate about the music program at Illinois Wesleyan. The job he created required him to call prospective students at home in the evening. Often, he got the parents instead. Most of them loved the opportunity to speak at length with a student in the very program their son or daughter was considering and get

If you're going to be serious about a career passion, you have to put in the time.

frank answers to their questions. Working a few hours a day, three or four days a week, he soon earned enough money for a down payment on a used car. Happy as he was, the school was even happier. Todd's initiative proved so successful, it's grown to be a program with six student recruiters headed up by a full-time faculty person.

His senior year at Illinois Wesleyan, Todd created another job—again taking note of an opportunity close at hand. Discovering that his cello needed a minor repair, Todd called the instrument dealer and was told he could easily do it himself. "He sent me the materials and basically taught me over the phone," he says, explaining that with the right glue and clamps, the repair was easy. It was also easy to imagine all the stringed instruments on campus that might need similar repairs.

Todd had two things going for him when he walked into the office of the dean of the school of music and proposed that he repair and restore the school's collection of musical instruments: He'd identified a need, and he had a track record. He'd already delivered on his previous initiative, the student recruiting program. "You can have the greatest idea in the world and present it well, but that doesn't mean you're necessarily going to get anywhere," he says. "Unfortunately, it's also who you know. You have to make connections and establish relationships and have a reputation. Then people listen to you."

> "Unfortunately, it's also who you know. You have to make connections and establish relationships and have a reputation. Then people listen to you."

Given the green light, he set up a workshop and charged fifteen dollars an hour. "I checked out every book I could find," he says. He essentially taught himself the skill of repairing instruments, often meticulous work with very small tools. Todd not only became curator of the college's instruments, he soon found himself entrusted with eighteenth- and nineteenth-century violins in the personal collection of Illinois Wesleyan's late president, Minor Myers, who, Todd says, "became a close friend and mentor and helped shape a lot of my future career."

"His big motto was, "Pursue your passion." Not just find your passion—pursue it. I think it's a natural process, because if you have something you're passionate about, you do apply yourself. President Myers loved to share his passion, and I was all over it." Under the wing of Myers, who invited him to play at trustee dinners, Todd learned about and then started making phone bids on instruments offered for sale at London auctions.

Offered a full scholarship to the legendary string program at the University of Southern California, Todd headed for California with a job awaiting him. Thanks to a glowing recommendation from President Myers, he arrived as curator of the school's stringed instruments, a position created especially for him. "My rates went up substantially," he says, explaining that while he pursued his master's degree, he worked five to ten hours a week repairing instruments. Many, including a famous golden period Stradivari violin, belonged to his fellow students.

As he would do later as an entrepreneur selling nationwide, Todd leveraged his growing expertise, staying ever alert for opportunities to do what he knew and loved. "At USC I was not just repairing but also appraising instruments, many of which were underinsured," he says, explaining that he learned their value in part by devouring auction catalogs. One day, through a friend of his roommate's, Todd was contacted by a California auction house, Butterfield and Butterfield, about possibly appraising an instrument for them.

He didn't get the job. But shrewdly, he saw past that single lost opportunity to something bigger. "I realized they didn't have a musical instrument department," he says. "They were the third-largest auction house at the time, and the first-, second-, fourth-, and fifth-largest all had musical instrument departments. I suggested they pay me a percentage of commissions, so there was no expense outlay for them." Thus, in the second year of his master's program, Todd added a second part-time job to his workload.

Musically, he was playing with the Long Beach Symphony and the Los Angeles Mozart Orchestra, gaining experience and adding additional lines to his already expansive resume. It came as no surprise that after graduation he was invited to play with the Los Angeles Opera's orchestra.

Nor was it surprising that Todd continued to pursue business opportunities on the side. His initial postgraduate foray was a business he started with a partner, which they named Sloan and Tucker. His friend provided the start-up money; Todd provided the industry expertise. The names of their maternal grandmothers provided an upper-crust veneer to the business, which bought and sold older stringed instruments. They sold a few, but without enough money to market themselves, they failed to stand out from others who moonlighted selling instruments.

In 1996 Todd bought out his partner and reinvented the business as a nationwide rental program. The concept: Provide quality instruments nationwide through string teachers who were frustrated that their students were often playing on what he calls VSOs—violin-shaped objects—that is, low-quality instruments with poor sound. Unable to find a violin workshop that produced what he wanted—a good quality violin that he could retail for around four hundred dollars and a cello that would sell for nine hundred dollars—he decided to design his own instruments and contract the actual creation to workshops he trusted. He called his new business StringWorks.

Taking out a second mortgage on his home, he started small, making a dozen violins in 1997, his first year in business. But he had big dreams. Financial independence topped the list. By then he'd been married two years. He met his wife, Heidi, in the USC master's program. After graduation she sang in the chorus with the Los Angeles Opera, then left for the business world, where one day she confronted the harsh realities of corporate America. Arriving for her job at a financial services company, she found the doors locked. Overnight, unannounced, the company had shut down. Her job disappeared out from under her. The lesson was not lost on Todd.

"There's no security in the corporate world; even if you're a senior executive, you're not the one at the top. If you own a business, you know exactly what's going on. You see what's going to happen before it happens. To me, there's nothing more secure that owning your own business."

By the time Todd started StringWorks, Heidi was working at a bank. Her income plus his salary from the Los Angeles Opera provided a financial cushion for getting his new business up and running. Seeking a low-overhead way to sell his wares, Todd turned to e-commerce. At the time, nobody was selling instruments on the Internet. He taught himself HTML and designed his own website and then watched his business take off, although very differently from how he'd imagined it in his business plan.

"I originally figured music teachers would rent the instruments to their students. We would send them, say, thirty instruments. They'd be our representatives, but students would have contracts with StringWorks," he says. "But as soon as we launched the website, we saw that most of our money was coming from sales, not rentals."

He changed gears, and his 1998 revenues of fifteen thousand dollars has grown to more than a million dollars each of the last few years. He has four full-time and four part-time employees—but not in Southern California, where he makes his home. His business is situated back where he grew up, in Appleton, Wisconsin, where he hired his mother as his first employee. One-week business trips back to his Main Street showroom and warehouse double as family visits, with his wife and newborn daughter, Ella, coming along. More multitasking on his part.

Ask Todd how many hours he spends on his business, and he laughs. "My wife, who's now a full-time mom would say, 'All day, all night on StringWorks.'" Working from home, he does stay up late many nights, but being his own boss, he can easily take a spur-of-the-moment afternoon or day off for family outings.

He estimates that he spends 70 percent of his working hours tending to business and 30 percent on rehearsing and performing professionally. "I feel incredibly blessed to be playing at the level I'm playing with the Los Angeles Opera. The people I'm playing with are true professionals, some of the best players I've ever met," he says, before zeroing in on the role that music currently plays in his life.

> "**S**ometimes, when you take something you love and turn it into a job, it doesn't always stay what you love anymore."

"The cello still brings me a lot of joy. I think that's because it's an avocation. Sometimes, when you take something you love and turn it into a job, it doesn't always stay what you love anymore." Todd first sensed that soon after graduating from USC. He'd joined an elite professional string quartet—and absolutely hated it. "We were rehearsing all this great music over and over and over again—pieces I once loved to play—but by the time I got to the performance, all I was thinking about was here comes the measure where I have to tune with the viola. It became technical, and the love I had for chamber music was gone."

What does fulfill and energize him each day are business challenges, like the ongoing challenge of running StringWorks. As others in the industry have joined him selling via the Internet, he's now seeking to expand his business by marketing in previously bypassed, traditional means. "Some 90 percent of those looking to buy a musical instrument don't use the Web for that purpose," he says, pointing to a large market that he can't reach through high-tech means.

As if not busy enough, Todd has also pursued other business ventures. He founded a second business, ISIS Services, on the concept of putting a scannable microchip the size of a grain of rice inside a musical instrument. Originally conceived as a way to prevent theft and also locate valuable stolen instruments at the time of resale, Todd soon realized his concept offered a second, potentially much larger revenue stream by judiciously tapping the marketing potential in the demographic information contained in the system's central database.

In lieu of making the necessary investment in money and time to run with the idea, he changed course and sold ISIS, becoming instead owner/partner in yet another fledgling business. This business, called Inovium Corporation, promises that its automated electronic bill present-ment and payment systems will save companies 60 percent by replacing paper invoices and manual check processing with cyber-sent bills and elec-tronic fund transfers. For now, Todd is mostly working remotely from his home on website design and marketing matters as the company's COO.

Where's the music connection with Inovium? There isn't one. "And I like that," says Todd, "I feel more like a businessman, more legitimate, I guess, because it's easier to work in a field you know. Here, I have to learn about new client bases and acquire different marketing skills, learn who the com-petition is, and learn about new technologies, and the whole business-to-business marketplace is relatively new to me. It's exciting. My wife, Heidi, tells me she hasn't seen me this jazzed in a long time."

Todd's uncommon dual life provides him very different career satisfactions. When asked what he does for a living, he says, "Most of the time I say I'm a cellist. It's more fun to say cellist than businessman," he says. "But it depends on who's asking. Sometimes I'll say I'm a cellist who owns a business in Wisconsin."

Todd's Smart Moves

- He created his own jobs in college, gaining entrepreneurial skills.

- He found a way to enjoy not one but two careers—simultaneously.

- He shifted one of his passions from vocation to avocation status and preserved his love for it.

Getting His Just Desserts

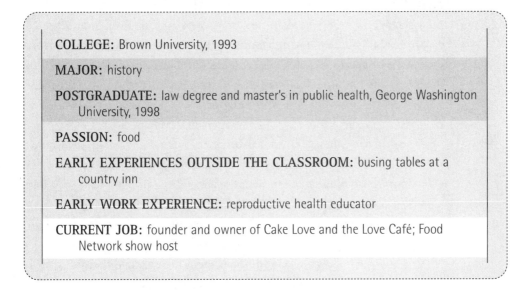

COLLEGE: Brown University, 1993

MAJOR: history

POSTGRADUATE: law degree and master's in public health, George Washington University, 1998

PASSION: food

EARLY EXPERIENCES OUTSIDE THE CLASSROOM: busing tables at a country inn

EARLY WORK EXPERIENCE: reproductive health educator

CURRENT JOB: founder and owner of Cake Love and the Love Café; Food Network show host

Warren Brown, president of the class of 1993 at Brown University, accepted his diploma and left campus with no idea at all as to what he wanted to do next. He couldn't know it then, of course, but not quite ten years later, after being profiled in the *Washington Post* and named one of *People* magazine's Fifty Most Eligible Bachelors, Oprah Winfrey would make him her lead in-studio interview on a show dedicated to finding one's passion in life. In 1993 though, Warren was about as lost as a college graduate could be. He returned home to the Cleveland suburb of University Heights worn out from college, and started a garden in the backyard.

Growing up in one of the few African American families in town and the son of a pathologist, Warren had known as early as junior high school where he wanted to go to college. He remembers seeing a feature on *Entertainment Tonight* about colleges. "The image I saw of students at

Brown, faces mugging for the camera, told me they were clearly having a good time," he says, adding that he also remembered liking the idea that a student there could create his or her own course curriculum. "That kind of freedom appealed to me, too."

Warren was a bit of a free spirit as far back as Catholic primary school, the type who in the fifth grade pressed the nun for answers about the Virgin Mary. With his sights on an Ivy League college, he attended a local boy's prep school. There, he earned mostly Bs, took no AP classes, and scored 1220 on his SATs. He got into Brown—and six of the seven other highly competitive schools to which he applied. He imagines, largely thanks to those so-called intangibles—his college essay, his interview, and, especially, his teacher recommendations. "Nothing in my high school record was particularly remarkable," he says. "It's my personality that stands out."

Some of the golfers he caddied for at a local country club were quick with advice for his upcoming years at Brown. "Your job is to go to class and learn as much as you can about a wide range of subjects," they told him. "Try different things. Get involved in as much as you can." Warren took that advice to heart, especially the part about extracurricular activities. "My biggest lessons," he says, "came outside the classroom."

At the urging of a counselor in the student life office in the spring term of his sophomore year, Warren became a volunteer member of a campus group called Sexual Assault Peer Educators. With others, he'd act out various dating situations and stay in character to field questions from the audience. "I enjoyed the role-playing and saying things that would direct the conversation to a teaching moment," he recalls, explaining that the sessions taught him a lot about listening skills and presenting skills as well as revealing to him one of his two great personal passions.

"Public speaking is one of the things I enjoy most in life," Warren says. "I think it's because you have the opportunity to look closely in the eyes of other people. You don't have to look away."

As president of his senior year class, he had numerous public speaking occasions when he helped organize events to bond the class more tightly. For the traditional, well-before-graduation party—for his class, ninety-three days in advance—Warren not only reprised his sophomore year

Mohawk haircut, he had the barber shave his class numerals, nine and three, on the back of his head. He was a charismatic leader who devoted long hours to his duties as class president.

"Not that I cut class or slacked off," he says, "but my classes were not a priority for me." Finding that he excelled outside, rather than in, the classroom, Warren concentrated his efforts where he found success. One of those areas happened to be at the stove, honing talents he'd begun to explore after working as a busboy and host the summer after his sophomore year. Warren pursued no internships while at Brown, though the summer after his junior year, he bought a Eurail pass and spent two months crisscrossing Europe. But the job at a country inn in Rhode Island opened his eyes to the inner workings of a commercial kitchen.

> **W**arren concentrated his efforts where he found success. One of those areas happened to be at the stove.

In addition to the partially choreographed, often chaotic ballet of the kitchen, which caught his fancy, Warren discerned, watching the cooks make vodka sauce for pasta or the spice mixture for the inn's signature tenderloin tips, that cooking wasn't all that complicated and looked like fun. So he bought a bunch of cookbooks and some pots and pans that he stored in a duffel bag in his dorm room back at school, and he started cooking for friends—fairly challenging meals for as many as six to twelve people. He pounded chicken breasts, then rolled them around a filling of basil, mozzarella, and sun-dried tomatoes. He tried Mexican dishes. He even roasted a turkey in the dorm kitchen.

Cooking struck a resonant chord for him. "I liked the preparation, the combinations of food," he says. "I loved being in the kitchen from four o'clock on, when the sun's going down, and listening to public radio, because it made me think of when I was a kid and the radio was on at home."

However, Warren did not perceive this budding passion as a possible career option as his days at Brown dwindled. Why? Looking back, he can think of two reasons. While he liked cooking, he wasn't so keen on what he'd seen of a chef's lifestyle. The hours were long and included weekends. And, frankly, he cringed at the occupational hazards, like burn-scarred forearms from grease splatters. Knowing himself to be accident prone, stories of knife accidents also gave Warren pause. But what really dampened his enthusiasm for a career in food was the well-intentioned advice of a man he respected. Visiting a

> **W**hile he liked cooking, he wasn't so keen on what he'd seen of a chef's lifestyle.

friend's house on a break from school, the friend's father asked Warren what he wanted to do with his life.

When Warren responded that he was thinking about maybe wanting to be a chef, he was counseled to set his sights higher. "Warren, you've got to be something bigger, something better."

The trouble was, upon graduating from Brown, Warren had no notion of what that something might be. As late as the spring of his senior year, he'd considered the possibility of med school, knowing he lacked the necessary undergraduate science courses. But when he found out it would take him another two years just to amass the necessary course credits, he nixed medicine. Law school? He was throwing career darts, hoping for a bull's-eye.

Warren took refuge in planting vegetables behind his parents' house back in Ohio. The activity was no doubt therapeutic, for he was both physically exhausted from his class president responsibilities and unsettled mentally, having not yet come to terms with the death of his junior year roommate, who died suddenly, shockingly, of meningitis. "I just kind of checked out," he recalls. " I didn't really want to deal with life at the time." His parents remained patient and didn't pressure him or pester him with questions about what he would do next.

Thankfully, Warren's postgraduation inertia lasted only a month. He returned to Providence, where he felt comfortable, found an apartment and a campus job to help pay his bills, and by the end of August, after regularly scanning the help wanted ads in the newspaper, he identified a job in a field in which he already had some experience. Hired by the Providence

Sometimes the advice you get may be dead wrong.

Ambulatory Health Care Foundation, he worked as a health educator for adolescent boys, focusing on sex and reproduction.

He worked in five community-based health clinics, teaching adolescent boys who came for vaccinations and physicals about sexually transmitted diseases and the importance of wearing condoms, and how to put them on, and answering their many questions about sex and male and female bodies. Most of the clinics were in lower-income neighborhoods, which opened Warren's eyes to a world very different from his prep school and Ivy League bubble. It was a good short-term job, a bridge to his future, which he was again thinking might emerge on the far side of law school. Warren admits he was as dazzled as many of his peers by the *L.A. Law* view of the legal profession. He, too, thought those TV lawyers had cool jobs.

Thinking he'd benefit from a radical change of pace and scenery, Warren decided to move to Los Angeles and get a job while he applied to law school. He moved in with an older sister and another housemate in a rundown Hollywood mansion once owned by Chuck Berry. Looking only for a yearlong job, Warren again turned to the want ads. Capitalizing on his previous experience, he quickly landed a post with the Northeast Valley Health Care Corporation as a reproductive health and antitobacco teacher in two Los Angeles high schools.

Unlike his previous job, which involved one-on-one counseling sessions, this one put Warren at the blackboard in front of twenty to forty students. He'd have them for a week of daily one-hour coed classes—frank discussions and question-and-answer sessions on human anatomy, including a demonstration, which employed a wooden penis, of how to put on a condom.

His presentation skills and techniques improved with each presentation. "I learned to measure success by the level of the questions the students were asking," he says. A full-time teacher at one of the schools commented, "I hear you're an all-star."

But law school beckoned. After being accepted by several schools, Warren selected George Washington University. His thinking? "You go to the college you want to and the best grad school you can get into." Looking back, he now sees various omens that his study of law would not go especially well.

The day he was supposed to take the LSATs, he flew over the handlebars of his bicycle, breaking several teeth and requiring eighteen stitches in his mouth. When he finally did sit for the LSATs, he came out to see that his truck had been towed.

Warren found many of his law classes intimidating. "I was very disillusioned. I didn't really like the curriculum. I didn't take to law naturally. I was confused and wasn't doing all that well grade-wise," he says. After his first year he enrolled in the school of public health and simultaneously pursued a graduate degree in public health, a field for which he had a greater affinity. That made for a terrible grind—law school classes during the day and public health classes at night. But he persevered and received both his law degree and his master's of public health in 1998.

His studying was far from over, however. Through the careers office at George Washington, Warren landed a job in Washington, D.C., with the federal Department of Health and Human Services. Passing any state bar exam would enable him to practice law in federal venues, and thinking he might sometime want to move to the Big Apple, Warren decided to take the New York bar.

"I know it sounds a little weird," he says, "but one of the highlights of my life was actually studying for the New York bar." Moreover, he feels that his mastery of the material really began after he attended a two-day Tibetan Freedom Concert that summer, a multigroup event at RFK stadium. Warren understood the refrain in one song to be "I ask myself." He started repeating those words to himself that evening and continued to do so, almost mantralike, in the weeks thereafter as a springboard to all manner of helpful questions. "I ask myself, Am I ready for the bar?" "I ask myself, Is this relationship right for me?"

He became more focused, and in concentrating on the bar review examples, suddenly his three-year legal fog lifted. He passed the bar on his first attempt.

Warren cut his dreadlocks, donned a suit, and stepped out into the workaday world of Washington, following what seemed his destiny at the time, a path he had created for himself. He worked hard at his job as a federal litigator practicing administrative law, in some instances bringing suits against individuals alleged to have committed federal fraud. But as the months passed, it seemed liked he'd disappeared. Shorn of his signature hairstyle, he'd lost, Samson-like, part of his vibrant personality. Warren felt like just one more federal employee in the nation's capital. Increasingly, he found his mind drifting to his growing passion.

A business trip to Los Angeles to take statements from witnesses became more of an occasion to take his colleagues to a hot new cake shop called Sweet Lady Jane. Afterward, at his desk in D.C., he'd sometimes work on cake recipes. Lunchtime often meant shopping for ingredients, like fresh raspberries, to adorn his latest two- or three-layer creation. His life changed forever in the fall of 1999 when he flew from Washington to JFK to see family in New York, and he carried a cake he had made for the occasion.

Lacking a box, he'd set the cake on a plate and wrapped it in plastic wrap. By then Warren had regrown his dreadlocks, and the sight of him carrying a cake through the airport caused quite a stir. People struck up conversations with him. And since the cake was obviously not store-bought, they asked whether he'd baked it himself. People smiled when he said yes.

It became clear to him, after reclaiming his cake from the plane's overhead rack and carrying his cake through the airport terminal at JFK, that he'd created a kind of magic under that plastic wrap.

Some nine months earlier, Warren had made a New Year's resolution to direct himself to greatness. It became clear to him, after reclaiming his cake from the plane's overhead rack and carrying it through the airport terminal at JFK, that he'd created a kind of magic under that plastic wrap.

As he sat outside the terminal waiting to be picked up, he recalled a lesson from his caddying days. "I'd learned, searching for lost balls, that often the best place to look was right under your nose, straight down," he says. He suddenly realized it was time to listen to his inner voice. "Look at what's happened today," Warren told himself. "Just make cake. That's all you need to do." Right in front of him, frosted in chocolate ganache, sat a sweet career epiphany.

As soon as he got back to Washington, he grabbed a Yellow Pages, tore out the page for bakeries, and started driving around the city to check them out one by one. Every shop he visited seemed stuck in the past. Few sold cakes. Nowhere in the city did he come across what he had in mind, a hip haven for raising cake making to new heights. For nearly a year he worked perfecting recipes, even boldly inviting seventy-five guests to his 750-square-foot apartment for a cake open house that featured no fewer than fifteen of his creations. To quickly learn some basic business principles, he took several business classes at a local community center a couple of nights a week.

By October 2000, Warren had lined up several restaurants that would buy from him, establishing a wholesale base for his intended retail business, and had located a small catering kitchen that shut down after lunchtime that he could sublease from 4 P.M. till 10 P.M. for $310 dollars a month. At that point, he arranged a leave of absence from his federal job and ran up a ten-thousand-dollar debt on his credit card.

He bought a double-door reach-in refrigerator, an electric convection oven with five racks, a twenty-quart mixer, an eight-foot metal worktable, and added to his collection of baking pans.

Day two into his new profession, Warren found himself at the counter of a gourmet food supply store, discussing, rather heatedly, some of the finer points of making buttercream frosting with one of the store's employees. When the exchange died down, a woman in line behind Warren struck up a conversation with him. They talked for a bit, and then she handed Warren her business card.

The card identified her as Judith Weinraub, a writer with the *Washington Post* food section. Chance delivered Warren a solid-gold opportunity, and he

It takes a lot of guts to jump into a high-risk venture.

> To quickly learn some basic business principles, he took several business classes at a local community center a couple of nights a week.

was savvy enough to cash in on it, coming up with an elevator pitch on the spot as he offered her a compelling reason to write about him in the *Post*.

He said he was just embarking on a dramatic career change—lawyer to cake maker. Intrigued, she suggested not just a story, but a long, behind-the-scenes profile that would follow his progress for three months. The result: An above-the-fold feature with a huge lead photo and a jump inside the food section to a full page with more photos.

Warren's phone did not stop ringing for two days after the story appeared. Sales doubled overnight. "I was a nobody in the food business, and all of a sudden I was on the map," he says. "People still come up to me and tell me they remember that story."

The story essentially legitimized his business. As often happens, it triggered additional media coverage. *People* magazine soon dubbed Warren one of America's Fifty Most Eligible Bachelors. Not long afterward, a producer for *The Oprah Winfrey Show* called and dispatched a film crew to shoot background footage. Warren's appearance on *Oprah*, initially scheduled for a program on the topic of quarter-life crises, was scheduled for studio taping on September 13, 2001. The tragedy of September 11 shelved the show, but Warren led off another show about finding one's passion in life, which aired on January 27, 2003. For that program he had 350 of his signature Crunchy Feet pound cakes flown to Chicago for the studio audience.

By then, he'd changed the name of his business from WEB's Cakes (he had employed his initials, which doubled as his nickname) to Cake Love and moved it to a six-hundred-square-foot storefront that he renovated on U Street, in the neighborhood where he lived, which was known as Washington's Black Broadway. The renovations and build out cost him about $80,000 of a $125,000 loan that he secured from a small community bank.

Ignoring the advice of his hired designers, Warren did not wall off the working side of the bakery, thereby keeping Cake Love's kitchen open to customers. "Why hide what I do?" he reasoned. "This is my work. I want people to see the baking. I felt I needed to evidence the value of the product. I wanted to see people, and I wanted them to see me."

Passersby can watch him frosting a cake through the big storefront window. Rather than being hidden in the back, Warren placed himself and his

Develop your elevator speech. It can really pay off!

work on stage and couldn't imagine why bakeries hadn't done this long ago. Nor could he figure out why more didn't specialize in cakes. "It's the highest-ticket item and the most profitable item in the bakery," he says.

He turned out other sweets as well, soon winning raves for his line of small specialty pound cakes made in fluted brioche pans, which he called Crunchy Feet. To simplify operations, Warren sold only baked goods at Cake Love, no coffee or bottled drinks. With only two stools at a tiny counter, business was essentially takeout. But the bakery was so bright and engaging and such a sweet-smelling haven that his customers clamored for drinks and seats.

So he expanded across the street, opening the Love Café in August 2003. This thirty-five-seat café, with three bay windows and custom-made, denim-backed booths, has become a neighborhood meeting place, a favorite hangout for students with laptops, moms with babies in strollers, and small groups having meetings. The café serves coffee and tea and bottled drinks, a wide array of sandwiches, and, of course, cakes and still-warm desserts from across the street.

"It's scratch-made baked goods," stresses Warren. "People love things made from scratch. And while I wouldn't expect or want to see people come in every day, there's nothing wrong with having a great piece of cake for a special treat."

Nowadays, with twelve employees in the bakery and another dozen in the café, Warren is spending less time pulling cakes from the oven and more on honing profit margins and fine-tuning the management of his intertwined businesses so he can open additional outlets. Franchising is one option. "I'm an ambitious guy," he says, "and I'd like to bring Cake Love to as many neighborhoods and communities as I can, other regions, maybe even other countries. And I'm always working on new products because I strongly believe that if a business doesn't grow, then it dies." Espousing entrepreneurial principles like that prompted *Inc.* magazine to include him in its April 2005 roundup of Entrepreneurs We Love.

He remains very much in the news, known on sight in Washington and occasionally approached by starstruck customers, an important component of his brand. He is also a frequent career day and motivational speaker in the D.C. schools, which he enjoys because of his passion for public speaking. Warren also spoke at his law school, sharing his story with students who followed him at George Washington University.

When asked, considering his current career, whether he feels like he squandered those three years at law school plus his time as a federal lawyer, Warren will tell you he did not. For one thing, he is convinced that he has created a far more successful bakery by not going to cooking school, taking an untraditional route.

"I'm an attorney," he says, stressing that his analytical training helps him think outside the box and innovate, as with the open floor plan at Cake Love. He believes traditional bakers have it all wrong, coming to work at 4 A.M. to ready the day's inventory of breads and cookies and pies. He says most people want to buy bread on their way home from work, for dinner, or sweets in the late afternoon, when their blood glucose level plummets. "So," he stresses, "you should bake then so you can have some of your products warm at four in the afternoon."

Warren also believes that had he not been a lawyer-turned-baker, he'd never have made it into the *Washington Post*. That story triggered an ensuing wave of media attention that has even catapulted him onto television. In the second half of 2005, Warren taped thirteen episodes as the host of a Food Network show called *Sugar Rush*. "It's been a lot of work, but also a lot of fun," he says of his TV gig traveling around the country and taping segments with some of the nation's top pastry chefs and candy makers. "It's fulfilling another dream of mine. I enjoy being in front of the camera. I like public speaking, I like presenting information to people, and this is another medium to do it."

The pay for a television host is surprisingly modest, but Warren hopes that *Sugar Rush* will be renewed for a second season. The exposure, he guesses, has increased sales at Cake Love and the Love Café by as much as 20 percent, and should help fill a second, larger Cake Love bakery that opened in January 2006 in Silver Spring, Maryland.

Publicity, Warren continues to discover, makes a very potent professional yeast. A budding TV career and a second retail bakery are not the only projects rising in Warren's busy creative realm. He's under contract to write a book and is also teaming with a candy maker, finalizing recipes and assisting with package design for a small box of specialty chocolates intended for gourmet food stores. Life is sweet, indeed.

As for that off-the-mark career counseling he received back in college—to forget about a career in food and become something bigger in life—Warren met the man who provided that advice at a wedding not long ago. The man knew, of course, all about the success of Cake Love and the café and Warren's stature as a baker/entrepreneur. He pulled Warren aside and apologized profusely and emotionally.

"I come from a generation that kind of just followed the party line," Warren remembers the retired insurance company owner saying. "We didn't follow our passion. We didn't set out to do what was in our hearts. You've obviously done very well and I couldn't be more thrilled for you."

Warren's Smart Moves

- Faced with career inertia after graduating from college, he sought a fitting short-term job before addressing long-range career goals.

- He listened to his inner voice to discover his passion.

- He looked before he leaped into his new career, conducting market research and taking some helpful classes to prepare him for an entirely new profession.

- He wasn't shy about marketing himself. When an incredible networking opportunity unexpectedly presented itself, he created an on-the-spot elevator pitch.

5

Taking
Your
Degree
Abroad

Starting a New Career Journey

COLLEGE: Iona College, 1985

MAJOR: communication arts

PASSION: travel and new cultures

EARLY EXPERIENCES OUTSIDE THE CLASSROOM: covering a Walter Mondale campaign speech for her college newspaper

EARLY WORK EXPERIENCE: ad agency secretary, public relations company account executive

CURRENT JOB: manager of communications at AmeriCares

Several times in her life, Beth Walsh has used her birthday as a landmark to pause and assess the status and alignment of her career and life goals. She did so in 1998, while having lunch with her best friend on a beautiful September afternoon, and she soon burst into tears.

Exactly why was she crying, she wondered? After a hard-earned start to her professional career in public relations, she'd settled comfortably into the best job she'd ever had. She was a partner in a small New York company with a good reputation and enough business to pick and choose its clients. Her job satisfied her yen for exotic travel. She liked her clients. She enjoyed her work. And yet . . .

She didn't feel fulfilled, Beth told her friend. A voice inside her was welling up, asking, "What next?" She was in the early stages of a major career change, and she made it after listening to this inner voice. This wasn't surprising, for she had been doing so since childhood with good results.

Beth grew up in Garnerville, New York, about forty-five minutes from New York City. Her father was a high school English teacher. Her mother was a nurse. "I think they both liked their jobs, but I don't think for either of them it was their passion. They were both very religious. My father left the seminary to become a teacher. My mother left the convent to marry my father. I think for both, their identity was being a member of the Catholic church," she says. "They were both concerned that I become a good person, but I didn't really get much career guidance from them." Her father did offer what he deemed pragmatic advice: "If you go into accounting, you'll make more money. What are you going to do with a liberal arts major?"

But the latter was her leaning. Shy by nature, Beth was happiest reading and writing, both for school and in a journal she kept, where the words flowed easily. "You see people who struggle with writing. I think math is hard. Put me in front of a sheet full of equations, and I want to run. But put me down with a blank piece of paper and tell me I have to write 250 words . . . that I can do," she says, calling herself "a word lover."

Beth first heard the rumbling of her inner voice when asked to fill out a survey in high school. In response to a question asking what she enjoyed, she wrote down "I like to travel." She was remembering a family trip to Hawaii when she was twelve. Her father, as newly elected head of the teachers union, was attending a national conference. It was Beth's first plane trip. Both her parents were from working-class families in Brooklyn, and Beth can still picture her mother standing on the balcony of their hotel room, tears of joy streaming down her face, happily stunned to have traveled so far. Beth was also joyous. "I felt like I was doing what I was supposed to do—see the world," she says.

"I remember making fun of myself at the time. 'Big deal. You've been on one trip. How can you say you like doing traveling when you don't do it very much?'" Beth says, explaining that she now understands she had instinctively identified not just an important personal interest, but ultimately a key career motivation.

The biggest influence of her childhood, however, was the death of her mother. Diagnosed with cancer when Beth was in seventh grade, her mother passed away Beth's sophomore year in high school. Her older brother and sister were no longer at home, so Beth took care of the house and did most of the cooking for her father and younger brother. When it came time to consider college, her father insisted that she continue to live at home, so she only applied to schools within commuting distance, deciding upon Iona College in nearby New Rochelle.

As it turned out, Beth did "go away" to school, thanks to her sister convincing their father that Beth should live on campus at Iona, rather than at home. Her father would pay for her first year of college; the rest was up to Beth. So her sophomore year, Beth took a part-time campus job, and that summer she waitressed at a local country club, working the lunch and dinner shift from Memorial Day to Labor Day. She banked enough money to pay for her junior year at Iona. In the fall, she continued to waitress on Friday evenings and weekends. The downside was that during vacations, Beth had no time for an internship that might have helped provide career insights as she pursued a communications major and wrote for the school paper.

At first, because of her shyness, she found it difficult to interview students and faculty members for the stories she wrote. But as students who noticed her byline came up to her and said, "Hey, I saw your story in the paper," she felt "a kind of confirmation of being pointed in the right direction."

Such was the case her junior year, when she was chosen to cover a campus appearance by then presidential candidate Walter Mondale. That meant getting fingerprinted by the FBI and mingling with the national press corps. Most memorable, though, was the feedback she got from a story she wrote in advance of a campus lecture by a Holocaust survivor. "Hers was a horrible story, about her family dying. There's a fine line between not wanting to hurt someone and having to ask the questions to get what you need," she says, explaining that after the story appeared, the woman's daughter wrote a letter to the paper praising the story and Beth's ability to perceive and vividly describe a look on her mother's face that she recognized immediately. "That was a big pat on the back," Beth recalls, and another validation of her talent as a writer and potential journalist.

She had, in fact, selected the journalism track of her communications major over radio, television, and public relations. She knew next to nothing, however, about the life or job requirements of a newspaper reporter, the typical out-of-college journalism job. "All this time I was studying, I didn't know anyone who did this for a living, and I don't think I'd talked to a real journalist," she says, admitting it came as something of a surprise when, junior year, a guest speaker in one of her classes explained from personal experience the sorry reality of entry-level pay for starting reporters. "I didn't have champagne tastes," Beth says, "but I didn't see how anyone could survive on ten thousand dollars a year.

"I had a friend on the school paper who was more career savvy. She'd had a couple of internships. She said was going to go into public relations, where you could write and make more money at it. Simple as that, I said, 'Me too.'"

Beth remembers campus recruiters interviewing business and accounting majors (her father was right!), but no sign-ups for public relations companies. She knew she wanted to work in Manhattan and started checking the want ads. With the help of a family friend, she did arrange for an informational interview with a senior-level corporate communications executive at Seagram's, and his advice proved sobering, but helpful. He said to her, "Look, it's great that you worked on the school paper, but there's eight million people like you in this city. The best way for you to get a job in public relations is at the entry level, as a secretary. Prove what a hard worker you are, and you'll advance."

Through an executive staffing agency, Beth interviewed for a secretarial job at Grey Advertising, one of the top ad agencies in Manhattan. She passed the typing test and took the job because it paid overtime, because of the "lovely man" who hired her, and mostly because she was assured that advancement was possible from the secretarial ranks. She was even introduced to someone who'd done just that. Beth was following the foot-in-the-door advice she'd recently been given. Unfortunately, in this case, things didn't play out as intended.

"I found out after a while, yeah, it happens," she says, "but it took forever, as long as eighteen months. I was organizing people's schedules, writing reports—all work that others had generated. I don't remember hating the work or feeling bored. You can learn a lot by typing people's correspondence. But I remember thinking, there's a limit on how much of this I'm willing to do." Her limit proved to be six months. Having learned that the realistic time till promotion didn't match her expectations, Beth quit. She did not tell her father. Nor did she have another job lined up when she left.

"I'd always worked. I wasn't worried about finding a job," she says, explaining that she slipped easily back into her old job waitressing while she looked for another secretarial job that might better act as a springboard to an account executive's job. This time she signed on with a small PR agency, one with about two dozen employees. Most importantly, the position Beth was filling had been vacated by a woman promoted to an assistant account executive position—precisely what she wanted to do. This company handled a lot of consumer electronics and technology accounts, business that didn't particularly interest Beth, but people at the agency worked well together, she liked the woman she reported to and, indeed, after a year, Beth too left the title of secretary behind—for good.

"After the first promotion, you want that second promotion, to account exec, which usually takes another year," she says. But as her second anniversary with the company approached, she spotted red flags. She was now reporting to two men, not the woman who had started as a secretary. Not only were her new bosses not looking out for her, one, in fact, was taking credit for work she'd done, "getting the *Wall Street Journal* to talk to one of my tech company clients." When she asked when she could expect a promotion to account executive, the vagueness of her boss's "a little while longer" triggered her departure.

"I thought the third time would be the charm," she says. "In some ways it was. In some ways it wasn't."

Beth's next job was at a public relations company. Although the same size as the company she'd left, this firm was owned by a husband and wife and the company culture was much more congenial. Her starting title was account associate, a level below account executive, but her salary exceeded that of her previous job. "The real carrot they held out was that I would be able to travel," says Beth, explaining that the agency concentrated on travel and tourism accounts.

"I didn't even know there were public relations agencies that specialized in this. It was a revelation," she says. By chance, not design, Beth learned that she could link her passion, her unrequited love of travel, with her work and compound her enjoyment.

The agency handled public relations for several Caribbean resorts and hotels. So instead of working on PR campaigns for electronics companies, as in the past, Beth was packing sunscreen and a bathing suit and flying, to the Dominican Republic, for example, to help a new resort publicize itself with a prepublic opening for travel writers. She'd found a happy niche, clients and a work environment that she loved, and a job she also enjoyed that fit her talents. "With advertising, you pay to get into the media. With PR, you're basically convincing editors to write those stories," she explains. "Public relations is the job of using your oral and written skills to persuade the media or the public to have a certain opinion about something. Essentially, you're a storyteller, and that's how I was using my skills."

She had no regrets about not pursuing a job on the other side of the press release, as a journalist. Not only was she still ferreting out the news, the angle, in her clients' latest offerings and telling their story, but as a public relations person, she had the luxury of something that journalists do not. She could, and did, develop close relationships with many of her clients. "I'm still friends with many of my clients from the early nineties, even though I haven't worked with them for years," she says. "I think that's part of my personality, building relationships."

At the company, Beth's clients requested and respected her opinions. And for more than a year, the work environment was equally rosy. Beth recalls, "I was totally in love with that job and thought to myself, I will never want to leave here."

She now knows that "never" can arrive very soon. The harmonious office suddenly turned tempestuous. "They started having financial problems, and in business, like love, money problems can color everything," Beth says, identifying the first cloud on the horizon as her boss, Laura, being fired.

Beth learned of the impending firing from the woman who was to take Laura's place—before Laura had even been told. "I thought it was horrible to treat her this way, to fire her behind her back. I was sick about it, and I called Laura from a client's office and asked her to have a drink after work that evening," Beth says. Beth had made a friend for life, and it wouldn't be long before the friendship proved invaluable.

The company began to implode. Some of the clients followed Laura out the door. The owners sold the agency to a British company, which invoked yet more cost cutting. The end of the line for Beth actually followed a promotion, of sorts. Her new boss offered her a fancier title and much more responsibility, but no boost in her salary of thirty-five thousand dollars. Beth consulted on the side with Laura, who advised her a job of that level merited a salary on the order of fifty thousand dollars. Beth's new boss actually laughed at her request, saying, "We're not going to pay you more money. You're lucky you have a job."

Beth felt anything but lucky. She was angry and insulted and started looking for a new job immediately. Fairly quickly she learned of a senior account executive opening at another Manhattan public relations agency that also handled travel and tourism accounts. Beth interviewed for the job, only to learn she narrowly missed out.

"I was really disappointed, as it had come down to the two of us," she says, explaining the importance of what she did next, which was to write to the woman who had interviewed her. "I said I was disappointed this didn't work out, but that I really appreciated the opportunity to meet with her and others at the firm. I wished her luck with the new piece of business they were getting and said please think of me again. I wrote promptly," Beth says. "I've always been queen of the note writers."

By being gracious in defeat she kept the door open, and fortunately so, for about six weeks later the job reopened. Beth accepted the position when it was offered and moved to yet another public relations company. She again enjoyed the work and the travel opportunities, which now took her to Arizona and Tennessee and throughout the Northeast. But once again management changes, this time following the merger of the company into another organization, spelled workplace uncertainty.

Flying back from a job in Phoenix on her twenty-eighth birthday, Beth used the quiet time aloft to take stock of her career. Mentally balancing a scale with the pluses of her career on one side and the minuses on the other, she realized she could no longer overlook the downside of working in an industry, then frequently disrupted by mergers and acquisitions, that consistently undercut her work satisfaction with management concerns. Before she landed, she'd vowed to make a change before she turned thirty.

Beth kept that promise. A year later, she left to become her own boss as a freelance public relations consultant working from her apartment in Greenwich, Connecticut. She placed one of her first calls to her old boss, Laura, who had by then started her own company, Laura Davidson Public Relations. "She was working with travel and tourism, for some of the same companies who fled the earlier company we'd both worked for. And she surprised me by offering me a job," says Beth. Beth initially deflected the offer, accepting only a freelance project from Laura. With two other jobs already lined up, she had plenty of work from the very start. But after only three months, Beth abandoned her solo practice.

"I joined Laura," she explains. "She wanted to pitch a new client but had been told they wouldn't give her the business unless she had someone else working with her full-time." Beth already knew the potential client, a major hotel chain. And she knew her former boss to be both a shrewd business-woman and fair, and they had worked well together in the past, and, as Laura stressed, had had fun working together. Moreover, the job came with two things Beth had forsaken: an office and health benefits. When she started, it was just the two of them plus a part-time intern. She and Laura could build the business together. Beth felt reinvigorated.

Together, they did expand the business, serving clients such as Marriott, the French hotel company Accor, and El Al Airlines, doubling revenues within two years and adding a staff member every year through the 1990s. Early on, Laura made Beth a partner in the business and offered to change the company's name. "I thought Davidson and Walsh sounded like a Jewish-Catholic law firm," laughs Beth. "And I didn't have this need to have my name on the door, so we kept the original name." Beth again traveled internationally, to Italy, to the Caribbean, and in April 1994 to Africa for the first time, beginning what she calls her "love affair" with Africa.

"I was so taken by the incredible beauty and simplicity of Tanzania," she says, explaining that business returned her to Tanzania in 1996 and took her to Kenya two years later. It was then, six years into this hugely successful career stint, that she heard more rumblings from her inner voice. She was again on an airplane, on the return flight from Kenya. "When you're on a plane, you're either going somewhere or leaving something," Beth says. "And there I was, leaving Africa again, for the third time in four years. I'm thinking, I should be thrilled to have this job that keeps me coming back here, and I am, but I'm also feeling like, maybe, the job isn't enough—that I'm missing something."

With new hotels to help open in Philadelphia and New York, the work remained exciting. But two years later, on her thirty-fifth birthday, during that fateful, tear-filled lunch with her friend, Beth said aloud what she'd been thinking for a while: "I have wonderful friends. I have my health, a nice apartment. No, I'm not Donald Trump, but work was never about becoming a millionaire. I love my job, but it's my life.

"Yeah," she shares now, "I was wishing to some extent that I'd get married and start a family, but I don't believe you can force those things, although a lot of people do. But that wasn't the driving issue. I was thinking, is this all there is? Am I going to do this until I die?"

These were big questions, and Beth promised to give them the consideration they deserved. To do so, she listened ever more intently to her inner voice. The key, she discovered, is "giving yourself the time to daydream, the time to do nothing—and doing nothing is not sitting home alone with the TV or radio on. You have to tune out all external influences. If you travel a lot, you have time on the airplane, but it's important not to pick up a magazine or start a conversation with a seatmate; it's important to really let yourself be." Beth has always lived near Long Island Sound. Her apartment now is about a half mile from the water. She often goes for solitary walks along the beach.

Over time, Beth fashioned the first leg of a new life itinerary. She recalled that, as far back as college, she'd thought about joining the Peace Corps. Thinking that might be her ticket to an extended stay in Africa, she attended an open house for potential Peace Corps volunteers in December 1999. Before Christmas, she turned in her completed application.

After the holidays, insomnia struck. For the first time in her life, Beth had trouble sleeping. Now in her eighth year with Laura, she felt like she was betraying her business partner by not telling her of her Peace Corps plans—and, of course, by planning to abandon her to start a new chapter in her life. Waiting until a quiet Saturday, Beth broke the news. They both broke into tears. Beth wouldn't leave until September, so there would be plenty of time for her to finish current projects and for Laura to plan for her departure.

Beth would report to the West African country of Benin. She hoped that during her stay, rather like a Polaroid photo slowly coming into focus, she'd get a clear picture of what she wanted to do with the rest of her life.

She found it liberating to give up her apartment and sell many of her possessions. She crammed the remainder into a seven-by-twelve-foot storage unit. At two hundred dollars a month, this cost more than her stipend in the Peace Corps—four dollars a day—more proof, not that she needed it, that her destination was all about fulfillment and happiness, not about money. Beth bid her friends good-bye, shut down her email accounts, and flew to Benin, one of the world's poorest nations.

Her destination was all about fulfillment and happiness, not about money.

After a three-month training period, she headed off to work in a village called Adjohoun, some twelve miles from the nearest paved road. Her task was to teach basic business skills to local struggling proprietors—tailors, mechanics, hairdressers—who were just emerging from communism. Peace Corps volunteers are encouraged to develop a secondary project on their own during their stay. Beth started a junior achievement program to teach business to teenagers, and she quickly found the village youth much more attentive students.

Beth finished her Peace Corps stay in Benin in December 2003, happy with the choice she had made except perhaps on one count. No sharp picture of her future had come to her while in Benin. She flirted with staying overseas, but after asking around, she learned that expatriates working abroad for international agencies typically hold advanced degrees in public health or nutrition or education. She didn't know exactly what she wanted to do upon her return home, but she had identified a new career thrust.

She assembled a list of international humanitarian aid agencies, and, recounting her Peace Corps experiences during lunches with friends and former clients, she asked everyone she spoke with if they knew anyone in those nonprofit circles. Much more aggressively than in her out-of-college career shopping, Beth sought informational interviews with the contracts that she had leveraged. "You introduce yourself and ask if you can meet with them for fifteen minutes. Usually, you'll get twenty or thirty. You ask, 'How did you get into this line of work?' And your last question is always, 'Is there anybody else I should talk to?'"

Beth's former business partner, Laura, graciously provided her with an office computer, a phone, and a copier to help her job search. Beth says, "Laura would have taken me back in a New York minute." Many of her friends expected her to return to her former career. "Oh, but you're so good at it," people told her. "Just because you're good at something doesn't mean you can't be good at something else," Beth counters. Her job search lasted six months, ending after a friend of a friend, hearing of her employment interest at dinner one night, asked if she'd ever heard of an organization called AmeriCares, headquartered in Stamford, Connecticut.

> **"In the Peace Corps, I learned that it all comes down to the human connection. I may not have changed anyone's life radically while I was there, but I may have given many people a small change in direction."**

Beth went straight to the Internet, saw that AmeriCares specializes in providing disaster relief and long-term humanitarian aid worldwide and, as luck had it, found a posting for a manager of communications—preferably one with overseas experience and bilingual skills.

"I've been here nine months now, and it's been great to see how a nonprofit works," she says. "I admire the way the agency works. There's an incredible collection of people here, in fact, a lot of people like me who were in private business, then wanted to do something more fulfilling on a human values scale.

"In the Peace Corps, I learned that it all comes down to the human connection," Beth says. "I may not have changed anyone's life radically while

People are rarely good at only one thing. Explore your talents.

I was there, but I may have given many people a small change in direction. That's what I want to be able to continue to do—make a difference in people's lives."

Beth takes heart from a Nigerian proverb: Wherever you fall down, that's where your god has pushed you. "I take that," she says, "as a way of saying, accept where you are and realize there's some bigger scheme in your life that you might not yet know. Working so much in the travel business has shaped my opinion of life as a journey. And it's taught me it's important to make sure you appreciate all the places along the way and not be in such a hurry to get to the end destination.

> "**I**t's important to make sure you appreciate all the places along the way and not be in such a hurry to get to the end destination."

"I feel like I'm in a slow time, a fallow period, right now. I haven't figured out yet how I'm going to get back to Africa, but I'm not in a big hurry. I'm confident it will happen."

Beth's Smart Moves

- She seeks quiet, distraction-free times to listen for her inner voice when making career decisions.

- She never misses a chance to cement a favorable impression with a thank-you note. After unsuccessfully interviewing for a job, Beth quickly penned a thank-you note—and six weeks later reaped the benefit when the job reopened.

- She cast a wide net when pursuing her recent career change and job search, asking friends and former business clients for contacts and leads. She owes her current job to a dinner conversation and a lead provided by a friend of a friend.

Fridays with Chaplain Crocker

COLLEGE: Dartmouth College, 2003

MAJOR: government

PASSION: foreign policy

EARLY EXPERIENCES OUTSIDE THE CLASSROOM: internship with a New York law firm, two government internships in Washington, D.C.

EARLY WORK EXPERIENCE: temporary research assistant, Research Triangle Institute

CURRENT PURSUIT: Peace Corps volunteer in Morocco

Chris Curran had already had three internship experiences—a summer on Capitol Hill with one of his two senators from Rhode Island, a spring term in Washington working for the Senate Foreign Relations Committee, and a winter term at a prominent New York law firm—but more consequential was Chris's internship the summer before his senior year at Dartmouth College, an overseas experience that found him one evening looking down on a bowl of bird soup.

The bird in the bowl looked back at him. "It was defeathered, but a whole bird, bones and beak, eyes and everything," he says, describing the very different food he encountered in the Chinese city of Jiaxing, where he was teaching English to Chinese boys and girls at a summer camp. How did the soup taste? "I ate it," Chris answers.

He may not have enjoyed the soup, but he had passed the test, measured up, by adapting to a very different local culture. Chris returned to campus in the fall with a much clearer picture of what he wanted to do nine months later, after graduation. He didn't yet know where or how, but he knew that he wanted to live outside the United States and continue to learn about other countries and societies.

An amateur psychologist might label this wanderlust a reaction to what Chris describes as a "childhood of excess stability." But a closer examination of Chris's path to this career-orienting decision shows nothing so simple or clear. He reached this decision via a true search, a search of self and an exploration of potential career fields and postgraduate landing spots. Chris, the son of this book's coauthor, has made many (though not all) smart moves in identifying and pursuing a career in line with his passion for foreign policy.

Chris grew up in the same house in Providence, Rhode Island, from the age of one on, and he attended the same school from kindergarten through high school, Moses Brown, a private coed Quaker school within walking distance of his home. Summers, from age ten through seventeen, he couldn't wait to claim a bunk at the same YMCA camp on Lake Winnipesaukee in New Hampshire.

His earliest career thought, at quite a young age mind you, had him working as a garbage man. "I thought it would be great to hang off the side of the truck," he laughs. At eight or so, he wanted to be an astronaut. By eleven, he'd set his sights on the presidency of the United States. By high school, however, these career aspirations had faded. He didn't covet his father's job as an attorney specializing in real estate finance, or his mother's job in human resources at Brown University.

A three-sport athlete—cross-country in the fall, captain of the wrestling team in the winter, and baseball in the spring—Chris also wrote for the school paper. He was a well-rounded middle-class kid, but by no means a slam dunk at getting into a top college. Chris realized he needed a hook. Grades wouldn't do it. He'd earned more B+ grades than As, and he had struggled in French, his chosen foreign language. Luckily, Chris discovered a knack for taking tests, and on his second sitting for the SAT, he scored an 800 on the math and a 720 on the verbal. He'd established his hook, and he snagged the school he'd fallen in love with, Dartmouth College.

Sometimes you know the general direction in which you want to go, but the specifics are unclear. The more experience you get, the clearer your objectives will become.

Neither parent, Chris says, tried to steer him toward any specific profession, but he did receive advice about the importance of internships in exploring possible career paths, establishing contacts, and adding lines on one's resume. "My mother encouraged me to do something useful with my breaks from college," he says. "Something other than flipping burgers for minimum wage."

After enjoying the government classes he took fall and winter terms of his freshman year, Chris settled on his major—government—and narrowed his search for a summer internship. He applied, albeit on the last possible day, for an unpaid internship on Capitol Hill in the office of Rhode Island Senator Jack Reed, a liberal Democrat. He did so online, via the Senator's website, and was hired after a telephone interview. Several weeks later, Chris's mother, now director of career services at Brown University, came to visit him at Dartmouth.

"How, exactly, do you plan to support yourself in Washington, Chris?"

Chris had no ready answer. But his mother had planted an important seed, so it wasn't just chance when he soon spotted an ad that Dartmouth career services had placed in the student newspaper, announcing a scholarship available to students who wanted to take unpaid internships in the field of government. Chris's parents agreed to pay for his Washington expenses provided that Chris apply for the award. Getting the funding was never the point. The lesson was to make Chris more aware of opportunities and available resources. As things turned out, the $2,500 grant he received from the Rockefeller Foundation just about covered his living expenses.

Like many internships, the work rarely rose above low-level tasks. "I led tours of the Capitol for constituents, which got boring after a while, and wrote letters to constituents," he says. "I'd look up what the senator had said about various topics, like softwood lumber tariffs, and draft a reasonable response, give that to somebody higher up to edit, and eventually it would get sent out.

"On balance, it was a very positive experience," he continues. "There were other interns from West Point, and through their connections I got to go up in a helicopter and fly near the White House. I got to see a bit about how Washington works—how constituents are dealt with, the influence of lobbyists and interest groups, and also the substantial amount of time the average elected official devotes to fund-raising, often as much as two to three hours a day. And that's when I started reading the newspaper every day."

Day one, however, he got off to a bit of a rocky start—and learned another Washington lesson. During his very first coffee break, he picked up a newspaper and started reading, only to notice a hush fall over the room.

Someone said, "What are you doing?"

"I'm reading the newspaper. Is there a problem?"

Chris's sin, he learned, was that he had picked up the wrong newspaper, the conservative *Washington Times*. "Not the paper you read in the office of a liberal Democrat from the Northeast. From that day forward, I read the *Washington Post*."

He got an instructive insider's view of Capitol Hill that summer. He came to the conclusion that this wasn't the place for him after graduation. "There were some jobs I'd gladly take, like legislative director or chief of staff," he says, acknowledging in the very next breath that "to get those positions you have to go through years and years of low-level jobs, where you're paid virtually nothing. I thought I could find a better use of my time."

Spring term of his sophomore year, he returned to Washington, this time taking government classes with other Dartmouth students who had all lined up local internships. With a budding interest in foreign relations, Chris landed a job with the Senate Foreign Relations Committee, basically answering phones and photocopying documents the first few weeks. During the second half of his stay, the work turned more substantive. Most memorably, conducting interviews and reviewing recent events, he helped update and rewrite a thirty-five-page government booklet for congressional offices on U.S. policy toward Cuba.

Now voraciously reading newspapers and keeping up with current events and hot Washington topics, Chris began to solidify his stance on various issues. Accordingly, he found himself motivated to respond to an op-ed piece in his college newspaper, the *Dartmouth*, which he kept up with online. "It had a fairly extreme pro-choice slant on abortion," he says, noting that at the time, Congress was debating legislation to protect unborn victims of violence

Unpaid internships can be worthwhile if they further your ultimate goals—even when they involve menial tasks.

that would make it a federal crime to harm a fetus. Chris wrote a response to the op-ed piece that mentioned the legislation (since passed) and his support for it. His piece was published. Encouraged, he followed with another op-ed page response, and upon his return to campus was tapped to be a columnist at the *Dartmouth*, the nation's oldest college newspaper.

One of his more controversial articles caught the eye of the new college chaplain, Richard Crocker, who emailed Chris with a slightly unnerving message, the gist of which was this: "Dear Chris, I read your recent op-ed article with interest. I think I disagree with practically everything you say, but I'd like to discuss it with you. Would you like to have lunch with me?" Intrigued but a bit nervous, Chris agreed to meet with him, making one of the better decisions of his college career. Friday lunches with Chaplain Crocker became a cherished part of Chris's college experience, a time for debate and discussion on everything from Chris's latest column to other issues of the day, careers, and life in general.

"We disagree about 85 percent of the time. He's on the liberal side, and I'm on the more conservative side," says Chris. "When you're writing an opinion piece, it's incredibly helpful to have the opposing point of view in mind when you're composing it, to think of the objections that could be raised, and then try to counter them.

Chris had found much more than a weekly lunch mate and political alter ego. He'd landed a champion, a mentor who would later provide helpful career guidance.

This [relationship] really helped clarify my thinking and made me a better writer." Moreover, in Chaplain Crocker, Chris had found much more than a weekly lunch mate and political alter ego. He'd landed a champion, a mentor who would later provide helpful career guidance.

Well into his junior year, Chris hadn't really gotten much of a handle on his career desires. "For the most part, at Dartmouth the only ones thinking that far ahead seem to be the econ majors," he says, "the ones who go on to be investment bankers." Winter term, seeking to fulfill the dual goal of enjoying ten weeks in the bustle of Manhattan and getting a glimpse of law—a potential fit with his government major—he checked leads in the careers office. He lined up an internship with a big New York City law firm and housing with an alumnus.

He loved working and living in the city. Earning fourteen dollars an hour and time-and-a-half overtime, he made good money. While Chris discovered that he liked the intellectual rigor of the law, he didn't care for the nature of much of the casework he saw in his area of litigation. "Ninety percent of the clients seemed to be multinational corporations guilty of doing something bad, and it was our job to try to help them escape with minimum punishment."

Nor did he perceive a future for himself on the other side of the courtroom. "As a prosecutor, you get paid about a third of what [defense attorneys] make," he says, acknowledging that he also lacked the necessary passion to justify a career as a government lawyer. Besides, he had decided that he wanted to expand his horizons beyond the United States and England, where he'd been visiting relatives, and law school would continue to keep him in the ivory tower.

It was this desire to look beyond the English-speaking world that led to Chris's fourth internship, his summer stay in China only a few months later, between his junior and senior years. A fraternity brother a year ahead of him had raved about his experience teaching English at a summer camp in China through a program organized by the US-CHINA Education and Culture Exchange Center. Chris also enjoyed his stay in China, returning to America eager for more foreign experiences and wiser about the importance of speaking the local language. In half-hour daily Chinese lessons, he'd picked up a vocabulary of maybe 150 to 200 words. "I could count and say hello and good-bye and where's the bathroom, but that was about it," he says. "I realized that I'd have had a much better experience if I could speak and understand Chinese."

Fall term of his senior year, Chris gave serious thought to life after Dartmouth. His column for the college newspaper and his growing interest in foreign affairs had him dreaming of writing the kind of influential op-ed pieces about world affairs that Thomas Friedman was writing for the *New York Times*. The trouble was, Chris considered this—and rightly so—"a long-

If you think you'd like a particular type of internship, check around to see if your friends have done anything similar. Listen to their experiences—positive and negative. You can save yourself a lot of time.

odds occupation, like becoming a pro basketball player," and he believed he had little patience for the typical long, hard climb up from break-into-the-business reporting jobs in small-town newspapers to a Friedman-like post at a major metropolitan daily.

Impatience with low-level, low-paying jobs also kept Chris from seriously considering a door that eased open for him in the political realm. This came, surprisingly enough, because of his membership in a fraternity. It so happened that an alumnus of the Dartmouth chapter of Sigma Alpha Epsilon had endowed a fund that brought a speaker to campus annually.

Chris learned, by doing, the arduous task of overseeing such a challenging event. Tasks ranged from booking the speaker (the first choice backed out) to reserving the lecture hall, renting chairs, hiring security, and placing ads in the local media to announce the appearance of senatorial candidate John Sununu. Chris delegated some of the work, but everyone turned to him in a crunch. After both the main program, which was held in a campus auditorium, and a more intimate question-and-answer reception in the fraternity living room, Chris became the recipient of the kind of leading suggestion that many a government major would jump at. "Chris," asked candidate (soon to be Senator) Sununu's scheduling person, "Have you ever considered doing advance work?"

In praising his work and suggesting an inside track to a job overseeing similar campaign trail arrangements, Sununu's scheduler boosted Chris several rungs up the Capitol Hill ladder. Chris didn't say no outright, but his "perhaps" didn't display a great deal of conviction. He was pleased to have successfully staged the Sununu visit, but sweating such myriad details week after week didn't particularly appeal to him, even if it might lead to a more prominent job on Capitol Hill. Chris's interests had changed, and he did not yet appreciate the downstream value of connections. What he really wanted to do now was find a way to live and work overseas.

He talked about this with the college chaplain during their lunch meetings. It turned out Chaplain Crocker had once passed the rigorous tests and the security check for a Foreign Service job, though a health issue with one of his children prevented him from taking his post at an overseas U.S. embassy. He encouraged Chris to apply.

Chris passed the written portion of the Foreign Service exam. The more difficult oral part would come in the spring. To provide himself with a backup plan should he fail to score high enough, Chris also applied for a job with the Peace Corps, despite the fact that it paid less than any position he'd ever considered. ("I live on two hundred dollars a month, if you don't count my rent, which is free," he says.) This proved to be a good thing, for he did not pass the oral exam, a grueling, daylong, three-part test that began with a conventional interview, moved on to writing a memo after digesting a forty-page report, and concluded with a group exercise centering on solving a particular issue.

Shortly before graduation, he learned he'd been accepted into the Peace Corps. His country assignment would come later, most likely in the next six months. So Chris had some time to fill. He discovered a helpful job lead thanks to a bit of opportunistic networking while standing in a line of students and parents at a pregraduation function. Talking with a classmate and the classmate's father, Chris explained that he was Peace Corps bound, but he wouldn't know the destination for a few months. The classmate's father suggested that Chris contact a friend of his at RTI International, a nonprofit research and technology development institute in Research Triangle Park, North Carolina. Overhearing the conversation, Chris's personal career advisor (aka his mother, and coauthor of this book), soon initiated the following dialogue:

"So, Chris, are you going to follow up with RTI?"

"I don't think so, Mom."

"Why not? It sounds like a good opportunity."

"Well, they do health care. I'm not interested in health care."

"Chris, you're only going to be in North Carolina for ten weeks. You have a choice—health care or McDonald's, McDonald's or health care. Which do you prefer?"

It wasn't subtle, but again, the seed was planted. And again, Chris responded. He shrewdly arrived for his RTI interview bearing not only his resume, but also a copy of a forty-page paper he'd written for one of his government classes. The paper, on presidential influences of going to war over the last half century, examined some twenty variables, including both

Networking doesn't have to be a big deal. It can even happen through spontaneous conversations with your friends' parents.

the electoral college and popular vote margins of victory, the state of the economy, and the extent of the president's party's control of Congress. Chris brought the paper to the interview not to prompt a political discussion, but rather to counter what he feared might be a perceived weakness in his job qualifications.

"I knew they were doing research, and I figured there's a perception that if you major in the humanities or soft social sciences, like government, that you're somehow incapable of doing quantitative research," Chris said, explaining that when that very question came up in the interview he pulled out his paper, which included charts and a written analysis of his statistical regression of the variables affecting the president's decision to go to war.

Chris brought the paper to the interview not to prompt a political discussion, but rather to counter what he feared might be a perceived weakness in his job qualifications.

As a college graduate temp in the department, great things weren't necessarily expected of Chris, who was charged with finding out which types of pharmacies and distribution networks proved most effective in persuading HIV/AIDS patients and those with tuberculosis to complete treatment. Though Chris began, frankly, by looking at the job mostly as a paycheck, he soon treated it more like a career, putting in many late nights to ensure he performed his tasks well. As a result, he has a standing offer to return to RTI whenever he wants. This offer he didn't brush off so cavalierly, for the job he'd thought of as health care proved to be about reading, researching, analyzing, and writing—skills that he'd developed through his liberal arts education.

Chris's two-and-a-half-month project ended, fortuitously, just about the time the Peace Corps contacted him with his country assignment. Just as fortuitously, Chris got his first choice: Morocco.

He'd hoped for this posting, two years after the events of September 11, because he was eager to try to understand the Arab world. "I think all of us wonder what would make someone choose to do the things that those hijackers did, and I wanted to get a glimpse of that society," he says. He also wanted to learn Arabic, which he has come to consider a beautiful language. "Those were my selfish reasons. My selfless reason was to do some good and help the less fortunate."

His job, in a town of some sixty thousand people north of Marrakech, centers on teaching English to mostly high school–aged students at a youth center. This time abroad, immersed in the local culture, living in rented rooms in a house in town, Chris has, out of necessity, learned Arabic quickly and proficiently, unlike the French he studied in high school and college and his quick brush with Chinese. He's found that not only have his perceptions of the Middle East changed, but his winding down, twenty-seven-month Peace Corps stint has changed his personality. "I'm more extroverted than I used to be," he says, explaining that his Western appearance and Peace Corps status make him a bit of a local celebrity. "Everyone knows who you are, so you have a lot of conversations on the street because it's virtually impossible to walk anywhere without starting a conversation."

Living abroad and making local friends has had its high points. Chris's students threw him a surprise birthday party, presenting him such gifts as a copy of the Koran, a brass plate, and a fez. As hoped, he also attained deeper looks inside the Arab world, as when a friend invited him to his mother-in-law's wake. Only upon arriving did Chris realize the extent of the honor. He expected to be the only foreigner. But talking to the other mourners, he soon discovered he was the only nonfamily member among the four dozen or so people packed into the tiny house. The women gathered in one room; the men, in long robes, many with long beards, assembled in a room with one exposed lightbulb hanging from the ceiling. "The men started singing the Koran from memory for forty-five minutes straight. I was so impressed by their commitment to their faith, the discipline to be able to learn to do that," Chris says. "I felt very welcome, and when I paid my respects they were very accepting of that."

Chris's success inside and outside the classroom in his Moroccan village led to his selection for a local good will visit from the U.S. ambassador and his entourage. From Chris's classroom at the youth center, the visit moved on to the home of one of Chris's Moroccan friends, where all enjoyed a meal of chicken and mint tea. "There were other diplomats with the ambassador, and over couscous we discussed the free trade agreement with Morocco, and I discussed the Sarbanes-Oxley bill with the ambassador's wife and Morocco in general with the ambassador. Such wonderful, intellectual conversations, I thought to myself."

Here he was, thousands of miles from home, in an exotic land, discussing foreign affairs and issues of consequence that he had informed opinions about. "Yeah," he reaffirmed mentally, "I'd like to be part of that world."

So Chris decided to retake the Foreign Service test. With his Peace Corps stint due to end in late 2005, he sought a different backup plan this time. Knowing he'd happily remain in Morocco, he applied for a Fulbright grant to study the effects of trade liberalization on different strata of Moroccan society. Again, he passed the initial written portion of the Foreign Service exam. But he wanted to increase his chances of passing the much more rigorous oral exam—especially since he had to come all the way from Marrakech to Washington to take it.

Help came in the form of the diplomat-in-residence at Duke University, whom Chris's mother invited to dinner. The diplomat personalized and supplemented the more general advice Chris unearthed at www.careers.state.gov. Listening to the former diplomat, Chris gained a better appreciation for what the examiners were really looking for. He also gained insight into the techniques examiners use to stress potential candidates, for example, withholding facial cues that would indicate how well you are answering questions. Consequently, Chris went into the exam better prepared mentally and with heightened confidence. And he performed well.

Chris ended up being the only one of the twelve people taking the oral test who received a passing grade. That was the good news; the bad news was that while he had met the requirement for administrative or consular work,

> **H**ere he was, thousands of miles from home, in an exotic land, discussing foreign affairs and issues of consequence that he had informed opinions about.

Chris's score wasn't quite high enough for his chosen career track of public diplomacy. He was told, however, that he could boost his score the necessary amount by passing an oral exam in Arabic within the next six months.

Once again, years after applying to college, he needed another hook. Ironically, his hook for cracking into the Foreign Service would be mastery of a foreign language, his academic black hole in high school and college. Although already reasonably proficient in the local dialect, Chris returned to Morocco fired up to improve his fluency in Arabic. Just before flying back overseas, he learned that his application for a Fulbright scholarship had been stamped waiting list, meaning his plan B had slipped to an unlikely option. But soon after returning to Morocco, he made it off the waiting list. In September he would move to Rabat, Morocco's capital, to start his Fulbright.

> **I**ronically, his hook for cracking into the Foreign Service would be mastery of a foreign language, his academic black hole in high school and college.

Then, in early June 2005, Chris learned that he'd succeeded with plan A as well. He'd passed the Arabic exam and received a conditional offer to join the Foreign Service. Assuming that he passed all the necessary security clearances and made it onto the placement list, a posting could become available about the time he finished his Fulbright scholarship. Everything seemed to be falling into place, and Chris couldn't have been more excited.

"I had this desire to see other cultures and visit other countries and be away from America for a while, and I haven't quenched that yet. It's still in me. There's a lot more that I want to see," he says.

"*In sha'allah*," Chris adds. "As they say in Morocco, 'God willing.'"

Chris's Smart Moves

- **He benefited from a mentoring relationship in college,** having Friday lunches with the college chaplain.

- He anticipated a perceived weakness in his qualifications for a job, and he brought evidence with him to the job interview that countered the weakness.

- He had a backup plan, a second overseas option (a Fulbright scholarship), in play should he not pass the difficult Foreign Service qualifying exam.

- He found a hook, a distinctive advantage when he was seeking a highly competitive position, a Foreign Service public diplomacy posting. His leg up was mastery of Arabic, which would add points to his qualifying exam score.

Returning to a Childhood Passion

COLLEGE: University of Chicago, 1988

MAJOR: Chinese language and civilization

PASSION: developing a business that promotes beauty

EARLY EXPERIENCES OUTSIDE THE CLASSROOM: street vendor in Taiwan

EARLY WORK EXPERIENCE: founded an international art company to promote cultural exchange

CURRENT JOB: stained glass artisan and co-owner of an architectural stained glass company

It is safe to say that Emily Carlson was the sole member of the University of Chicago class of 1988 to arrive at her tenth reunion on Rollerblades. Emily was then living and working in the Windy City, though her job at the time, at a small, technology industry–recruiting firm—her first (and likely last) office job—belied the unconventional, free-spirited nature of her career path.

Few, if any, of her classmates swapping postgraduation stories could match her decadelong string of exotic jobs. By then, Emily had acted in a Chinese TV commercial, peddled paintings and jewelry on the sidewalks of Taipei, and even staged an American art show in the Far East. She had no way of knowing it, but she was about to embark on an entirely new career as a stained glass artisan, a fine arts job that has circled her back to a creative passion of her childhood.

Once a city girl, always a city girl, sums up Emily's bred-in-the-bone craving for the vitality of metropolitan life. She remembers most vividly the second of her father's two very different vocations as a Chicago antiques dealer who bought and sold and often restored vintage furniture. Schooled as an engineer, he'd walked away from a secure but frustrating job as a steel mill foreman to be his own boss. When Emily, the younger of two girls, reached school age, her mother returned to the workforce as an executive assistant, first for a magazine in Chicago's Loop, then as executive assistant to the chairman at Sara Lee. Emily loved traveling downtown with her family to go out to eat and to the theater. Until the age of twelve, that meant heading north from the family's home in a changing neighborhood on Chicago's far south side. But after her mother was mugged walking home from the train station, the family moved to Downers Grove, a suburb west of the city, where Emily attended middle school and high school.

"You're smart. You're beautiful. You can do anything you want," her parents told her.

As a young girl in elementary school, art was what she enjoyed most and excelled at. Not only was Emily the one chosen to create the hall bulletin board for her class, but she did it so well that other teachers asked her to decorate theirs as well. To this day, the family summer cottage in Michigan bears a mobile she made in a fifth-grade quilling class, a fish fashioned of spiraled paper.

Emily effectively doused this artistic flame after taking a high school drawing class. Here, she did not shine. She saw other students sketching much more realistic faces and still life scenes. "I looked around me and thought, I'm never going to be that good, and I made a very conscious decision," she recalls. "I'd heard too many starving artist stories and figured, without that kind of natural talent there's no way I'm going to make it as an artist."

Forgetting her past successes in other mediums and defining art so narrowly, Emily prematurely closed a career door. So, like most of her classmates, she found herself college bound with only a vague notion of what she might like to do with her life. After she'd been accepted at the University of Chicago, she remembers a favorite high school social studies teacher asking her what she planned to study. "Maybe French," she replied, saying she'd love a career where she'd get paid for traveling. Her teacher told her, forget French, suggesting instead Chinese, Japanese, Arabic, or Russian, languages increasingly in demand for all manner of jobs. "That's what opened me up to Asia, to studying Chinese," Emily says.

She did, indeed, major in Chinese language and civilization at the University of Chicago. She did not, however, study abroad. "I don't think there was a program available back then," she recalls, "or I really wasn't aggressively looking for one." She did have a makeup plan. Emily intended to immerse herself in Chinese culture and improve her speaking skills by living in Taiwan after she graduated, as soon as she could earn the necessary seed money. To do so, she waited tables in a Chinese restaurant, which she originally imagined would help her polish her language skills. Though she interacted mostly with English-speaking customers, she made decent money. In nine months, living at home and saving her tips, Emily banked enough for a round-trip ticket to Taipei good for one year, and for initial living expenses.

Foreign language proficiency will become increasingly important in a global economy.

But she had no real plan of action, no job waiting for her, no place to live once she arrived in the foreign land. "I am Taurus, the bull. And Year of the Horse," she explained. "When I get my mind set on something, don't bother trying to persuade me otherwise." Her parents were supportive, and, in fact, role models, inspiring Emily's bold venture with their own self-reliant actions—her father's courage to leave the steel mill to start an antiques business and her mother's pluck at venturing far from home at an early age. At eighteen, in the 1950s, her mother left her conservative, Bible Belt upbringing in Missouri, headed west to Los Angeles, and found work as a secretary.

Tears streamed down Emily's face as she headed down the jetway at O'Hare Airport to board her plane on March 11, 1989. She remembers that day like it was yesterday, packing a huge antique steamer trunk, then leaving for the airport. She'd bid her boyfriend good-bye and hugged her parents and was about to fly halfway around the planet. Was she crying about what she was leaving behind? Or the uncertainty of what stood in store for her? She wasn't sure.

She did have someone to meet her on the other end. "Never underestimate the importance of networking," she says, explaining that during her waitressing stint she'd made a fortuitous connection at a fraternity party back at the University of Chicago. Talking with one of the fraternity brothers, who was Taiwanese, Emily told him she was saving money for an extended stay in Taiwan. "Oh, I have to tell my father you're coming," the student graciously offered.

The boy's father, a prominent lawyer, arrived at the airport with his chauffeur, offered Emily an apartment to stay in for a few nights, and introduced her to one of his friends, who happened to own the largest English-language school in Taiwan. This connection led to a job and a place to live, a dorm room at the school, smoothing her entry into her foreign stay.

Her job was teaching English to adults—and she hated it. Most of her students had signed up for the class because their employer had made them. Because they weren't motivated, Emily's enthusiasm likewise lagged, and she soon quit. Lacking any real sense of direction, she began a will-o'-the-wisp assortment of jobs. She taught private English lessons. She did a bit of modeling, unglamorous work being little more than a human mannequin in a wedding gown factory. She earned fifteen thousand new Taiwanese dollars, the equivalent of about six hundred U.S. dollars, acting as a mother in a fabric softener commercial for Chinese television.

Lacking regular work, Emily pressed a family connection back in Chicago and secured a spot in a management-training program at a new Hyatt hotel that was about to open in Taipei. She learned, about a week in, that she'd taken the place of a more qualified local. That troubled her and she quit.

She had no more direction than a sailboat without a tiller. An American she'd met named Mark could see that. Talking with her one day, he asked Emily a number of questions: "Why are you here? Are you wasting your time? What are your dreams?"

Because Mark was a friend and because she realized, about six months into her stay, that these were questions she should have been asking herself, Emily didn't answer sarcastically, her usual defensive mode.

"I don't really know why I'm here. I'm trying to figure that out," she said. "Am I wasting my time? Probably."

When she hesitated at Mark's last question, he interjected, "Well, what are your interests?"

"I've always been interested in the arts," Emily heard herself saying, and as the two continued to talk, she got an idea for a mission that would justify her Asian stay. Why not use the arts to foster better cultural understanding between Americans and the Chinese and help erase prevailing stereotypes, she thought. "Many Chinese think that Americans are just like in the soap operas. We all have money and nice homes, and everybody is sleeping with everybody else," she says. "And, as far as many Americans are concerned, the Chinese are all black belt karate experts." Emily's idea? "If I'm not going to be a great artist myself, then I can help other artists. That's when the idea of representing artists first came to mind."

But her notion remained just that, an idea, for quite some time as she explored ways to make it happen, and began to make connections both in Chicago art circles on holiday trips home, and in Taiwan, while she struggled to support herself as, of all things, a street vendor.

Attracted by a sidewalk display of Egyptian papyrus paintings, Emily had struck up a conversation with the vendor, a Brit, who mentioned he'd be leaving Taipei in a couple of weeks. Would she like to take over for him, selling the paintings on consignment? She said yes. End of job interview.

She did pretty well selling the glittery images, some as large as fourteen inches by twenty inches. A couple of evenings of five-hour sidewalk stints might put as much as twelve hundred U.S. dollars in her pocket, half of which she got to keep. Here she was, a University of Chicago graduate, selling paintings on the streets of Taipei. Emily still takes perverse pride in that disconnect.

Nor were her street vending days anywhere near over. Befriending a Canadian named Alan, who peddled Thai jewelry across the street from her, Emily soon graduated to sterling silver rings, bracelets, and necklaces. She even sold the jewelry on return visits to Chicago, wiring money back to Alan in Bangkok for the desired merchandise, which she sold stateside until it started to show up in American stores.

Meanwhile, Emily continued to work on her art exchange concept, establishing a corporation in 1991, which she later renamed Solstice Art

Art can build bridges between cultures.

229

Source, to handle what she hoped would grow into a brisk business of international art sales. Scouting art fairs and galleries in Chicago and working through artists' agents, Emily lined up works of art to be shipped to Taiwan on consignment. "Hi, my name is Emily and this is my idea," she'd begin. The originality of her idea caught people's attention, but her sincerity and enthusiasm won them over.

More challenging was the Asian end of what came to be called the American Art Festival. "Here I was, a single, female American, starting my own business, alone, in the art world, which is a tough industry, and doing so internationally," she says. "How could I have stacked things any tougher against success?" Lacking local connections, Emily jumped into a partnership with an American woman who professed to have them, as well as access to money to get the business going. The woman shared Emily's Midwest roots, but not, Emily would later discover, her heartland values and ethics. The highlight of this business relationship and Emily's goal of brokering art internationally came just before the two-week art festival in 1993. Emily stood outside the American Institute in Taiwan's Cultural Center as the first of some two hundred works of American art were unloaded. Watching nine canvases, averaging eight feet by eight feet, emerging from an enormous crate, she thought, "How cool is this. I did it." She'd made her dream happen.

> **The originality of her idea caught people's attention, but her sincerity and enthusiasm won them over.**

Culturally, she had succeeded. American art made it on display in several Taipei venues, including a department store. But Emily's partner had not made good on her marketing promises. One press conference and a single small newspaper article failed to attract many visitors to the festival. Sales suffered. Only five small pieces sold. The partnership, which was fraught with other issues, dissolved in acrimony, lawyers' fees, and court appearances.

In January 1995, her dream dashed and her spirit broken, Emily repacked her steamer trunk and returned to Chicago. At age twenty-eight, she moved back in with her parents. "I didn't feel worthy. I had no energy to present myself in a positive light in job interviews," she says, describing the onset of a three-year depression.

During that time, Emily gradually regained her self-confidence and her former willingness to challenge herself. A couple of make-work jobs helped get her out of neutral. She did medical billing and office work for a reconstructive surgeon.

At a party at the doctor's house in late 1997, she met the owner of a small Chicago recruiting company that specialized in the technology industry. By then, Emily was looking to reenter the mainstream workforce and asked about a possible job. "I don't have anything right now," Carl told her, "but if you want to come in and use our computers to look for a job, please do." Shrewdly, Emily took Carl up on his offer; hanging around the office becoming a familiar face, she was soon offered a position. Her job, which involved phone interviews of candidates who'd submitted resumes, paid twelve dollars an hour—enough for her to afford a one-bedroom apartment in a far north Chicago neighborhood. Living on her own and working in an office with young, interesting coworkers, Emily continued to mend.

When her landlord announced a rent increase, she went looking for and found a condo, which she purchased with a $4,500 down payment, getting help from her parents and sister. Not long after moving in, returning from a trip to the hardware store for picture hooks, Emily decided to explore her new immediate neighborhood instead of walking straight home—a small, seemingly insignificant decision that would change her life.

Turning an unfamiliar corner, she came upon a stained glass studio, paused to look in the window, and then pushed open the door. Looking at some of the works in progress and watching the owner bent over a project, Emily felt a dizzying wave of emotion. "It was like seeing a long lost friend," she says. Eying the restoration work on old windows, she thought of her father and his love of antiques. She saw the creativity and beauty, the mystery in crafting a window of stained glass. She saw, as an adult, what she had missed as a high school student: an absolutely fascinating craft with a long and distinguished history that didn't depend on realistic renderings, a hands-on creative profession that just might satisfy her long-dormant artistic yearnings.

Emily chatted with the owner a bit and then asked, "You wouldn't be looking for an apprentice, would you?" Her tone was half joking, but her question was almost primal in its urgency. She had turned a street corner . . . and seen her future. Of course, she had to be alert to it, ready for it, and willing to act.

Emily started working on Saturdays and Sundays at the stained glass shop, at first for no pay, learning from the shop owner, a man named Bob. Meanwhile, she continued to work at the recruiting company, keeping her "day job," while she tried on this potential new career. Having become friends with Carl, she told him about her new passion early on, and after a few months, she asked if she might squeeze her forty-hour workweek into four days so she could work a third day a week with stained glass. Happy to support her newfound interest, he readily agreed.

In April 2000, after about seven months of working the two jobs, Emily spent a week's vacation from the recruiting office working in the stained glass studio. She'd pretty much made up her mind to concentrate on her new career, but she wanted to make sure first—as she put it, "To see if I could handle the change from an office of wonderfully dressed, though casual, women and gay men, interesting and intelligent and cultured coworkers, to a shop with pinups on the wall and ball-scratching guys."

Achieving your goal often requires bold initiatives.

Asking herself the kinds of questions her friend Mark had put to her years before in Taiwan, Emily realized how much she needed to be stretching herself with something creative. That meant a new job. While she enjoyed the camaraderie of the recruiting company and her boss's support, she realized she was "becoming a worker bee instead of a director." Carl gave her his blessing. "He knew how important creativity was to me," she says. "He's been my biggest cheerleader ever since."

Ed, a friend she started dating at the time, watched her personality change the more Emily got into stained glass. "I got happier," she says. "I got back to who I used to be." Emily stayed at Bob's shop about a year and a half, all told. She left when the work dropped off and her suggestions for developing the business seemed to threaten him.

She struck out on her own in late 2000, resurrecting her old business name, Solstice Art Source, only now she represented her own works. Carl, with whom she was still in touch, referred someone to her. That referral turned into a one-thousand-dollar commission. A couple of Emily's friends requested windows from her. Word of mouth brought her biggest commission, a three-panel dining room window. Each of the panels measured nineteen-by-sixty-one inches. From design to installation, which she did herself, the four-thousand-dollar job took a month. "I don't do 'sun catchers,' decorations that hang in front of windows on hooks that you can move from window to window. I do architectural windows," she explains. "My windows are waterproof and made to fill a hole in a wall, cathedral-like stained glass."

Emily was doing this without a studio of her own. She worked mostly in the basement common room of her condo, moving the fume-generating part of the job to a garage down an alleyway. Eager to progress to the next level, to be a more of bona fide business, she enrolled in a ten-week night course on small business development. The course cost three hundred dollars, but anyone who turned in a business plan at the end of the course got one hundred dollars back. Emily was working on her business plan when a friend sent her a brochure for Bill Klopsch Stained Glass, a well-known stained glass studio in the nearby suburb of Skokie. "I met this guy at dinner," the friend wrote. "You should go see this guy."

Emily remembered the name from her time at Bob's studio. They had contracted out a painting job to Bill Klopsch. She picked up the phone, and in her rediscovered bold manner she introduced herself and announced, "It's time you got to know me."

She needed a place to work and, despite her growing abilities, she knew she had much, indeed, a lifetime of learning ahead of her. They talked. "He didn't ask as much about my skills as he did about my personality, my drive, my integrity about fulfilling commitments, and my willingness to work hard," she says. Emily explained about her nearly complete business plan.

"It was a good thing I was sitting down," she recalled. "Because he says, 'Why go and start your own studio when you can take this one over?'" Why, indeed? Here was an established name, an established clientele— much of it in the affluent northern suburbs of Chicago. Emily started at Bill's studio a couple of days a week in February 2002. By June, she was working full-time. On sunny summer days, she commuted the five and half miles to work on her Rollerblades. She still does, and loves her work as much as she does getting there.

But it's not just the hands-on act of creating stained glass windows that appeals to her and occupies her as much as seven days a week. Emily is equally wrapped up in the challenges of building the business that she and Bill are in the process of figuring out how to transition to her.

"My passion now," she says, "is to grow a business that promotes beauty." Terming Chicago "a huge architectural Mecca," Emily feels that by preserving a part of its colorful past, she will fulfill a noble mission.

"I'm in a good place now," she says, alluding not just to Bill's studio, but to this juncture in her life. Not one to regret past decisions, Emily is quick to also point out that her Asian experiences, for better and worse, "are now part of the core of who I am." They are, she says, part of her life's story, determinants of what has followed. "Had someone said to me when I was young, 'Why don't you try stained glass?' I probably would have answered back, 'Yeah, what's your point?' I needed to go through everything I did before walking into Bob's shop to get to the point where I was ready for that day.

"And I'm convinced," Emily continues, "that I took Chinese for a reason. Who knows, long term I may have a studio and a gallery over there, perhaps a space for my own work."

> There's something about living and working abroad that changes who you are and often who you want to become.

Emily's Smart Moves

- **She wasn't afraid to take bold steps,** such as heading to Taiwan with no place to live and no job, or founding her own international business.

- **She learned to ask herself pointed personal questions to validate her career moves.**

- **She tried on a new career via an unpaid apprenticeship** while keeping her existing job.

- To finally satisfy her need for a creative job, she circled back to a mistakenly abandoned childhood passion.

Filling Her Competence Gap

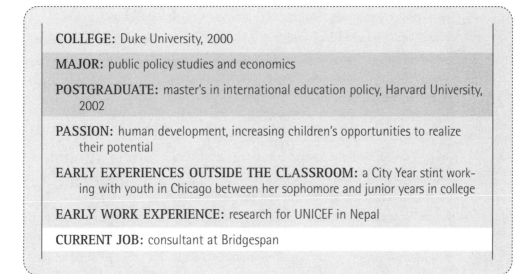

COLLEGE: Duke University, 2000

MAJOR: public policy studies and economics

POSTGRADUATE: master's in international education policy, Harvard University, 2002

PASSION: human development, increasing children's opportunities to realize their potential

EARLY EXPERIENCES OUTSIDE THE CLASSROOM: a City Year stint working with youth in Chicago between her sophomore and junior years in college

EARLY WORK EXPERIENCE: research for UNICEF in Nepal

CURRENT JOB: consultant at Bridgespan

Harpreet Singh opened the Duke University course bulletin with a new sense of excitement. She perused the course offerings, circling those she wanted to take. The circles clustered in public policy. That became her major.

Anyone walking in on this process with no knowledge of Harpreet's upbringing or nature or how she'd spent the previous year would have deemed her selection method rather haphazard. It was anything but.

Harpreet didn't do anything of consequence in a cavalier fashion. She had been making informed choices for years; for instance, while still in high school she worked on genetic research in a microbiology lab to explore a possible scientific career. Now, thumbing through the course bulletin, she had just returned from another exploration. After her sophomore year at Duke, Harpreet had decided to take a break from college, a so-called gap year experience. She'd chosen a job with an AmeriCorps organization called City Year, and her experiences working with youth in a poor, gang-filled Chicago neighborhood had opened her eyes to new career possibilities.

Indeed, Harpreet was turning her career search into a series of bold, personal explorations, rather like a frontier-exploring homesteader pushing ever onward in the search for an ideal place to settle. Unafraid to push beyond her comfort zone, Harpreet's first two postcollege jobs would take her to Nepal and Tajikistan to plumb her budding interests in international development. She was, at her very core, an introspective self-explorer, having come to terms with her bicultural upbringing at an early age.

Harpreet's first two postcollege jobs would take her to Nepal and Tajikistan to plumb her budding interests in international development.

The youngest of three girls, Harpreet was raised in the religion and culture of her parents, both Sikhs from the Punjab region of India. When her family moved to Cary, an affluent suburb of Raleigh-Durham, North Carolina, they were one of only a dozen or so Sikh families in the entire state. "Weekends," she says, "we might drive an hour and a half to a dinner party with other Sikh families."

While her school friends took flute and clarinet lessons, Harpreet practiced on the harmonium, an accordion-like instrument commonly played at Sikh religious festivals. "I grew up not being allowed to cut my hair. I always had the longest hair of anyone in my class," she says, looking back on what she now deems, on balance, the formatively helpful experience of standing out as a distinct minority, even one subject to discrimination. Because of their required turbans, Sikh men, and thus also their families, stand out virtually anywhere in America. "I think it made me become more self-aware, think more about who I am, and made me respect diversity and differences of opinions more," she says.

While clearly not a typical American teenager (her curfew, through high school, never exceeded 10 P.M.), Harpreet was raised biculturally, climbing trees, playing basketball and baseball, working as a candy striper at the local hospital, and traveling with her high school chorus to tour Spain in

1992 as part of the five-hundredth-anniversary celebrations of Christopher Columbus's voyage. She found that three-week trip exciting and exhilarating, further evidence, beyond that provided by her family's generally biannual trips back to India, of how multicultural the world really is.

Visiting India, she had her first glimpse of developing-world poverty and villages teeming with the uneducated. Both of her parents had been the first in their families to attend college. Her father was a nuclear engineer for Bechtel. Because engineers and doctors were respected in the other Indian families they socialized with, Harpreet's earliest career leanings were toward becoming a doctor. She loved science and pursued it beyond her high school classes. At a science and math camp she attended after her sophomore year, she created a mathematical model of Stonehenge. The following summer she landed an internship doing genetic research in a molecular biology lab. A career in scientific research or medicine seemed there for the taking.

Harpreet envisioned heading off to Brown or Penn, but her senior year in high school her father was diagnosed with ALS (amyotrophic lateral sclerosis, or Lou Gehrig's disease). Consequently, she applied to Duke to stay close to home (her father died her first term on campus). She immersed herself in a freshman seminar program on medieval and Renaissance studies while delving yet deeper into the scientific world by landing, even as a freshman, a coveted job in the immunology lab at Duke's medical school. Her job rewarded her in much more than dollars. While doing research on a possible genetic cause of lupus, she discovered, even more clearly than with her past research experience, that talent alone doesn't necessarily point to the right career path.

Talent alone doesn't necessarily point to the right career path.

"While running gels in the lab, I learned that while genetic research sounded like a fascinating and worthwhile career track, the nuts and bolts of it did not interest me at all," Harpreet says. "Toiling away in the lab, working on one or two chromosomes, was too micro level for me. I realized I love being around people and doing things that affect more than one gel, one chromosome. I'm so glad I found that out my freshman year,

Build your understanding of your own culture, and then try to understand how others see you.

Just because a career is "acceptable" to your family doesn't mean it's right for you.

237

rather than in my junior year, after having already decided to major in biology."

Harpreet's next big exploration came at the end of her sophomore year, when she chose not to return to Duke in the fall, but rather to take a year off from her classroom studies. In Britain, and increasingly in America, this student sabbatical goes by the name of "gap year," and while most often interposed between high school and college, such a creative change-of-venue year can prove equally valuable during one's college years, as Harpreet discovered.

"I had spent my entire life in an upper-middle-class enclave in suburbia and at an elite private university," she says, explaining that volunteer work in high school (related to AIDS education) and at Duke (teaching underprivileged students in Durham) had previously shifted her gaze to those less fortunate than herself. "I knew that life is not about a test on a Wednesday. It's greater than that. People are struggling in dire poverty and structural inequality, and I wanted to explore more of that and challenge my thinking."

> **"I knew that life is not about a test on a Wednesday. It's greater than that."**

Taking time out gives you the opportunity to assess what's important in your life.

Harpreet had never lived in a big city, so the metropolitan-based experience offered by City Year appealed to her. Her mother initially disapproved of her daughter's plan because it veered from the accepted track of going straight through four years of college and on to graduate school. Nonetheless, Harpreet pressed on, aided by a supportive email from a dean at the university. "Colleges love it when students take a year off like this. My dean said, 'This is great. More students should take the opportunity to explore before or during college.' I showed that to my mom. It took a couple months and help from my sisters, but I did leave with her blessing," she says.

As intended, Harpreet's gap year succeeded in thrusting her out of her comfort zone. She was assigned to an eight-person team charged with running a youth leadership development program for sixth- to eighth-graders called Young Heroes in the city's North Lawndale section, a rundown, African American neighborhood west of the Loop, where the gleaming home stadium of the Chicago Bulls rises incongruously above the gang-crossed streets. Dressed head to toe in her City Year uniform—hat, red coat, khakis, backpack, and Timberland shoes—most items emblazoned with the identifying words of her nonprofit organization, Harpreet felt safe. "You've got City Year written all over you," she says, explaining that the organization and its efforts are respected on the street. "An addict might point at you and say, 'City Year.'"

Harpreet's gap year succeeded in thrusting her out of her comfort zone.

She was less comfortable, initially, with her level of responsibility. Though the youngest member of her team and one of only two non-African American members, she was made executive director of her project. Harpreet recalls, "There was one middle-class guy from Texas. Most of the team members were urbanites from Chicago. Several were high school dropouts who had been raised on welfare. Some were past drug abusers. One team member, who ended up becoming a good friend, had been a crack dealer. I had never been exposed to the issues that many of them had grown up with. Talk about a challenge. The City Year built skills that I hadn't had the opportunity to build before: communication skills, negotiation skills, and, especially, learning how to manage a diverse team."

Of course, her City Year stint taught her much more. The Young Heroes program took her into the community on Saturdays. Weekday mornings, she and her team planned programs for the Young Heroes to do the upcoming Saturday—neighborhood cleanup days, perhaps, or door-to-door canvasing to increase attendance at school board meetings. In the afternoons, Harpreet tutored low-income students at a government-subsidized after-school center.

Harpreet was assigned a dozen middle schoolers in the Young Heroes program. Though she only saw them on Saturdays, she kept in touch during the week. "I tried to call the parents every week to try to build a relationship. Many had no phones or were moving all the time or the fathers were sort of 'out and about,'" she says, thinking back on an indelible memory. "One boy really rocked my world."

One eighth-grader's mother confided in Harpreet the reason that her son had to miss a Saturday meeting: he was in a courtroom, on trial with several others on serious charges. Because of the incident, the boy was ostracized at school, only aggravating his serious deficiencies in reading and writing. His needs were obvious. Although the children weren't supposed to arrive until 9:30 A.M. on Saturdays for that week's program, this student would show up well before Harpreet and the others from City Year. Seeing him waiting for them, they soon invited him to join their meetings. But when Harpreet learned of his brush with the law, she worried. "I'm sworn to secrecy, but he's a potential risk to others in the program," she said when she sought guidance on how to handle this situation at City Year's downtown headquarters. "Trust your gut," one of the directors told her. Harpreet decided that the boy was not a threat, and by the time he graduated from the Young Heroes program, he'd been acquitted of the charges. "His principal," she says, "came to the City Year graduation ceremony and afterward said, 'I had no idea this kid could do any good to anyone. Thank you for showing me that.'"

Often, transferable skills will come from outside the classroom.

City Year not only provided Harpreet with a street-level view of urban social and educational issues, it also afforded some more-elevated glimpses of public service and public policy work. As one of several City Year corps members chosen to represent AmeriCorps at a national conference of mayors held in Chicago, Harpreet shared some of her experiences and talked with some of the mayors about education policy, learning in some instances about cutting-edge middle school and high school reforms. She found the discussions galvanizing, for they took her City Year experience to another level, that of politics and policy.

"My interest has always been on human development, increasing children's opportunities to realize their potential," she says. "I was starting to realize that perhaps as a policy advisor, I could have more impact on a larger scale, make decisions that would affect hundreds of kids, not just one or two at a time." Unlike micro-level work in a science lab, Harpreet recognized the attractions of such a job. "*That*," she told herself, "I could do as a career."

She headed back to North Carolina ready to shop for a new major to replace psychology, which she'd selected her sophomore year at Duke.

Harpreet hit the ground running. She took two economics courses that summer, and with a much clearer picture of her future in mind, she roared into her final two years of college.

> **"I'm glad that I did that exploring while I was in college, rather than getting out and having no idea what I wanted to do."**

Some of her classmates didn't understand her decision to leave Duke for a year. "A lot of students want to graduate with the class they started with. It was not the norm to do what I did," she says. "But I'm glad that I did that exploring while I was in college, rather than getting out and having no idea what I wanted to do."

Harpreet's gap year experiences enriched many of her classes, such as child policy. For this class, in fact, she wrote her final paper on that troubled City Year student. She also became involved in diversity issues on campus, including Duke's first celebration of Martin Luther King Jr. day as a school holiday. As chairman of that committee her senior year, she represented her university on a panel discussion at the American Council on Education annual conference on diversity in education.

"Though they may seem somewhat random, the various career options I explored were actually very interrelated," she says. "I'd moved on from that very micro-level scale of biology and developmental psychology to studying human development policy and the economics behind it and applying it." She arranged for the latter by landing a summer internship in New York City after her junior year.

Through the campus careers office, Harpreet got a job with the Community Resource Exchange (CRE), a management-consulting firm that helps nonprofit organizations strategize and grow. Observing CRE's dynamic executive director, a woman named Fran Barrett, Harpreet discerned a key reason for the organization's success—the web of relationships Barrett had established—noting "how she really built a community around herself and CRE." The internship also reaffirmed Harpreet's growing personal preference for "working in scale." She notes, "Some of the nonprofits I worked with helped forty kids. I realized I need to reach more people to feel sated."

Senior year, working with her counselor, Donna Harner, in Duke's careers office, Harpreet helped start a pilot externship program for undergraduates to explore nontraditional careers. "The program was called Venturing Out because we wanted undergraduates to venture out of the traditional consulting/banking/law/medicine career routes and consider careers like advertising and journalism that do not have clear recruiting efforts and are therefore more difficult to learn about," says Harpreet. "I interviewed careers office staff at other universities that had a similar program, then combed through the Duke alumni database and learned about the plethora of career paths that Duke alumni had previously taken."

Meanwhile, Harpreet had begun narrowing down her own options. Writing several research papers on education policy in India, she decided that she really wanted to go abroad after graduating. Talking about her intentions with a friend led her to that person's best friend, who told her, "You need to talk to this woman who's doing educational development work in Bangladesh." Harpreet not only recognized the person's name, but knew quite a bit about the woman, Shamse Hasan. She'd written a paper about Hasan's much-heralded work heading an NGO (nongovernmental organization) running schools in poor Bangladeshi villages. Harpreet learned that the United Nations had lured Hasan to Nepal, where she was overseeing the agency's south Asia education efforts.

She contacted Hasan in February. By April, Harpreet was told she'd likely have a job. The contract finally came in June, after she'd graduated. But she wasn't just looking one step ahead. Harpreet also read about the postgraduate program in international education policy at Harvard, then visited the school to talk with some of the professors. Before leaving for Nepal in October 2000, she paved the way for grad school by taking the GREs.

In Kathmandu, Nepal, Harpreet stepped into a regional UNICEF office of some three dozen employees. The office researched and evaluated the impact of UNICEF's educational projects in eight countries: Afghanistan, Bangladesh, Bhutan, India, Maldives, Nepal, Pakistan, and Sri Lanka. Harpreet traveled some within Nepal, but not, as expected, to other countries. "It was a year of unrest in much of south Asia, and that was also the year of the big Indian earthquake," she says. Much of the work, while

Share your knowledge and your passions with others. If you see something missing in a career program, do something about it.

Always think one step ahead, and you'll be better prepared for your career.

confined to reviewing written reports, collecting best practices, and evaluating various educational programs, was nonetheless enjoyable. "It was fascinating for me to look at things at scale, to comparatively study how different countries approach issues of social opportunity," she says.

After a few months, her boss invited Harpreet to move in with her. "We became very close," says Harpreet. "She became like a second mother to me." And, it goes without saying, an influential mentor. For Hasan's work, clearly, stretched Harpreet's sights even broader than before. "Shamse Hasan worked at scale—her program reached 750,000 children in Bangladesh by the time she finished.

"We know a lot about what works. We know how children learn, how to get children into schools. That research base has been proven," she continues. "But we've had a hard time implementing programs or implementing the necessary changes because the politics and policy fields are so difficult to navigate. That requires certain management skills and skill in diplomacy."

So when Harpreet learned in February of 2001 that she'd been accepted into Harvard's master's program of international education policy for the fall of that year, she already had her sights on her next postdiploma job: project management. "Sort of what I'd done in City Year, but on a broader scale and a bigger, international stage. Yet I knew my skill set wasn't there, so I also took classes at Harvard Business School, one titled Corporate Diplomacy, the other called Leading Teams.

> **"I learned the importance of strategizing in advance and building relationships with key people. When I got to Tajikistan, that class really helped me."**

"That Corporate Diplomacy class was one of the best classes I've ever taken. It was all about mastering the art of complex negotiations, and not just in the for-profit sector. We also looked at the Middle Eastern conflict because our professor had been involved at several points during the negotiations between the Palestinians and the Israelis," she says. "I learned the importance of strategizing in advance and building relationships with key people. When I got to Tajikistan, that class really helped me."

Tajikistan it was, after Harpreet spotted "the most beautiful job description I've ever read" in Harvard's careers office. She interviewed first on the phone, and then flew to the former Soviet republic for a second interview. Though uncommonly experienced at the age of twenty-four, Harpreet was still young. Her boss at the Aga Khan Development Network wanted to meet her before putting her in charge of more than a dozen employees as project manager of a broad educational reform project. For her part, Harpreet wanted to ensure that not only was the job for her, but that she'd feel safe there.

"They speak Persian in Tajikistan. Persian is similar to Punjabi, the language of where my family is from," she explains, noting that an additional attraction of the job was the opportunity to become fluent in another language—a rare weakness in her otherwise glowing academic portfolio.

By nonprofit standards, her job paid exceptionally well and flew her back to the States three times a year. She first lived in a nice apartment, then moved into a house with two roommates, a cook, and a security guard. With the cost of living minimal, Harpreet was able to save a significant amount of money during her year and a half stay in Tajikistan—money to help retire her grad school loans. Working with government officials across many different agencies proved challenging, as did managing employees native to the war-torn region.

"It was one of the most politicized jobs I've ever had," she says, explaining that the country still clung to many of the ethnic tensions of a recent civil war. Soon after she arrived, she discovered one of her assistants had been embezzling funds. Her initial thought was to fire him immediately. Her boss, wiser in the local ways, advised her otherwise, counseling that the guilty employee was part of a prominent family and that it was best to proceed more cautiously. "We did fire him two or three months later, but not until we built coalitions with individuals from his family so they understood that the firing was not an ethnic issue."

In essence, Harpreet was now living a case study. "It was a very intricate, complicated way of working, because you needed to get clan input into your strategy, and everybody was very nervous because of ethnic tensions. If you spoke with one person in the ministry of education—who is from one ethnic group—the next day you might be speaking with someone from another group who has a rivalry with the person you spoke with the day before. I learned about the importance of tact, diplomacy, and negotiation in making change."

> **"I learned about the importance of tact, diplomacy, and negotiation in making change."**

While she enjoyed much about her job, especially the responsibility, Harpreet left after eighteen months. She missed her family in North Carolina. Tajikistan really was a world away from home. Communication with America was difficult, and flying back was a two-day ordeal. "My sister was getting married. My grandfather was getting older. I decided it was time to come back," she says. "I'd learned an awful lot, but I was risking burnout if I stayed much longer."

Harpreet returned home in December 2003 and spent the first few months relaxing and reflecting about what might come next. She describes this time between jobs as a sabbatical. "I'd had an amazing amount of experiences, and I wanted to write about them and reflect upon them," she says. While the memories were still fresh, she wrote narrative descriptions of experiences that had made a big impression upon her.

The biggest decision she faced was whether she wanted to continue to work internationally. Looming larger than any philosophical reservations were geographical ones. Her older sister's marriage wasn't far off, and Harpreet wanted to be part of the wedding preparations. "I want my kids to know my sister's kids and have a close relationship with my mother. I was raised within a close family. I do want to have more roots," she realized. "I don't want to move around every couple of years." She'd seen most of her colleagues in international development moving to a new country every two or three years. "Can I," she started wondering, "do international work based in America?"

What I love about international work is what I loved in my time at City Year," she says. "I love working closely with government officials, community members, and nonprofits to improve educational opportunities for all."

Harpreet's next move was an interim job, following a common pattern in the working world. Someone you've worked well with in the past, who has moved on elsewhere, contacts you and asks you to come join them at

> Always try to speak the language of the community in which you live, regardless of how bad you think you are at languages. It's the only way to get close to people.

their new agency or company. A woman who'd formerly served as a Geneva-based senior advisor for the Aga Khan Development Network, and who knew of Harpreet's work in Tajikistan, had taken a job in Atlanta as director of education for CARE USA, one of the world's largest private international relief and development organizations. CARE had just received a $28-million endowment earmarked for girls' education in developing countries, and the woman needed to hire a technical advisor to help with strategic planning.

The job seemed to fit Harpreet's coalescing career requirements like a glove: international development based in the United States. Harpreet signed on for a six-month contract as a technical advisor, knowing that she wanted to explore opportunities outside international development. "I loved the people I worked with. CARE's an impressive organization that even has an internal university for professional development," she says.

Working at CARE, Harpreet discovered a key weakness in her work experience. "I wanted to hone a more analytical skill set, including modeling, costing, data analysis. I'd taken classes that covered these topics but hadn't had the opportunity to apply them in my work," she says. "So I decided to move into strategy consulting. I felt that with a job like that, I'd get the mentoring and coaching and professional development, and some of the team-based work and skill sets that I wanted—and that would help me in the future in other jobs like the one I had at CARE."

While still employed at CARE, Harpreet zeroed in on the world of strategy-consulting firms, limiting her search to firms that served government agencies and nonprofit organizations. Taking advantage of one of the perquisites of her graduate degree, she was able to search potential leads through Harvard's and Duke's alumni databases. "I wrote short, concise emails to alumni asking targeted questions so they'd have something to respond to, not just, 'Tell me about your job.' I introduced my background very succinctly, thanked them for their time, and soon started having conversations with people," she says, while admitting that she garnered one productive response per about fifty emails.

"This is where your alumni network, your friends, past colleagues, come into play," Harpreet continues. "For a while it seemed like every one of my

If you're not satisfied with a particular situation, ask yourself whether you can achieve your goals in a different way.

friends had a friend who had worked for or was currently working for a company called Bridgespan." Bridgespan, a small, Boston-based nonprofit organization dedicated to assisting nonprofits, ended up being one of two firms she interviewed with as her six-month contract with CARE began winding down.

During this job search, Harpreet also sought help through a careers website called Vault.com. It helped her polish her resume for a new field and prepped her for her upcoming interviews, which she knew would involve demonstrating her problem-solving skills in an on-the-spot case study. "They give you an actual problem from a past case the company had, and you have to show them how you'd approach it. Do the math, the finances, the costs, essentially think out loud in a forty-five-minute session," she says.

Harpreet joined Bridgespan as a consultant in early 2005, turning down an offer from the other company, which would have paid her a significantly higher salary. She did so because Bridgespan offered a close-knit working environment and seemed to be mindful of something she craved at that point in her career—professional nurturing, which she had missed out on in her overseas nonprofit work.

In her first few months at Bridgespan she began with two cases. Her initial work supported a teen pregnancy nonprofit organization that had just received more than ten million dollars from two foundations and wanted Bridgespan to help focus their business plan. The second case was on behalf of a nonprofit dedicated to education reform, which was seeking better results by breaking large urban schools into smaller ones. "Both nonprofits," she says, "are high-profile organizations that address cutting-edge issues."

Through Bridgespan's team-based culture, Harpreet is getting the mentoring she desired. "Now, I share the draft of my presentation with my manager, who gives me feedback. There have been a lot of improvements I've had to make, which is great. I've learned so much getting that coaching."

As she continues to build her skills as a nonprofit-strategy consultant, Harpreet will likewise keep one eye on another client: herself. Will she continue to work at and perhaps head a nonprofit organization? Or will she remain a consultant, furthering the efforts of many organizations? Will she remain in America? Or will the broad impact, the scale that she hungers for, take her back overseas?

If you're interviewing for consulting firms, make sure you practice the case study interview technique long in advance.

All feedback—positive and negative—is good feedback. Learn from it.

Harpreet isn't sure. She does know that she's still building her career foundation and striving to do better things in the future. As she goes forward, she's guided by two voices. She repeats the advice of a good family friend who told her before her City Year experience, "Pursue your passion." That's her yang. Her yin comes from her father, the engineer, who counseled her to always be practical. Harpreet says, "I think it's important to strike a balance between passion and practicality, and I think I've learned to pursue my passion and be practical at the same time."

Harpreet's Smart Moves

- **She tried on her intended scientific career field before choosing her undergraduate major.** She did so via an internship while still in high school and with a job her freshman year in college.

- **She took a year off midway through college.** She spent a gap year working for a nonprofit organization, which not only refocused her undergraduate studies but redirected the path of her life.

- **She's continually challenged herself, stepped out of her comfort zone—** first seeking a big city experience, later taking jobs in Nepal and Tajikistan.

- **She's often looked more than one step ahead on her career path;** for instance, she planned for graduate school before heading to a distant country for her first job out of college.

- **She awarded herself a short sabbatical between jobs** to allow time to reflect on her previous experiences and thus better direct her next career move.

- **She continually assesses what skills she needs for the jobs and career moves she envisions—and considers whether she possesses those skills.** If she finds herself lacking, she looks to plug those gaps.

- **She networked in search of career guidance and job leads** via the alumni directories of both her undergraduate and graduate schools.

Following Her Own Compass

> **COLLEGE:** Lewis and Clark College, 1988
>
> **MAJOR:** English
>
> **POSTGRADUATE:** master's in education, international development department, Boston University, 1996; master's in teaching, Tufts University, 2000
>
> **PASSION:** "Besides chocolate? Travel and social justice."
>
> **EARLY EXPERIENCES OUTSIDE THE CLASSROOM:** founded a catering company while in high school; college study abroad in Kenya and Italy
>
> **EARLY WORK EXPERIENCE:** paid internship in Kenya with the United Nations High Commissioner for Refugees
>
> **CURRENT JOB:** seventh- and eighth-grade teacher at a private day school

What kind of a woman would negotiate an Internet Age dot instead of a hyphen to finesse the "your name or mine?" question when getting married? The same kind, it turns out, who swapped her college biology text for a case of upscale beer and, years later, redirected twenty thousand dollars intended for graduate school into a start-up boutique hotel in Zanzibar.

> **"My biggest problem was deciding what I *wasn't* going to do—because I wanted to do so many different things."**

"Some people can't decide what to do with their lives," says Jennifer Kay.Goodman. "My biggest problem was deciding what I *wasn't* going to do—because I wanted to do so many different things." Unlike many of her

249

college classmates, who focused their career choices with five-year plans, Jennifer's footloose approach to her future included no such proscriptive career planning other than what she told her mother. "My plan," she announced not long after graduating from Lewis and Clark College in Portland, Oregon, "is to have as many careers as I can before I die."

She's off to a fast start. A peek at her untraditional resume shows the following work experiences: caterer in Denver; United Nations refugee program evaluator in Kenya; chef and hotel manager in Zanzibar; evaluator of eco-friendly hotels in Central America and Mexico; and executive assistant with a Boston-based aquarium, zoo, and museum design firm. Now a middle school teacher in Cambridge, Massachusetts, Jennifer can, in hindsight, actually discern a common theme running through her colorful career mosaic, which, like most of her life decisions, has been driven by a childhood-inspired passion.

While she can thank her father for her entrepreneurial streak, Jennifer has her mother to thank for her deep-seated love of travel. The youngest of three children, Jennifer grew up in the well-to-do Denver suburb of Greenwood Village, where her father moved the family after leaving Proctor & Gamble to start his own records retention business. "He left the house every day very early and came home at 6 P.M. every night, beeping his horn twice to let us know he'd pulled in the driveway," she says. Her mother, an art enthusiast and photographer, volunteered as a docent at the Denver Art Museum and traveled frequently to Mexico to pursue her particular interest, Mexican folk art. As Jennifer grew older, she accompanied her mother on some of those trips and began learning Spanish and developing her love of foreign travel, which from the beginning has had less to do with seeing the sights than with meeting the locals and getting to know their culture and way of life. Her first study abroad came the summer before her freshman year in high school, living and learning in the quaint, cobblestone town of Guanajuato in central Mexico. "Travel," she says, "was liberating and educational and challenging. I liked having to speak a different language and liked the different food."

> "Travel was liberating and educational and challenging.

Being a good writer, she considered journalism as a career, perhaps humor or travel writing—or teaching. She recalls raising that possible career with her mother but being counseled otherwise. "You don't want to be a teacher," her mother advised, pointing out the discrepancy between teachers' salaries and her daughter's professed lifestyle.

At fourteen she worked for her father as a receptionist. Her demanding job required her to answer the phones for twelve different salespeople, take orders, and do filing. "That taught me what it was like to work in a lower white-collar job, and taught me I needed an education so I wouldn't have to be a receptionist for the rest of my life," she says, adding, "It also taught me I like working, like having money and being independent."

Her next high school job was for a Jewish catering company that did mostly kosher weddings. She started on the serving side, but disliking the French maid's uniform she was required to wear, she talked her way into the kitchen. "That was ultimately much more fun. You didn't have to have on a happy face. And I really liked the creative side. And cooking was something I already liked."

She liked it so much that she and three friends started their own business, Gopher Catering, printing up cute pink business cards bearing a gopher wearing a bow tie and the line "Small party specialists, but we'll Go-pher anything." Specializing in hors d'oeuvres and Mexican dishes, they hired classmates as needed to help them staff the parties they helped host. Jennifer remembers being flattered but a bit bemused when friends taking a business class at her four-thousand-student high school interviewed *her* for tips on starting a business. "I always thought the class was kind of silly, because if you want to open up a business, you just go do it."

Jennifer marched to a bit of a different drummer than the rest of her 850 classmates—not to mention faster. Finishing her course requirements a semester early and wanting to earn the money for a second summer of scuba camp in the Cayman Islands, she landed a job as a bookkeeper for a pedodontist. At seventeen, she was not only responsible for his billing but also helped computerize his accounts. She had a great boss who sang for and entertained his young patients, and she liked being treated, even as a teenager, like one of the team. But again, her job was clerical, reminding her that eventually she would need something "a little more creative that would make me use my brains more." With three jobs while still in high school, Jennifer had made an early start in identifying some of her career parameters.

Jennifer chose Lewis and Clark for several reasons. She'd loved the campus when she visited her oldest brother, Rick, there. She, too, wanted to go away to school, and after attending a large high school, she sought a small college. But the key attraction was the school's popular travel program. "My brother had studied in Nepal for six months. I knew I could study somewhere far away, too," she says.

Her scuba diving experiences had Jennifer thinking that she might want to be a marine biologist. Until, that is, she took her first college-level biology course and realized, staring into a microscope, that biology at the cellular level held little appeal for her. She bailed on her upcoming bio courses, trading her three-term biology textbook for a case of Henry Weinhard beer, and settled into a more comfortable major, English. Jennifer considered this "a bit of a cop-out, because it was easy." But she also saw it as a pragmatic choice. "I knew that having good writing skills would be important no matter what I did."

> **She bailed on her upcoming bio courses, trading her three-term biology textbook for a case of Henry Weinhard beer.**

Her study abroad programs started the summer after her sophomore year, when she arranged through her college to live with a family in Costa Rica. January to June of her junior year she spent in Kenya, passing over Greece, a country she longed to see but figured she'd be more likely to visit later. Then, fall term of her senior year, she headed off to Italy. She loved reading Italo Calvino and learning about Italian wines from her professor, when book discussions occasionally continued in a nearby wine bar. This was her idea of foreign travel—an extended-stay immersion in a local culture. She found the slow creep of acclimation not only enlightening and empowering, but also comforting.

Her final term in college, she took one course on campus and one off—earning her mixologist's license at a Portland bartending school on the

Columbia River. She can't resist dropping the school's name for fun, proudly announcing that she graduated from Columbia, *pause*, School of Bartending.

When, inevitably, her four years of college dwindled down to the last few weeks and many of her classmates felt anxious, perched as they were on the edge of the cliff from campus to real world with no idea yet of what they wanted to do with their lives, Jennifer had no such senior career anxiety. "At twenty-one, I'd lived in a mud hut in Africa sleeping beside a goat," she says, explaining that her travel experiences had taught her to enjoy the unfamiliar.

"I remember being completely lost in Rome, feeling at first, oh my god, this city is so big and overwhelming. But then, instead of being scared, I remember walking down the street realizing that soon enough I'd see something familiar and find my way back. It's like when you get a new job, and at first you don't know the place and you don't know the rules and you don't yet know the people. You just need to know that soon enough, you will. It was really cool to become cognizant of this at twenty-one, when I learned to love the excitement of the unfamiliar."

Craving more travel experiences and figuring she'd earned some time off before focusing on career matters, Jennifer decided to work for six months to bankroll a yearlong round-the-world adventure. Along the way, she figured she'd choose between two very different postgrad options she had in mind—pursuing a master's in international affairs or enrolling in cooking school, possibly in France. Jennifer already knew Spanish and Italian, and from her stay in Kenya, she knew a good bit of Swahili. Having set a goal of someday speaking seven languages, adding French to her verbal repertoire seemed enticing.

The summer after college, she returned to Denver and undertook not one, but two jobs. With the help of a friend of her father's, she got hired as an appetizer cook on the line at what was then one of the city's top restaurants. The kitchen's pace was stressful and the hours ran long, from late afternoon till about 1 A.M., which left little time for sleep before reporting to her second job, with a caterer, which began at 7 A.M. After a couple of months, she left the restaurant job in favor of a less stressful, though similarly long double shift with the caterer, both working in the kitchen and serving out front.

In January 1989, Jennifer began her travel odyssey. She started in London with a childhood friend named Keith. They spent time in Paris and Bordeaux, then split for a while. She traveled to Spain; he continued on in France. Later, they met up in Barcelona, then moved on to Italy, parted company again, then got back together in Cairo, where they sailed on the Nile in a felucca. Next came Kenya. Then Jennifer changed travel mates and continued on with a college friend to Uganda and Ethiopia. There she learned a bit of Amharic, the local language, enough she says, that she can "shop in five languages." Then back to Kenya. Her original plan had been to make it to Asia, then cross the Pacific and return to the United States. But tired of "moving so much," Jennifer decided to remain in Kenya, where she'd previously studied, and would have stayed on in an internship position that summer had she not come down with malaria.

She walked into the Nairobi office of the United Nations High Commissioner for Refugees in June 1989, explained she been accepted as an intern two years before, and asked about a job. She started the next day. The agency's mission centered on interviewing people claiming to be refugees and verifying or disproving their refugee status. Jennifer's first job was evaluating various education programs and helping build a database of refugees living in Kenya. A UN driver took her to villages as far as several hours away.

"It was an amazing learning experience," she says. "I learned more in one summer in that job as a UN intern than in an entire year in school. It was eye-opening because of all the different nationalities, the disparity between the international staff and the local staff, and how poorly the local staff was treated—and how inept the system was." She also saw corruption that siphoned off valuable resources.

> **"I learned more in one summer in that job as a UN intern than in an entire year in school."**

Within months, she went from program evaluator to working for a non-government agency, or NGO, the Kenyan Catholic Secretariat, which ran the education programs. "At twenty-three, I was in charge of evaluation programs for refugees. It was pretty amazing," Jennifer recalls, allowing that she benefited from being in the right place in the right time. But she also stresses, "The reason I got that job was I wrote an amazing report for the UN."

She credits her liberal arts background with providing her the necessary writing and verbal skills to succeed in any manner of profession. She had, after all, walked in unannounced at the United Nations agency and been hired on the spot. She would do likewise several years later, landing a job with a for-profit company. "Yeah, I walked the talk," says Jennifer. "But isn't that what you do in [college] discussion classes. Arguing your point of view, you learn how to articulate your ideas. That's a big part of liberal arts."

> "Arguing your point of view, you learn how to articulate your ideas. That's a big part of liberal arts."

Work permit issues brought Jennifer's Kenyan stay to a close in March 1990. A good friend joined her, and the country hopping began anew: Zimbabwe (and Victoria Falls), Malawi, then Tanzania, the latter because her friend wanted to go to the nearby island of Zanzibar. That's when fate, in the form of a man wearing shorts and pink socks, strode into Jennifer's life.

She spotted him in the airport at Dar es Salaam. Like herself, he was waiting out a long rain delay for the flight to Zanzibar. The man introduced himself as Emerson Skeens and said he planned to open a hotel in Stone Town, Zanzibar's capital city. "You'll need a chef," Jennifer announced, and reaching into her briefcase, she handed Skeens a resume and stressed her catering and cooking experience. "The third or fourth night we were in Zanzibar, this cute Italian invited us to a party and it turned out to be at this guy Emerson's house," Jennifer says. She restarted her "job interview" there.

"He wanted a two-year commitment. I told him I had to return to the States to take the GREs but would come back in January and work until grad school in the fall. He said no. I said yes. He said no."

Long story made short, Jennifer went to Zanzibar for a week and stayed the better part of four years. She did return to Denver, did take the GREs, and did apply to graduate schools to study international affairs, her UN work having tipped her decision in that direction. She lived with her father for six months, working as a volunteer intern with Jewish refugee immigrants, but as promised, she returned to Zanzibar to help her new friend and business partner get his hotel up and running. And there, in a formerly socialist country just beginning to welcome private enterprise, she enjoyed the kind of unanticipated professional joy impossible to foresee in any five-year career plan.

The work was all seat-of-the-pants, learn as you go. Jennifer had to obtain official permits, like tax clearances, riding her bike two miles in the equatorial heat to a government office—again and again, because she never seemed to produce the correct papers. Finally, she burst into tears. "Within five minutes I had the tax clearance," she says. Not to mention a lasting insight: "Being a go-getter American woman wasn't necessarily always the best strategy."

Be ready to take advantage of the unexpected.

The hotel, with eight guest rooms and a rooftop restaurant, opened that summer, and by fall, it filled to capacity most nights. Jennifer had by then invested some twenty thousand dollars meant for graduate school in the high-end, boutique establishment. Whenever Skeens was back in the States, she ran the hotel while also heading the kitchen. She had to train not only her cook, but also the waiters who carried food from the first-floor kitchen up five flights to the restaurant's ten tables. "Izam [the cook she trained] and I did all the cooking. I did most of the shopping, going to the market every morning, seeing what was fresh and designing my menu around that," Jennifer recalls.

Often she'd plan her menu sitting in the hotel lobby, where she could also greet guests. "What's for dinner?" asked one woman, as it happened just as the restaurant's fishmonger arrived with the day's catch—a shark nearly as big as he was, thrown over his shoulder. There was no backdoor to the kitchen. Shark and seller passed right through the lobby as if on cue, and not missing a beat, Jennifer answered the woman: "Looks like shark."

Always hungering for a job that required her to use her brain, she loved the daily, unexpected challenges of running a business in such an exotic locale. "Every day, there was always something to learn, like going to work and having my chef not being able to speak because his voice had been taken by an evil spirit," says Jennifer. For three days she had to communicate in writing with him. "I finally got the local Italian doctor to write me a receipt for three thousand shillings or so, about ten dollars, saying he'd seen my chef, so that my bookkeeping would make it look like a legitimate medical fee. But in fact, I gave him the money to see a local witch doctor, who cast a spell upon him and sacrificed a goat, and his voice ended up returning."

Before long, many of Jennifer's dishes started showing up in some of the other local restaurants. Food and travel magazines covering the hotel interviewed her, as did a reporter from the BBC. She had found a perfect niche—a wonderfully appropriate confluence of her overlapping interests: international affairs and food. Much of her time at the hotel was spent in training—teaching people who'd never had paying jobs before.

"One of Emerson's goals was to make sure each employee ended up with enough money to buy his own house. He would help them get the deeds. I went to so many weddings of my staff. They made enough money to get married. My fishmonger, who used to ride his bicycle around with the fish strapped to his back—a few years later he was riding a moped because he'd made enough money to upgrade." The hotel and restaurant, she stresses, were a boon to both the employees and the local economy—and a model for other new businesses on the island.

Which explains why Jennifer didn't return to America and head off to graduate school as planned. All four of the schools she'd applied to had accepted her, but she told them all no. Her reason for getting a master's degree in international affairs was to get a job overseas. Well, she already had a job overseas, one that to her mind seemed to be making a more pronounced impact on local communities than the problem-riddled, aid-driven programs she'd seen firsthand. There'd always be time for graduate school. She was already living a life that fulfilled her—professionally and personally.

Jennifer stayed at Emerson's House Hotel until January 1993, leaving due to management differences with her business partner. She took the time to write a cookbook about her African adventures. Each recipe has a story behind it, like the shark passing through the hotel lobby. Though as yet unpublished, the project provided Jennifer with a means of exploring her journalistic talents, a career itch she has more recently continued to scratch with an article for an Internet food site and a few capsule restaurant reviews.

Back in the States in mid-1993, waiting to hear from a second round of graduate school applications, her phone kept ringing with calls from Zanzibar. Jennifer was asked to open a pizzeria and run a retail spice shop. She named a sky-high salary (for Zanzibar, anyway) of two thousand dollars a month, assuming their solicitors would say no. She assumed wrong. She accepted the job and moved back to Zanzibar.

There will always be time for graduate school.

The spice store required travel to the mainland, which she liked, and opened a new window for her—running a retail shop—which also appealed to her. To open the Italian restaurant, she had to hire no fewer than fifty-five employees. Here, unlike at Emerson's House, where she shared the often ill-defined management responsibilities with the hotel's namesake, Jennifer was the sole general manager. Again, she walked the talk. She got the new pizzeria and spice shop up and running.

September 1994, six years after graduating from college, she returned to the United States and the classroom, selecting Boston University for her master's in international affairs because of its specialized program on sustainable local development. Her thesis topic reflected both her experience overseas and her career aims: she planned to design a culinary school with a working restaurant that would train chefs and cooks, paying them modest salaries until they graduated to other local restaurants. She met with United Nations officials to help mold her idea into a fundable project, and also traveled back to Zanzibar, to Stone Town, where she planned to establish her demonstration culinary school. Jennifer successfully earned her master's degree in January 1996, but unfortunately, her culinary school never got off the ground. Zanzibar's first elections did not go well according to the United Nations and the rest of the world community, which pretty much pulled the plug on international aid, dooming her project.

Once again, Jennifer had a diploma in her hand and no specific idea of what to do next. Feeling a second round of postclassroom exuberance, she soon headed off on a lark—a twelve-day road rally and scavenger hunt from Virginia Beach to Costa Rica that a friend organized to raise money for endangered rainforest frogs. She had meanwhile heard about a company called Ecotels, which evaluates hotels on a wide range of environmentally friendly parameters, awarding a rating of four globes to the best. She contacted the company, first by phone, then online, and eventually in person at company headquarters on Long Island. Jennifer announced she was headed to Central America, where, she pointed out, they were lacking qualified eco-friendly hotels. She had experience in the hotel business, she told them. And she promised, "I'll do twenty hotels for you in the next three months."

They gave her a job, earning one hundred dollars per evaluation, plus free lodging at the hotels she evaluated in Costa Rica, Belize, Guatemala, Honduras, and Mexico. In early June, back in the States, she had just turned thirty and felt the time had come for some career stability. "My resume was fascinating, but I worried I was becoming unhirable because it looked like I had no staying power."

Indeed, interviewing with the head of a Boston firm that designs aquariums, museums, and zoos, for a job as his executive assistant, she had to address exactly that question. The man scanned her resume and then asked, "Zanzibar? Costa Rica? How can you convince me you're not going to just take off on me one day? Why should I invest in you? Why would you want to stay in Boston?"

Because," she responded, "I just bought a couch."

Jennifer got the job, which did enable her to sink her roots more deeply into an American city. But the job proved disappointing. The week after she started, she traveled with her boss to Amsterdam, but that would be her only international travel in her year-and-a-half stay with the company. She did get to use her Spanish on the phone when the company built an aquarium in Barcelona, but as an executive assistant she made very few decisions of any import and faced few mind-stretching challenges. "I'd run companies, been an entrepreneur, been the subject of a BBC interview, and suddenly I was a different person, sort of like a little beginner in this company."

She left in the fall of 1997, after getting a call from a company in Vermont that ran international programs for university students studying overseas. Jennifer had sent her resume to the company nearly two years earlier and been told they'd keep her on file. "I assumed," she says, "that meant the circular file in the corner that gets emptied at the end of the day." But in this case, her blind job application had paid off, and the offer of a job as an academic director in Zanzibar, while belated, came at a perfect time. She was more than ready to leave her executive assistant's job.

Her boyfriend in Boston protested her move back to Africa. "He spent most of 1998 emailing me to come back to Boston," says Jennifer. Her new African job involved setting up local "experiential outings" (like snorkeling in the Indian ocean), arranging lectures by local professors, and chaperoning two dozen or so students. Sitting in on one such lecture in Dar es Salaam about conservation and the law, she had a flash of insight. Teaching American students about conservation in Africa, she realized, paled in significance beside taking the message back home to the United States, where a disproportionate percentage of the world's resources are consumed. "I wanted to get to kids at a younger age," Jennifer says, explaining that her seemingly disconnected string of jobs suddenly shared a similar theme, effectively pointing the way to her next career move, one that would reunite her with her boyfriend.

"I'd always known I'd wanted to be a teacher," she says, explaining that her rear window view of her life so far showed that "looking back, most everything I did had to do with education. My UN job was evaluating education programs. Then I ran education programs. The hotel was all about training people. I even got my master's in international affairs through the school of education."

Jennifer returned to Boston in the summer of 1999 and started classes toward her master's in education at Tufts University. The following year she got married, graduated, and took a job as a middle school teacher at the Cambridge Fayerweather Street School, a private school in Cambridge that teaches kindergarten through eighth grade. Her second year of teaching was interrupted by the birth of her son, Henry. When she returned to work after eleven weeks, her husband, Brad, stayed home with their son until summer. Teaching, with its frequent vacations and summers off, has offered her a family-friendly new career.

It's also a career that Jennifer enjoys. Teaching seventh and eighth grade English and history in one of the nation's most liberal cities, she's led field trips to the local jail, where her students learn "how trials work and don't work." To reinforce a curriculum on immigration, she has taken her class to Harvard Square to ask people where they're from. She has also taken them to a swearing-in ceremony for new citizens.

"I know in my heart that the best teachers are the ones that had other careers," she says, admitting that while she's very happy now, she's not at all sure she'll remain a full-time teacher for the rest of her working life. The summer of 2004 she took her husband and three-year-old son with her to Africa as she led an educational safari in Tanzania.

"I always felt at home in Africa and was happy," Jennifer says. "But I came to feel that something was missing; having the family to go through those experiences with me would be the ideal. I think my ultimate goal is to take my family with me and do some new journeying.

> **"It's hard to imagine five years from now what I might be doing. And I like that."**

"Kids are hard work when they're little," she says, describing the burden of teaching and being the sole income earner with a two-year-old to care for when her husband went to grad school. "My twenties were all about doing whatever I wanted, and here I was in my thirties totally trapped," she says, explaining that the trip to Africa was therapeutic for her.

While a bit amazed, she takes pride in the fact that she's held the same job for five years. "It's hard to imagine five years from now what I might be doing. And I like that," she says.

"Maybe I'll want to go back to traveling the way I like, which is to go live in a place for a couple of years," she says, adding, "I think my son will definitely spend some of his childhood in a different country."

Jennifer's Smart Moves

- She envisioned her life unfolding not in so many five-year plans, but rather as an ongoing series of career discoveries.

- She learned, traveling abroad, to enjoy the challenges of the unfamiliar.

- She traveled with a resume at the ready and wasn't shy about on-the-spot job applications.

- She didn't rush right into graduate school. She waited until her life experiences better directed her course of study.

- When the time came, she found a job that enabled her to balance her career with starting a family.

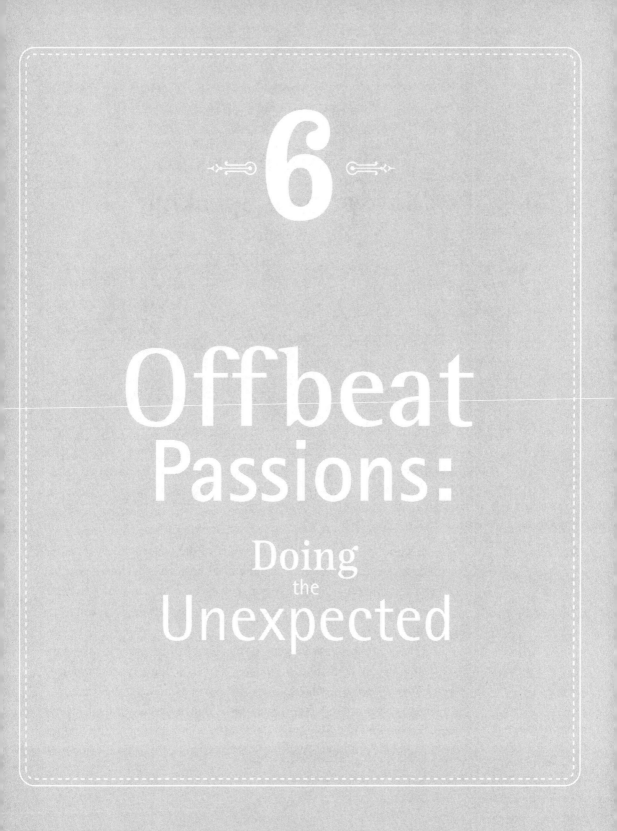

6

Offbeat Passions:

Doing the Unexpected

From Mountains to Motivational Speaking

COLLEGE: University of Arizona, 1987

MAJOR: communications

POSTGRADUATE: MBA, Duke University, 2000

PASSION: combining adventure travel with philanthropy

EARLY EXPERIENCES OUTSIDE THE CLASSROOM: new product pitch person at Toy Fair; marketing internship at Mattel

EARLY WORK EXPERIENCE: sales jobs—for a pager and voice mail company, then with a pharmaceutical firm

CURRENT JOB: motivational speaker, founder of the Climb High Foundation

Anyone wanting an unforgettable reminder of the importance of initiative in making career opportunities happen need only consider the night that University of Arizona student Alison Levine took an unscheduled break from her off-campus job as a restaurant hostess to make a spur-of-the-moment purchase.

The concierge from the nearby Westin Hotel had just called. "I'm sending twelve people from Mattel over for dinner if you can accommodate them." Alison said no problem. Then she quickly lit out for 7-Eleven. The toy company, she knew, had just launched a line of Masters of the Universe action figures and had a big promotion going with 7-Eleven, promoting the toys on plastic drink cups. Thinking she'd have some fun, Alison came back with a dozen cups and made sure they were used as water glasses for the Mattel executives.

Long story short, the execs loved the special attention and asked who was responsible for the cups. Alison had an opportunity to present herself and was offered temporary work representing Mattel at several toy fairs. She parlayed those into a summer internship with the company in California, which helped jump start her steady rise in the business world. In 2004, Alison started her own motivational speaking business, Daredevil Strategies, and founded the Climb High Foundation so she could better pursue her passion in life: combining adventure travel, such as climbing the highest mountains on all seven continents, with philanthropy.

So who was this enterprising college student bound for high places? Until that life-changing night at the hostess stand, Alison was a communications major from Phoenix with a heart defect and very little idea of what she wanted to do. An honor roll student in high school and active in student government and community theater, she might have considered a career in the arts except for her mother's disapproval. "My mom was very much into bragging rights. It used to really bother me, but I just laugh at this now," Alison says. "Doctor. Lawyer. Being in finance. Trust me, when I took a job at Goldman Sachs she was in hog heaven. And when I quit the job to be a motivational speaker, she went around telling everyone I was making a huge mistake."

Alison's father, an FBI agent turned lawyer in private practice, just wanted his three children to be happy and have fun. That's basically how she approached college, choosing the University of Arizona and devoting as much time to extracurricular activities as to her studies. She chose the University of Arizona partly because it was in state and inexpensive and partly because escalating health problems took precedence over college applications and visits. During a weekend ski vacation her senior year in high school, Alison collapsed and was hospitalized. She was diagnosed as having a heart defect. Doctors tried to surgically correct the problem. When that didn't work, they prescribed medication, which Alison took only sporadically because it gave her headaches and dry heaves and caused a ringing in her ears.

Alison wore a medical alert bracelet in college, and stabilized on medication, she returned to normal activity and filled her free time with plenty of extracurricular activities. She was rush chairperson at her sorority, volunteered at the university hospital, and ran a small T-shirt, hat, and sweatshirt business out of her campus room, creating designs for parties or special occasions and contracting the silk-screening work elsewhere. She worked hostessing and later waiting tables on Thursday, Friday, and Saturday nights. "In a couple weeks," she says, "I could cover my five-hundred-dollar tuition for the semester."

Having spread herself so thin, Alison admits she sought classes she was naturally good at—subjects that came easy to her. She chose to major in communications and took some journalism courses. Mostly, though, she took classes on negotiation, organizational behavior, and small group communication, where she honed her skills in debate, argument, and advocacy. But she didn't always make it to classes outside her major, borrowed notes from friends, and generally pulled all-nighters writing term papers. "I still pull all-nighters all the time for work, more often than I'd like to admit. I'm a huge procrastinator," she says.

She figured—correctly—that her major would assist her in whatever career she later pursued. "No matter how smart or experienced someone might be, if they can't communicate—in a job interview, or marketing a product, or trying to get funding for something—they're lost. You have to be an effective communicator."

> "No matter how smart or experienced someone might be, if they can't communicate . . . they're lost. You have to be an effective communicator."

There's no questioning her communication skills with that table of Mattel executives. After getting their attention with the cups from 7-Eleven, Alison used the sudden opportunity to explain that she was a marketing minor in addition to a communications major. The executives were in Tucson to host potential buyers at a local toy show. They asked whether she'd like to help them at the trade show in Tucson, demonstrating some of the new products.

Alison skipped classes for a few days in December to join them. In her free moments, she peppered those she worked beside with dozens of exploratory questions. How did they get their job? What was their background? "I learned they'd all gone to prestigious undergraduate schools and business schools," she says. "I met one woman, a product manager for large dolls, who took me under her wing."

Mattel's next presentation was in Phoenix, where Alison was headed home for winter break, and she worked that gig as well. There, she earned an invitation to the International Toy Fair in New York in January and a pinch-me-is-this-really-happening paid trip to the Big Apple with a room at the Grand Hyatt Hotel. Her creativity, poise, and initiative had turned a glimmer of an opportunity into an instant internship. After earning praise from the Mattel marketing people at Toy Fair, Alison landed a more traditional internship at company headquarters in Southern California the summer before her senior year.

Day one she was thrown a bit of a curve. She walked in the door as employees walked out carrying boxes of belongings. Alison's arrival coincided with a big corporate restructuring that cut jobs—including the paid intern program. She opted to stay as an unpaid intern, covering a good portion of her living expenses by finding work as an extra on the set of an HBO series called *First and Ten*, starring O. J. Simpson. As is often the case with internships, Alison learned more from the people she worked with than from the actual job. Her easily followed strategy: Pretend you're behind the wheel approaching an eight-sided traffic sign. Stop, look, and listen.

"Pay attention to everything around you," Alison stresses. "Ask as many questions as you can in order to learn as much as possible about the path you need to take to get to where you want to be. Once you figure out what your goals are, talk to as many people as you can who are in a position to help you, and let them know what you aspire to do."

She spent time getting to know the marketing directors and realized these were the people hiring product managers. "I started knocking on doors and saying, 'Can I have ten minutes of time with you? I'm an intern studying marketing at the University of Arizona, and I want to be a product manager. Tell me what I need to do to make that happen.'"

Taking initiative pays off in the most unexpected ways.

She heard a similar refrain. "Our best product managers come to us through the sales force because salespeople tend to understand the customer best." Accordingly, when Alison graduated a semester early from the University of Arizona (and despite all her distractions, with a 3.5 GPA), she had a clear sense of her first career step after college. She'd start in sales.

In her first job, back in the Los Angeles area, Alison sold pagers and voice mail systems for a division of a big telecom company. Before her first anniversary in the job she was looking elsewhere. She'd found she didn't believe enough in her products to enthusiastically sell them to others. And also, she needed wheels. Her car was dying and she didn't have the money for a decent replacement, so she started scanning the help wanted ads for sales jobs that offered a company car.

A longtime friend from home suggested that she contact the company where she worked in pharmaceutical sales, a company called Allergan. Unlike her friend, who had studied to be a vet, and most other staff members, Alison had no science background. But she had a year's sales experience, her time with Mattel on her resume, and her buoyant personality going for her. In her job interviews she made it clear that she'd happily start in sales but stressed her goal of soon moving into marketing. A Ford Taurus came with the job that she accepted.

Alison had to study hard to learn sciences she had bypassed in college, like anatomy, physiology, biochemistry, and pharmacology. She shocked herself by earning the highest score on an advanced training exam given one year after hiring. However, she was still eager to move into marketing. And in 1990 she did, earning a promotion that would take her to the corporate headquarters in Irvine, California. In 1991 she changed divisions and moved to work as a product manager in the company's medical equipment division. Four years later, she accepted a temporary assignment in Singapore, this time in a business development role. Thinking she'd spotted greener pastures soon after her return stateside, she left Allergan in 1996.

She'd been contacted by a former Allergan employee who had started a small ophthalmic laser technology company. He offered her a good bump in salary, future stock options, and an upcoming IPO. Dreaming of financial independence, it wasn't hard to ignore the traffic on her daily commute from her San Francisco apartment to the Mountain View offices of the thirty-employee start-up. "But the stock did a reverse split, and shortly after the IPO my options were totally underwater," she says, explaining how quickly her hopes of a financial windfall vanished.

Suddenly the traffic seemed much less bearable; the job less alluring. "The medical laser industry is a very technical field that I wasn't extremely passionate about. It wasn't like I wasn't doing cartwheels down the hallway about our semiconductor technology. I found it hard to put my heart and soul into the job," she says. "What kept getting me by was that people liked me. I was enthusiastic and I could present well." Alison gave thought to her quality of life. The hours were long and now the money wasn't there to justify them. Plus, after a decade in the world of business, she'd started thinking that perhaps she didn't always want to work for someone else. Maybe she'd want to start and run her own company sometime. The trouble was, she had no formal business background. That shortcoming she could remedy. She applied to business school.

But before she took her seat in a graduate-level class at Duke's Fuqua School of Business, Alison treated herself to a month's trip to Africa to climb Mt. Kilimanjaro. Medical advances had offered a new procedure to correct her heart defect, and with a newfound ability to challenge herself with outdoor pursuits, Alison chose an exotic locale and a high (nearly twenty thousand feet) but not terribly steep ascent for her first mountain. She climbed with a local guide, which is required on Kilimanjaro. "I liked being away from the craziness. No cell phones. No email. I liked the calm, the view, and the realization that you don't need very much to get by in life. You can be happy sleeping on the ground in a tent. And," she adds, "I knew that I wanted to do more of that."

Alison returned to the States mentally refreshed for her business school classes—and immediately hit a wall of confusion and self-doubt. "I cried the whole first week," she says. "I thought I'd made a huge mistake. I felt too old to be going back to school. I thought I wouldn't fit in with my classmates. I felt like everyone was so much smarter than I was because most of my classmates already had an understanding of accounting, finance, and statistics; that stuff was all new to me and it was a struggle." She credits

Being your own boss brings many benefits.

her classmates who tutored her with getting her through that first year and on to a summer internship, which for her meant a stint on Wall Street at Goldman Sachs.

In choosing Wall Street, Alison ignored her classmates, who'd seen her creative and funny side in skits and when she emceed events. They told her she seemed much better suited for a marketing job at a company like Procter & Gamble. She held fast to her business school mission of plugging the holes in her business education.

"Wall Street was so far out of my comfort zone, and I wanted to stretch myself, try an area that would really challenge me instead of falling back on the skills and areas where I already had a successful track record."

Most days began before 7 A.M. and ended with business dinners that might not finish until 11 P.M. That summer, Alison worked with equity analysts who research companies and learned about trading stocks and derivatives. She shadowed various employees at the firm and spent time on the trading floor. She liked the fast pace of the business and the people. "They were bright, great people to work with, team oriented. I was in awe of the people who worked there," she says.

Look for challenges that will stretch your capacities.

In the fall, soon after returning to Duke, she got an offer from Goldman Sachs to join the firm as a new associate after graduation, and she promptly replied yes. "A job at Goldman offered the chance to work with the best and brightest folks out there, but what I loved most was that the Goldman employees were not only incredibly intelligent, but also some of the most accomplished people on the planet—Olympic athletes, Navy SEALS, concert pianists, people who'd started and run and sold companies. Bob Rubin left Goldman to become secretary of the treasury, John Corzine to become a senator," she stresses. "Working alongside that level of talent was the kind of opportunity I couldn't pass up."

Having loaded up on classes, Alison had enough credits to graduate without taking fourth-term classes her second year of business school. Eager to climb another mountain, she again packed her climbing gear. This time she headed for Tibet. "Back to the simple life, carrying everything you need on your back," she says. The trip's challenge was a peak called Cho Oyu, a twenty-six-thousand-footer. Alison spent a month on the mountain and got to within two thousand feet of the summit before bidding her fellow climbers good-bye and heading back to business school graduation.

"But you've come this far. You only have another two thousand feet to go," they said. Alison explained she wanted to make it back in time for her business school graduation. She had realized the importance of friends in her life. "This mountain will be here forever," she said. "This is my last chance to be with that group of people. I'm heading down."

Alison was approaching her one-year anniversary as a Goldman Sachs associate, having transferred from the New York to the San Francisco office, when she clicked open an email that would change her life. Although still establishing herself in the financial world, she'd already made a name for herself in climbing circles. The email invited her to be part of the first American Women's Everest Expedition, a climb set for the spring of 2002—only eight months out.

Asked to serve as team captain, the challenges started long before she stared up in the direction of the world's tallest mountain, for Alison needed to find sponsors to fund the trip, plus she'd added a charitable component to the expedition. Wanting the Everest climb to take on additional meaning, she dedicated the ascent to cancer research. A longtime basketball fan, she chose the V Foundation (started by former college basketball coach and ESPN announcer Jimmy Valvano, who died of cancer in 1993) as the recipient. Close to seventy thousand dollars ultimately flowed through the nonprofit organization she established, the Climb High Foundation.

Early on, Alison struggled in her efforts to find corporate sponsors for the expedition. "I'd been getting all these nos, doors slammed in my face. It was just after September 11, a difficult time to get companies' attention," she says. Eventually, a single phone call made all the difference.

A former Goldman Sachs partner named Janet Hanson introduced herself. She'd heard about the American Women's Everest Expedition, and she explained that she ran a networking organization of former and current female Goldman Sachs employees called 85 Broads (a play on the address of Goldman's corporate headquarters at 85 Broad Street in Manhattan). "You have three minutes to tell me what you want to do," she said to Alison.

Surrounding yourself with talented people inspires you to higher levels of achievement.

Alison described the project and her desire to simultaneously raise money for cancer research. On the spot, Hanson offered ten thousand dollars.

"Suddenly there was a glimmer of light. Someone believed in us," says Alison. Encouraged, she pressed on. A friend from business school who worked with Ford Mercury helped her circulate a sponsorship proposal throughout the Ford Motor Company, which eventually led to the brass ring—the company came aboard as the sole underwriter of the expedition.

Managing all these efforts plus working at her job at Goldman Sachs left few hours in the day for Alison to train. She found a gym that was open around the clock and hit the cardio equipment from midnight to 2 A.M. "With my eyes closed, I'd try to convince myself I was both sleeping and working out." Then she'd catch a couple hours in bed before heading off to work that morning. When it came time for the climb, Alison took a two-month unpaid leave of absence from work.

The Everest ascent proceeded according to plan, up the Nepal side of the mountain. Then the weather turned. Alison and her team got to within about 260 feet of the summit. Visibility dropped to zero. The group spent the night at twenty-six thousand feet in difficult circumstances and the next morning turned back down the mountain. Though disappointed, they were overjoyed at what they had accomplished, which included the construction of two schools in Nepal thanks to the money from the 85 Broads network. With Ford underwriting the entire trip, Alison had suggested a different use for Hanson's generous offer of ten thousand dollars, and the idea had been warmly received. Alison didn't yet know it, but she had staked out her next career path.

When she returned home, she started making formal presentations about the trip, initially to various divisions of Goldman Sachs, soon to other audiences in a variety of industries. "Wow, you're the best speaker we've ever had," she was told after one such talk. "We had a guy come speak to us last year. We paid him thirty thousand dollars, and he wasn't nearly as good." In March 2003, she joined several speakers, including former NFL great Lynn Swann, on the dais at a spring training charity dinner hosted by the Anaheim Angels. Afterward, Swann complimented her. "You could do that full-time, make a living as a speaker," he told her.

Hone your elevator speech. You never know when you may be called on to deliver it.

It didn't take an MBA from Duke to get her thinking that maybe she should become a motivational speaker and start charging for her speeches.

She knew that if she remained at Goldman Sachs she wouldn't be able to pursue her growing dual passion, that of combining her love of adventure travel with raising money for worthwhile causes. The job was too demanding, and she could hardly keep asking for extended leaves of absence. As a motivational speaker, Alison could command her own schedule—take speaking engagements that fit her expedition schedule.

One reason she'd acquired her MBA was to be prepared if she ever started her own business. The business would be her speaking services—a business with no inventory to manage. You don't need to warehouse enthusiasm and well-chosen words. No employees to hire. No office to rent. She could work from home. It seemed she'd been preparing for this all along. Her communications major, her time in sales and marketing, her MBA, and her brief finance career all made the leap to motivational speaker possible.

> **I**t seemed she'd been preparing for this all along. Her communications major, her time in sales and marketing, her MBA, and her brief finance career all made the leap to motivational speaker possible.

"I totally customize every presentation for the particular audience and industry. Because I went to business school, I know to do the research and figure out industry trends and analyze the competition," she says. She starts with, "'How climbing Mt. Everest is like working at . . . (whatever company).' If the company has undergone a reorganization lately, the theme might be dealing with a changing environment. If they've had to cut resources, you talk about doing more with less, learning to get by with just the necessities, like in the mountains, you get by with what you carry on your back. If you're talking to an investment bank, you talk about managing risk and return and using good judgment and knowing when to walk away from a deal." Like she and her team did on Mt. Everest, prudently turning their backs on the summit. And like she did when she left a secure job in finance.

In early 2004, after leaving Goldman Sachs and serving as deputy finance director on Arnold Schwarzenegger's gubernatorial campaign, Alison took on the new challenge of building her own speaking business. "It was pretty scary at first," she admits, explaining the importance of her low cost of living. She lives in a rent-controlled apartment and she's been driving the same car for seventeen years. The odometer on her BMW froze years ago at 126,000 miles. Top speaking engagements can earn her as much as fifteen thousand dollars for a single one-hour speech. For those gigs, she flies business class and stays in nice hotels. But those engagements are few and far between.

Alison is now beginning to achieve success as a motivational speaker. That's a good thing, because she's using the money for a cause that's very important to her: helping the women in the regions where she climbs. "In 2005, I went to the Rwenzori to help train local women to work as porters in the mountains so they can establish themselves in a sustainable career and can become financially independent," she says, explaining that she took along a documentary filmmaker to record those efforts. "We hope the film, which follows seven local women who are working in the mountains for the very first time, will bring more awareness to the struggle of Ugandan women. Women there have no land rights, no property rights. They are actually considered to be the property of men."

To edit and produce the film and hopefully premier it at a film festival, Alison explains, first requires raising as much as one hundred thousand dollars, and for that she needs a trailer, the film world's equivalent of a demo reel. "It's really challenging trying to get a documentary film made because I've never done it before," she says. But as with starting a new career as a motivational speaker, she's brimming with confidence. A big success, like the Mt. Everest trip, she agrees, sticks with you, empowers you for future challenges.

> **A** big success, like the Mt. Everest trip, she agrees, sticks with you, empowers you for future challenges.

"I think I'm in a very good place right now," Alison says, assessing her new solo career with its long start-up hours. "I can't remember the last time I went out on a Friday or a Saturday night," she says. "My new boyfriend is like, 'Wow, you're really busy. Is your life always like this?'

"I have this disease," she continues. "I can't say no to people. She confesses to days with two breakfast meetings, two lunch meetings, a dinner meeting, and maybe an evening meeting over coffee.

"I'm going to have to start learning the art of saying no," she says. But in the very next breath she admits she finds it hard not to assist those who ask for advice. She remembers, not that long ago, during her internship at Mattel, asking the very same, career-starting questions.

Alison's Smart Moves

- **She effectively created her own summer internship,** adroitly showcasing her communication skills to a dozen Mattel executives she seated in the restaurant where she worked as a hostess.

- **Trying to find the best path to a job in marketing, she showered questions upon those with marketing jobs:** How did they get their job? What background should she have? What skills would be most helpful?

- **She has continually sought experiences outside her comfort zone**—both job experiences and recreational pursuits. Succeeding at major challenges has imparted a glow of confidence that she transfers to other endeavors.

- **She has reoriented her career, becoming her own boss, to better pursue a newfound passion.**

Say "Cheese"!

COLLEGE: Yale University, 2000

MAJOR: American studies and art history

PASSION: food

EARLY EXPERIENCES OUTSIDE THE CLASSROOM: summer internships at MOMA in New York and a direct marketing firm in Washington

EARLY WORK EXPERIENCE: marketing consultant for a dying dot-com

CURRENT JOB: director of wholesale and importing, Murray's Cheese Shop

As a high school student, Liz Thorpe portaged through forested wilderness and braved raging rapids while canoeing in Canada. But now, nearly two years after graduating from Yale, her spunk and self-confidence seemed to have left her.

After the first of two unsatisfactory Internet jobs, she had looked deep inside herself, plumbing for what grabbed her interest, what gave her pleasure, hoping to discover a career that might overlap those interests. In fact, she found something, explored some options, and even got a job offer. But then she backed off. "Common sense," she says, led her to ignore a budding, unconventional choice and sign on with another Internet firm. She took the "easy" choice, the desk job in an office cubicle, "the vision of work that's presented to most people." In other words, she took the road more often traveled. And here she was, unhappy once more, feeling stuck and unable to address her stagnating career, until her boyfriend invited her to dinner.

"There's this restaurant I really want to take you to," he said, "but they only had a reservation at ten o'clock, so I also made another reservation at another place in case you want to eat earlier."

Liz was thinking, "There's only one restaurant in New York that I'd wait until ten o'clock to eat at." As if reading her mind, her boyfriend named it—the city's latest hot new eatery, Artisanal. "I hear they have a lot of cheeses," he said. "I thought you might like it."

"We went, and it was incredible," Liz recalls. "We had just wine and cheese for dinner until about 12:30. One cheese was Wabash Cannonball, made by Judy Schad in Indiana. I liked it so much we bought some to take home." That evening changed her life; it captivated her, motivated her, and helped empower her to grab for that career thread she had previously dropped. "I decided," says the current wholesale buyer at Murray's Cheese Shop in Greenwich Village, "to take a stab at cheese."

There's plenty of food for thought in Liz's zigzag, faltering, but ultimately successful path to what she now views as a dream job. Her story begins in North Haven, Connecticut, where she grew up as the only child of parents who worked for and then owned a small publishing company aptly named the Shoestring Press. "Books were the standard form of entertainment [in my house]," Liz recalls. "We had one broken-down television and no cable." She started reading on her own at three or four and always did well in school.

She did so well, in fact, that she qualified for a cooperative study program at nearby Yale University while still in high school. Given the thick Yale class guide to choose from, Liz picked a Renaissance and religious studies class her junior year and followed that with a survey course on literature her senior year. She found the experience liberating, enlightening, and initially a bit frightening. "I remember feeling sick to my stomach, being scared I would sound stupid," she says, "but it never crossed my mind not to go."

To the extent that she thought about possible careers in high school, Liz kicked around two options: lawyer and college professor. "Law seemed exciting and slightly glamorous but also sort of intellectually respectable. It's all about talking and writing—and I was good at those things. A professor was an intellectual; I'd teach and write."

Sometimes you need to overcome your insecurities to truly develop your potential.

She did, however, know how she wanted to spend her high school summers. She had such a good time during two weeks at a white-water canoeing camp in Maine that she returned the next summer for four weeks and the following summer for eight weeks. That summerlong trip, in canvas canoes made at the camp, took her to Indian reservation lands in Quebec so remote that supplies had to be periodically dropped in by airplane. "It was incredibly bare-bones. We carried everything and had to portage. It was very physically and mentally demanding," she says. She remembers being in the stern of a canoe facing a set of rapids. Four canoes in front of her had already attempted them—and tipped, dumping paddlers and gear into the cold rushing water. Liz exchanged a quick glance with the boy in the bow of her canoe and said, "Let's go."

She picked the route. They paddled safely through the rapids. She learned then a lesson that has helped her later in life making job and career choices: "Trust your gut. Take risks. I'm aware that something is difficult or a risk,

"Trust your gut. Take risks."

but I just do it if it feels right. I think that's part of my personality. My parents never suggested there was anything I could not do."

After deciding to attend Yale, an easy choice, Liz studied what interested her, double majoring in art history and American studies. Graduation and the notion of a career seemed far off. But one summer Liz did find an internship in a relevant field. Visiting the websites of several New York City museums, Liz identified summer openings at the Guggenheim, the Whitney, and the Museum of Modern Art. She called, sent in her resume, and went for interviews. She accepted an internship at MOMA.

There, she helped with educational programming for visiting high school students, doing everything from alphabetizing slides to developing materials for teachers who brought visiting classes. Keeping her eyes open beyond her rather limited work responsibilities, Liz learned something important that summer—that the inner workings of a museum, the politics didn't appeal to her.

The following summer, after arranging to house-sit in the nation's capital, she turned to the careers office at Yale to help her find a D.C. internship.

Thumbing through a binder full of offerings, she spotted a direct marketing firm that specialized in helping nonprofit organizations raise money. "Marketing means writing. I can probably do that," she thought. The world of direct marketing did not capture her interest, but Liz nevertheless considered the summer a valuable experience.

"You get glimpses of things," she says, speaking of internships. "I knew I was a good writer, but that summer I learned I could write in different applications." A small point? Hardly. A couple years later that knowledge would act like a booster rocket on her career.

But senior year at Yale, in her mind the word "career" still looked like this: career????

"Basically I hit panic mode," she says. "The way our society works is, up until you're twenty-one or so, everything is laid out for you. After second grade you go to third grade. After middle school comes high school. Most kids want to get into the best college they can. The next step is always very clear. Then, all of a sudden, you're on the cusp of graduating from college—and what do you do? And how do you know what you might want to do? How do you understand what your options are?"

Like many of her classmates, Liz reflexively interviewed with several New York consulting firms. She did know that she wanted to work in New York City after she graduated. But she'd heard from friends in consulting jobs that the hours were long, and the idea of making PowerPoint presentations didn't excite her. An Internet company job she learned about at a career fair in the spring seemed much more to her liking. The Philadelphia-based company was about to open a Manhattan office. In the spring of 2000, Internet companies were flying high. Liz recalls, "It was all about smart young kids who were not playing by the rules, playing foosball in the office, having bagel Fridays, and functioning independently and creatively while making insane amounts of money."

Liz was promised stock options. Her starting salary of fifty thousand dollars was more than her mother earned as head of the family's publishing company at age fifty-seven. (Liz's father died when she was sixteen.) But Liz hated her job. Her faltering company had no new clients. She had virtually nothing to do from the time she arrived in the morning until she

> The word "career" can be really scary. It's important to realize that first jobs do not define your future.

left at the end of the day. "Hey, enjoy it while you can. It's going to hit the fan any day, and you'll be working till 2 A.M.," her coworkers told her.

Liz soon grew tired of surfing the Net all day at work, spending much of her time at a wedding site called TheKnot.com. She and her boyfriend had been talking about getting married, but as the months dragged on, they began to fight as she grew bored, unchallenged, and increasingly depressed and testy. *He* was moving up in his job, doing website work at a law firm. *She* was going nowhere, doing nothing.

"I was like a deer in the headlights. I felt like my glory was fading. I had no idea what was going on, what to do. When you're a high achiever and not achieving . . ." she pauses. "I was embarrassed that I was not succeeding. I felt like something must be wrong with me."

Liz's lack of workplace experience swirled these thoughts in her head: "What I'm used to is going to class for three hours a day and hanging out with my friends. Now I have to get up at 7 A.M. every day and sit at a desk until 6 P.M. Everybody says work sucks. Maybe this is what it's like to work. Maybe it's really horrible."

Six months after being hired, Liz lost her job along with everyone else in the office. "It was a blessing because I probably would have stayed another six months," she says, admitting that inertia kept her foolishly hoping that things might get better instead of looking for another job. "Making a change in your life is incredibly hard, especially when you don't know where to go. It's like being in a bad relationship. Even if the status quo makes you feel depressed and demoralized, at least it's familiar."

> "Making a change in your life is incredibly hard, especially when you don't know where to go.

She received two weeks' severance pay and started interviewing with other dot-coms. With more hours in the day to call her own, Liz found herself taking great pleasure in shopping for food—meat at the butcher's, bread at the baker's—in her largely Italian neighborhood in the Cobble Hill section of Brooklyn. As a young girl, she'd enjoyed grocery shopping with her father. They'd split the list in two and each fill a cart. Saturdays often meant a slow-simmering pot of homemade tomato sauce on the stove. Those rituals, those smells, had became part of her. In college, Liz had shopped for and cooked most of the meals at the off-campus apartment she shared with three other girls. Senior year, she threw lots of dinner parties. "We'd have wine, a wonderful meal, and stay up late and talk," she says. Such memories, along with in the food capital of America, got her to thinking. "I really like this. Maybe I could do this somehow for a living. But how? She wasn't really even sure what *this* was. Only that it had something to do with food.

Buying some cheese at a well-stocked counter at one of her local markets, Liz picked up a book called the *Cheese Primer* by Steven Jenkins. Jenkins, she knows now, "is the person who 'made' cheese in America. He's to cheese what Bill Gates is to computers." But she didn't yet know that when she impulsively reached for the phone and called Fairways Markets, Jenkins's base of operations, and left a phone message, something along the lines of "I recently graduated from Yale and was just laid off from work. I think I might be interested in cheese. Can I come talk with you?"

> **"I recently graduated from Yale and was just laid off from work. I think I might be interested in cheese. Can I come talk with you?"**

> It's a challenge turning passions into careers, especially if they're off the beaten path.

Amazingly, Jenkins returned her call and invited her to his flagship store on the Upper West Side. He spent about forty-five minutes with her and showed her the store's legendary cheese counter. What was Liz expecting? What was she hoping might happen?

A bit of Cinderella, actually: "I think I was hoping he'd say, 'You young, smart, enthusiastic person, let me take you under my wing, and you can learn about cheese.'" Minus the fairy-tale glow, that's pretty much what he did say. Jenkins offered Liz a job behind the cheese counter at minimum wage. Liz thanked him and told him she'd get back to him.

"I like to say that I declined because of the college loans I had to pay, but I totally panicked." She admits, thinking, "This is so wrong. You don't go to an Ivy League school, have your parents shell out $120,000, and then work behind a counter for minimum wage with a bunch of middle-aged men. That wasn't where someone like me was supposed to end up."

Where she did end up was at another Internet firm. The company, Thought-bubble, specialized in online promotional work for the TV and film industry. Liz sat in on strategy meetings to land such high-profile jobs as *Buffy the Vampire Slayer* and the Smithsonian's Air and Space Museum, and then she helped write the proposal to land the business. "The company was run by incredibly

> **"You** don't go to an Ivy League school, have your parents shell out $120,000, and then work behind a counter for minimum wage."

smart people who did really excellent work," she says. "But they expanded too quickly and had more employees and space than business to support it." As at her previous Internet job, there wasn't enough work, and though she survived three rounds of layoffs in her year and a half with the company, Liz knew that she needed to get out.

She had applied to graduate school when her boyfriend took her out for that memorable dinner, prompting her to call another New York cheese icon, Rob Kaufelt, owner of Murray's Cheese in Greenwich Village. She hadn't been to Kaufelt's tiny shop, which specialized in fine cheeses and other gourmet food items. But she knew of the store's reputation as a foodies' mecca. When she met with Kaufelt, he asked her why she didn't bring a resume with her.

"Because I didn't come for a job. I came to learn about cheese," Liz answered.

"Well, if you want to learn, there's an event in two hours in Union Square," he told her. "We're providing some cheese for a wine and cheese tasting. You can go work it if you want to." She said yes. And a good thing, too, for on the way to the event she called home, only to learn that she had been rejected from graduate school.

"This is smoked ricotta from the Veneto," Liz said that evening, passing out samples and enjoying the work, which she found exciting and glamorous. Kaufelt offered her a job—working behind the cheese counter for minimum wage. And this time, Liz accepted.

Rejection from graduate school is not necessarily a bad thing. It can send your career in a whole new direction.

What was different? A bit more seasoned in the workplace, she felt less averse to starting at the bottom, to paying her dues. She also eased into the job by starting part-time, working a few days a week at Murray's, and supplementing her low wages by working a second part-time job. Her boss at Thoughtbubble had moved to CNBC and asked her to work for her in the ad sales department. So Liz split her days between the two jobs.

She quickly began to master the wide array of cheeses at Murray's. For example, there's no such thing as just cheddar. "Is it Montgomery cheddar or Grafton cheddar? American cheddar or English cheddar? How long is it aged? Is it pasteurized?" She learned about the cheeses, how to cut them properly, and how to deal with the steady stream of customers. There was plenty to like.

"I loved not being at a desk," she says. "I loved walking into this cramped little space where the smell of three hundred cheeses cohabited in a pervasive cloud: meaty, milky, nutty, toasty, stinky, all hanging out together. I loved talking to people. There was something liberating about it. To this day, one of my greatest joys is going to work in jeans and a top and sneakers. There's classic rock on the radio. You don't have to posture. There's not your professional self and your personal self."

Her job at CNBC provided a safety net while Liz pursued this educated risk. The cushion was psychological as well as financial, for Liz had yet to fully accept the disconnect in an Ivy League graduate ringing up cheese by the quarter pound. At parties, if someone asked her what she did, she'd mention first her CNBC job then add she was "sort of learning about cheese on the side."

By June 2000, after a couple months of part-time status at Murray's, Liz reached a crossroads. Her boss at CNBC would be happy to bring Liz aboard full-time at one hundred thousand dollars a year. Or she could work full-time at Murray's, fifty hours a week, for about one-fourth the money. Following her passion, and not what she'd previously considered common sense, Liz took the rockier, less well-worn road, and as in the Frost poem, that has made all the difference.

That's not to say there haven't been bumps along the way. In fact, Liz lasted only six weeks working full-time at Murray's before, exhausted and

Sometimes you just have to pay your dues.

Your work environment is important. Choose wisely.

minus a social life, she switched back to part-time. All those hours on her feet were tough. So, too, the erratic nature of her schedule—rarely two days off back-to-back and work on weekends, when her friends were off. She'd discovered how much she valued and missed predictability and structure in her life.

Before long, thanks to a combination of her own initiative and simple good fortune, she transitioned into a different role at Murray's that gave her both predictability and structure and confirmed her bold career move. Late in the summer of 2002, she overheard Kaufelt talking to another employee. Kaufelt had been invited to speak at a conference about the naming of American cheeses, and he needed someone to do some writing for him.

Passion trumps money any day.

Spotting an opportunity, Liz researched the topic, writing about names like a Connecticut farm cheese called Hooligan, which fits its soft, runny, sticky nature, and Old Chatham Camembert, whose name she deemed a poor fit since it diverged from the traditional French variety. Kaufelt liked what she presented. With that success duly noted, Liz soon began writing descriptions for new cheeses at Murray's.

Know your strengths well, cultivate them, and reap their benefits.

She enjoyed the challenge of writing about cheese, putting her growing knowledge into words. "I know I'm good at that," she says, "but he didn't know. No one at Murray's had seen me write." In so doing, Liz distinguished herself from others behind the counter, showing her potential for other jobs. Kaufelt talked about training her to be a store manager. Liz, however, did not aspire to manage a

> **Liz distinguished herself from others behind the counter, showing her potential for other jobs.**

counter crew. Meanwhile, she kept reading her way through the store's shelves of cheese books and educating her palate, learning deeply in one area, a lesson from college, all the while thinking about possibly opening a wine and cheese bar back in New Haven.

In late January 2003, she caught a career break—and jumped on it immediately. The woman who had run Murray's wholesale department was headed back to France. Liz volunteered herself. "Why don't I run the department?" she suggested. Selling to restaurants would not only be more glamorous than standing behind the cheese counter, but with its more predictable, normal workweek schedule, it would eliminate her still-vexing issue about full-time employment at Murray's.

About a month later, Kaufelt agreed and told her to start training with the interim wholesale manager, the former second-in-command, who was herself about to leave Murray's to become a cheese maker. "Ninety percent of it was luck and 10 percent having the guts to say I wanted it," she says.

Liz's satisfying career in food had suddenly revealed itself. She has been happily running Murray's wholesale department ever since. As such, she oversees a small staff that sells to some 150 restaurants nationwide, about two-thirds of them in New York City. She conducts training sessions for the kitchen and waitstaffs of some of the top restaurants in the nation. In September 2003, she spent a week in Spain visiting cheese makers, eating in three-star Michelin restaurants, and serving as the lone female and only American judge at a prestigious local cheese competition. "That was pretty cool," she says, acknowledging that those dues she paid behind the counter are now paying dividends.

Liz has found a niche that she's good at in a field she enjoys. From 2003 to 2004, she helped increase Murray's wholesale business 20 percent. From 2004 to 2005, she boosted sales 35 percent. Continually leveraging her abilities, she has become increasingly in charge of buying decisions. At her urging, the entire staff tastes and rates newly arrived cheeses on a scale of one to five. Liz tallies the ratings and generally decides which varieties make it behind the counter and on the wholesale menu.

Her newfound responsibilities and challenges even include a book contract. As Kaufelt's coauthor, she's the wordsmith behind the pocket-sized *Murray's Guide to Cheese*, which describes and cross-references some 250 cheeses of the world in a Zagat-like presentation.

She discovered cheese just as America did. "I got in just as the wave was starting to build," she says, noting that when she started at Murray's, she was one of twelve employees, only two of whom were women. "It was like an old-school deli. Now there are two stores [the second in Grand Central Station] and forty-five employees, practically all women, mostly under thirty-five, middle- to upper-middle-class backgrounds, with liberal arts educations. It's totally different."

She speaks excitedly about her next European trip—to Italy. "I love talking with cheese makers and farmers and love travel," she says, stressing how much she loves her job at Murray's. Down the road, who knows? Now an experienced and still-learning authority in her field, Liz can see the outlines, if not the specific careers moves that might await her. "There's an infinite number of things that can be done, for instance, exporting American cheeses to Europe."

Asked to rate her current job on the same scale she uses to assess cheeses, she thinks but a moment. "Sure, there are days when I'm really tired and don't like my job, but everybody has those days. Really," Liz says, "I'd give it a five."

Liz's Smart Moves

- She has not forgotten a lesson learned while white-water canoeing: trust your gut; take risks.

- She swallowed her pride and paid her dues, accepting the low-wage entry-level job demanded by her field of interest.

- She tested the waters in a new career with a part-time job and added the safety net of a second job.

- She took the initiative at work, volunteering for a project she knew she'd be good at, thereby showcasing skills not demanded by her current job assignment and helping further her career.

Not His Father's Career,
Not by a Long Fall

COLLEGE: Duke University, 1992

MAJOR: math and economics

POSTGRADUATE: master of arts in teaching, Duke University, 1994

PASSION: performing stunts; coaching and teaching kids

EARLY EXPERIENCES OUTSIDE THE CLASSROOM: IBM summer
   internships

EARLY WORK EXPERIENCE: Midwest consulting firm

CURRENT JOB: performing as Indiana Jones at Disney-MGM Studios; president
   of Superior Marching Band Enterprises

"I've been a real challenge for my parents to understand," laughs Ray Eddy, who is simultaneously pursuing his third and fourth careers since graduating from Duke University in 1992. His father, by contrast, worked for the same company for more than a quarter century.

Ray grew up in the upper-middle-class community of Rochester, Minnesota, a company town made prosperous by two thriving institutions, the Mayo Clinic and IBM. Ray's dad worked as a systems engineer and later as a manager at IBM, retiring after twenty-seven years, from the very company that paid him his first postcollege paycheck, as did many Fortune 500 white-collar executives of his generation.

A straight-A student in high school, Ray felt the expectation to do well—to get into a top college and go on to a lucrative career—as surely as he felt the bracing, annual chill of a Minnesota winter. Unknown to his family and friends, however, Ray harbored a dream he'd had since he was a little boy, when he'd watched a documentary on public television about Hollywood stuntmen, a profession that seemed like so much fun it was hard to believe you also got paid to do it. His dream did not square with his parents' expectations or his plainly evident academic abilities. Besides, it seemed so untenable, like hoping to become a pro football player or a rock star.

So Ray let his dream go dormant. He'd gotten into Duke and won a prestigious IBM Watson scholarship to help pay the way. The scholarship included summer jobs at IBM. Ray's first summer job, at a couple bucks above minimum wage, found him on the assembly line in the plastics department making hundreds of small converter pins each day. "The pins," he recalls, "turn the angle of charge as energy flows through the converter board." He recalls the unvarying, repetitive nature of the work just as clearly. "It was mind-numbing."

But following summers, his jobs were more challenging. Assigned the next year

> **R**ay harbored a dream he'd had since he was a little boy, when he'd watched a documentary on public television about Hollywood stuntmen, a profession that seemed like so much fun it was hard to believe you also got paid to do it.

to a company graphics center, he helped design internal and external sales materials. He did so well that the next summer he headed the graphics center. Dressed in a suit and tie, he instructed two employees wearing jeans and T-shirts, one his own age, one about twice his age, where to put the machines, machines he'd ordered, when they arrived. "Who am I to be in charge of these guys? It was kind of a weird feeling," Ray says. Weird, but also empowering. "A synapse fired. I realized I've impressed the right people and have been given a level of responsibility and amazing opportunities."

Many days he ate lunch with his father, and he became accustomed to people saying how much he looked like his dad. Not surprisingly, Ray began envisioning as an himself "IBM guy" like his father. "I started thinking maybe my plan was to graduate and work for IBM."

Ray had always had an aptitude for math, and he also enjoyed it— especially the black-and-white nature of its unambiguous solutions, the clarifying power of its logic. He'd talked with his father about possibly becoming an engineer. But that first summer at IBM he'd watched engineers fixing broken machines. "I saw guys doing what I was theoretically planning to do and realized, I don't know if I want to do that and sit behind computers designing stuff," he says.

So his sophomore year, Ray changed his major from engineering to math, and later on, realizing he'd taken enough economics courses to be only a few short of a major in that field, pursued a dual degree, feeling it would look good on his resume and give him a leg up in job interviews. That process revved up in the spring of his senior year when corporate recruiters set up booths in the student center. As if drawn to a familiar, friendly face in a room full of strangers, Ray strode straight for the IBM booth.

He exuded confidence. And why not? He'd won a prestigious IBM scholarship, had four summers of IBM experience on his resume, and had a dual major from a prestigious university. The recruiter noted all that and Ray's career leanings on the technical side of marketing, and then, as politely as possible, dashed his hopes. IBM had begun a major restructuring as it switched from its long-standing focus on mainframe computers to desktop models. The only current job openings, the recruiter explained, called for engineers and programmers—not the kind of positions Ray wanted to pursue.

"I had all my eggs in the IBM basket," he realized, feeling almost sick. "Now what?"

Several consulting firms also had prominent booths in the student center. Ray wandered by and listened to their pitches, his deflated sense of self-worth assuaged by prestigious names, good starting salaries, and on-the-job travel opportunities. He explored jobs at four different consulting companies, received offers from all four, and hired on with Hewitt Associates in the Chicago suburb of Lincolnshire. His parents were pleased. "It was their assumption and mine," recalls Ray, "that I was going to be there for the long haul."

In July 1992, Ray began a monthlong training period. Life was good. He was living in a townhouse. He'd bought his father's late-model Acura. He took advantage of all the city of Chicago had to offer: Cubs games, Bulls games, museums, plays, great restaurants. His job was to create databases to test the benefits programs that Hewitt Associates offered its clients. His math background stood him in good stead as he laid out spreadsheets, changing variables, putting the company's programs through their paces. He was working sixty-hour weeks, earning a reputation as an overachiever, and realizing he'd made a big mistake.

"This is it?" he asked himself before the leaves had even started to turn on the trees that first year. "I'd finish a tough project, but driving home I'd feel no euphoria. Only, yeah, the program's ready. I felt no joy in the accomplishment."

The job lacked variety, and it lacked something that did bring him satisfaction—looking people in the eye and helping them, like he'd done at Duke as a residence hall advisor his junior and senior years.

"I loved it," he says. "I liked being a resource, liked being someone who could help people out." In fact, during his short stay at Hewitt Associates, Ray volunteered to tutor math after hours to two employees studying for associate's degrees. Ray remembered the words of his department advisor at Duke: "You can always teach math."

He took out a clean sheet of paper. One side he headed Staying Here. Beneath it he penciled in the pros—money, stability, neat city, like the people—and a single con, but a big one—don't like my work. On the other side of the paper he wrote Master's in Education. A few pluses of teaching were interacting with people, every hour a new class and a new bunch of kids. "I craved that. I realized I'm too active to sit all day at a desk," he says, having identified a glaring problem with the dynamics of his job at Hewitt Associates. Ray gave his employer several months' notice.

"I've decided to go back to school and become a math teacher," Ray's parents didn't understand. They felt he was senselessly abandoning a stable career and the financial security that had anchored their lives and those of

Don't put all your eggs in one basket. Things change that are beyond your control.

If you don't enjoy what you're doing, move on.

their children. From their vantage point, it didn't make sense. They would come to better understand and support his decision, but it took some time.

When word got out at work, a couple of Ray's colleagues stopped him in the hall to tell him they wished they could follow his lead. "I really envy you for this decision to find a new career that you'll be happier with," said one. "If I could leave and go to grad school right now, I would, but I've been here for six years. I have a wife and two kids and I'm the sole income provider. I can't leave my job right now."

Unencumbered by such responsibilities, Ray returned to Duke. Student teaching math classes two hours a day in a nearby high school as part of his master's degree requirement, he learned he both enjoyed being a teacher and had a knack for it. Someday, he says, he may actually return to the front of the classroom. But after applying to three private schools and getting offers from all three, he turned them all down. Why?

The short answer: Extracurricular interests. While working on his master's of education, Ray simultaneously pursued two other passions. Again, he signed on as a residence advisor (RA), this time with the added responsibility of overseeing eight other RAs. More significantly, Ray returned to a long-standing love—the drumline in a marching band.

In high school he quit the football team because he liked playing drums in his school marching band even better. His junior and senior years, he was captain of the band's drumline. As an undergrad at Duke, strapping on a five-drum tenor set, Ray again served as captain of the drumline. He valued the camaraderie, the discipline, and the orderly nature of a well-schooled marching band. Knowing he could get kids to listen to him, he volunteered to help teach the drummers at Riverside High School, the school where he was student teaching. "I also asked if I could help with the Duke marching band," he says, "The drumline instructor there also taught at other schools, and I would go with him and listen to those rehearsals and see how he taught." Ray was starting to fashion a career strategy that offered options, lots of eggs instead of merely one in his career choice basket.

Thanks to these additional experiences, Ray learned that as much as he liked teaching kids in the classroom, he enjoyed working with them even more outside the classroom, on life issues. This was certainly the case in the

You are the architect of your career. Don't expect your parents to understand.

dorms as an RA, where he helped with roommate issues and all manner of personal problems, even counseling bereaved students when a classmate drowned while swimming in a nearby quarry. The drumline, in Ray's mind and in his lessons, had always been about much more than music and marching. "Being in a marching band drumline is not just about playing drums. It's about dedication and responsibility and integrity and teamwork. It's about life lessons," he says. "It's nice to see students who may be floundering a bit, academically or socially, work hard and then realize they can find success in other areas."

So when he applied for teaching jobs, Ray added a wild card job to the mix. He applied for a student affairs position, living in a dorm and supervising RAs, at the University of North Carolina at Chapel Hill. When he was offered that job, he chose it instead of teaching math, in part because its more flexible hours would allow him to continue as a drumline coach.

While working at UNC Chapel Hill in the fall of 1994, Ray took over for the just-departed drumline instructor at Duke and also commuted to Riverside High to instruct the drumline, this time being paid for his work. Word of his prowess spread in marching band circles. The following year he added two more schools, moonlighting in a hectic but rewarding fall schedule. Come the summer of 1995, as many as ten band directors inquired about his services. Far too many to accept, in light of his student affairs job at UNC, but more than enough to get him wondering, "What if I just taught drumlines? Could I make a living at that? How much would I have to charge? Maybe if I also put on summer camps and tutored math..."

With those thoughts knocking around in his head one day while on the Duke campus, he saw a flyer that stopped him in his tracks: Hollywood Comes to Duke. "It was all about how do you get a career in the film industry," he recalls. An actor, a cameraman, and a scriptwriter would be speaking. As he had at several career junctures, Ray thought about his simmering dream of being a stuntman, replaying his still-vivid memory of a scene from that PBS documentary he'd seen when he was just in elementary school.

"There was a guy on a horse riding next to a train, and he jumps to the train and climbs on top and starts fighting with a guy in black, who's thrown off the train and rolls down a hill," he says. "The director yells, 'Cut.' They pull the camera back, and the stuntman gets up and brushes himself off. Somebody says, 'Nice take, good work.' It was the coolest thing I'd ever seen."

All the speakers were former Duke students, which made it easy for Ray to identify with them. When the agent spoke, Ray felt an immediate connection. "I realized I had to give it a shot."

So he switched careers again. In January 1996, Ray left his job at UNC and set up a business called Arrow Percussion, which at first was just him instructing drumlines at various schools. Late summer and fall were especially hectic as he shuttled between eight schools—Mondays and Wednesdays, three to five o'clock at one school, seven to nine at another; Tuesdays and Thursdays at other locations, seven days a week. "I was driving about a thousand miles a week," he says.

That summer, he became even more entrepreneurial, testing the waters with a summer drumline camp at Duke, where he had contacts. Hiring Duke and UNC students as his instructors, Ray offered two overnight, three-day drumline camps. He also held a camp in Arkansas, near where his parents had moved so he could spend time with them—and save a bit on expenses. He's continued with the summer camps, switching to day camps and adding flag corps instruction in addition to drumline sessions. Summer of 2003, by then operating as Superior Marching Band Enterprises, Ray held fifteen camps in Rhode Island, California, Florida, North Carolina, and Virginia, hosting some four hundred students.

"It's still a work in progress," he admits. "But if it expands as rapidly next year as it did this year and I have forty to fifty camps, then I'll feel like I've figured a way to make this work." He means the band camps. For Ray has long since achieved his long-deferred career goal of becoming a stuntman, which he pursued on the side, especially during the slower winter and spring months, with the safety net of his own business.

He learned all he could about the stunt business and started training, working to get in shape and taking private lessons in martial arts and stage combat from a certified fight director. Although living in North Carolina, far from Hollywood, Ray networked his way to a number of fruitful con-

If a dream still simmers after ten years, take it off the back burner.

tacts, often making helpful connections by simply talking about his dream of becoming a stuntman with almost everyone he met.

At the gym one day, he met an actress who told him how to get head shots done and suggested finding an agent. At the photo session for his eight-by-ten glossies, Ray talked with the photographer, who put him in touch with a stuntwoman who told him to get his name on the North Carolina Film Commission list.

Yet another connection led to a precision driver job as an extra on the set of a TV show, *Rescue 911*, which was filming in North Carolina. Ray drove his own car in a high-speed highway chase scene (at all of about thirty miles per hour—they speed up the film), making around one hundred dollars a day for his two days of work. His car, if not his face, made it on TV. More important, he got to talk to the stuntmen on the set, learning they probably weren't his entrée into the field.

"Most stuntmen really don't want to help a new stuntman," he says. "If I do a good job on the set, maybe they hire me the next time instead of the guy who got me the job. In the entertainment field, if you can't handle that kind of stumbling block and constant rejection, don't bother," he says. In his case, having a career to go home to helped counter the closed doors, the rejection, and the steepness of the learning curve.

Ray's first film job was as a stuntman on a very low-budget independent film. He gladly worked without pay, for the experience, figuring he'd get a line on his resume and some action shots to demonstrate his work. He figured wrong. "It's a vampire film," the director told him. Dressed as a zombie, Ray dodged out of the way of a moving car. As a human, he tumbled with a vampire over a couch. When he finally received a copy of the finished film, he was shocked. "Practically every other scene in the movie that didn't involve stunts was soft-core porn," he laughs.

> **"In the entertainment field, if you can't handle constant rejection, don't bother."**

Not long afterward, Ray talked his way into a contact that helped bring him to his current job. He was helping a friend who'd started a catering business, working a party, and found himself in a free moment talking to a young woman about his dream of becoming a stuntman. "I know a guy who knows a guy who plays Indiana Jones at the Disney-MGM Studios stage show," she said. By now well-versed in the it's-who-you-know school of Hollywood hiring, Ray didn't hesitate to call him up.

"I know someone who knows someone who knows you," Ray began, then asked the stuntman, Todd Warren, if he had a few minutes to tell him about the job and what the auditions were like and how he might best prepare for them. "He's the nicest guy in the world," says Ray. "I watched him do the show three times, learning some of the nuances of it. He told me the techniques they used for high falls and their philosophy of stage combat, which is different in a live show as opposed to film or TV. On stage, every action has to be huge: huge backswing, huge follow-through."

So Ray got the job on his first audition? No, nor on his second audition, when he made it past the strength test (ten pull-ups) and agility portion (shoulder rolls, dive rolls, pratfalls, and a high fall), only to be cut before stage combat. His third audition, after again traveling to Orlando, ended before it hardly began when he heard the dreaded words "thanks very much," this time before even breaking a sweat, after merely standing still for the body typing. That day, inexplicably, he didn't look enough like Indiana Jones.

This rejection stung the most. Ray considered tossing in the towel, but fortunately, a friend in the entertainment business told him to stick with it, try again. So Ray auditioned a fourth time, in the summer of 2001. This friend, a writer for *Law and Order*, he met through his hairstylist. Again, Ray talked about wanting to be a stuntman. The barber had another regular customer who wrote TV scripts and connected the two. Says Ray:

"Ray says, I was quiet about my dream for a long time. I was kind of embarrassed to talk about it. It seemed kind of silly. I thought people would laugh at me, tell me, 'You can't be a stuntman.' I realized later that I'd made some terrific contacts just by talking about it. The lesson here is simple. If you have a dream, especially if it's a difficult one to achieve, tell everybody about it, because someone might know someone who knows someone, and all of a sudden you've got a great contact."

On September 12, 2001, Ray got a call from Disney. They offered him a role as one of the several stuntmen who play Indiana Jones in the long-running stage show. "I couldn't believe it," he recalls. "The whole world was crashing down, and I was one of the few people in the whole country with something to be happy about. My lifelong dream was coming true."

It's not Hollywood. Ray can't see himself on the big screen, but he's getting paid to do something he truly enjoys. And while he still thinks of trying to break into film work, he's happy where he is. "I love the Indiana Jones show," he says. "It's fun. I'm doing stunts every day. I'm being chased by a giant boulder. I'm jumping off a building. I'm fighting a huge guy, being beat up while a plane is turning around right above me. It's such a great character. Every day I put on that hat and grab the whip, I think I'm the luckiest guy in the world. This is the coolest job ever. I feel like I've been successful in my quest to be a stuntman. I've made it."

> "**E**very day I put on that hat and grab the whip, I think I'm the luckiest guy in the world. This is the coolest job ever."

He's hands down the most educated stuntman in his show. He says his liberal arts education allowed him to pursue his ultimate goal because it gave him the skills to make that happen. "The math and economics helped me figure out a way to make a living at this," he says, explaining that he worked twenty hours a week on the Indiana Jones stage (with summers off to run his band camps) before stepping up to full-time in December 2004.

The marching band business also provides a fallback position, another job he enjoys, should the show be canceled or should he incur a serious injury. He's suffered a sprained foot (when the plane ran over it) and a partially dislocated shoulder, and had to have his scalp stapled back together after a prop ax parted more than his hair. "I don't tell my parents when I get hurt, generally not until weeks afterward," Ray says, adding that after they realized he was making it on his own, they finally stopped worrying and now support his career decision.

On the Indiana Jones stage, the performers have a backup plan should certain effects fail, for instance, if the trapdoor isn't going to open to drop

---

The more difficult the career path, the more persistent you need to be.

Indy's giant foe safely beneath the whirling propeller as pieces of torn clothes are blown skyward, simulating a bloodless demise. If sensors don't detect the trapdoor opening, an alarm (heard only on stage) sounds. That signals the actors to switch to plan B. "Instead of disappearing from sight, the giant picks me up and throws me aside," says Ray, "and from inside the cockpit of the plane, Marion fires a fake gun and the giant pretends to be shot."

Ray, too, has a plan B, and plans C and D, if you will. Knowing that Disney could at any time decide to shut down his stage, and also feeling that after four years of cracking Indy's bullwhip it might be time to consider moving on, Ray has auditioned for a role in one of the Blue Man Group companies.

"Blue Man Group is a combination of percussion, which is obviously a passion of mine, and performing, which I love, and there are comic moments in it, so it's fun and interactive. Every show's a little bit different. People from the audience come on stage and you're improvising. It's really the only show I would leave Indiana Jones for," he says, continuing, "not because I don't like Indiana Jones. I love it there. But it's coming up on four years now. I don't want to stagnate. I want to keep it fresh and always enjoy my work. I'd be sad to leave that stage because I love my friends and I love the work. I love being able to be with the kids who think you're really Indiana Jones. You're not Ray; you're Indy. It's very moving, sometimes, to have that interaction with kids."

After four auditions, Ray has made it past the body typing and the drumming portions of the Blue Man audition. He's now taking acting classes to improve his chances of making it into one of the four current American Blue Man troupes. He considers that plan B.

Plan C would entail devoting more time to his spare-time business. Plan D looms a bit further off in the future. "The marching band business has real potential for expansion. I have some new ideas to make it more successful and profitable," he says. "And I feel like in later years I still might want to teach high school math. If nothing else, I'll be the teacher who has really good stories—especially if I get banged in the head a few more times. I can already hear my students: 'Hey, just ask about when he was Indiana Jones, and he'll talk the whole hour away.'"

Ray's Smart Moves

- He heeded wise words from others—first from his mother, who told him never to settle for less than his best.

- He learned from his summer jobs and extracurricular jobs. He discovered not only what he liked, but also the kind of work that he didn't like.

- He made prompt career corrections.

- He networked to increase his opportunities. He talked about his dream with almost anyone he met and followed up with the contacts those conversations turned up.

- He pursued multiple interests, sometimes simultaneously, giving him choices and fallback positions.

Take Me Out to the Ball Game

COLLEGE: Haverford College, 1994

MAJOR: English

POSTGRADUATE: MBA, UCLA Anderson School of Business, 1999

PASSION: baseball

EARLY EXPERIENCES OUTSIDE THE CLASSROOM: market research externship at Reebok International

EARLY WORK EXPERIENCE: marketing coordinator, the Rockport Company, helping launch their website for promoting and selling walking shoes

CURRENT JOB: senior director of baseball operations for the Colorado Rockies

Thad Levine had been building up the courage for this conversation with his father for days. "I knew it was time," he says, "when I looked into the eye of the giraffe." Thad's father had flown to meet him in Cape Town, South Africa, where Thad had just finished a foreign study term he'd arranged as part of his second-year MBA studies at UCLA's Anderson School of Business. He had shown his father around South Africa for about a week before the two took off on a safari in the neighboring Republic of Namibia. They'd finished eating dinner outdoors and were venturing on a short walk, when one of the continent's many four-legged wonders stopped them short. Only fifteen feet away stood a giraffe, which slowly turned and looked at them. Riveted there in a stand of trees, Thad figured it was time to stick his neck out, too—time to break the news to his father.

"Dad," he said, steeling himself for the worst. "I've got something I'd like to talk to you about, and it may shock you. It's about my future, but please hear me out before you react because I've thought about this long and hard."

Only a few weeks earlier, Thad's future could not have seemed more certain, more gilded, more secure, nor his father and mother any happier. Thad had been notified by email that his recent summer internship at Coca-Cola headquarters in Atlanta had resulted in an offer to join the company when he graduated the following spring. One of America's premier corporations wanted him to come aboard and was offering a nice signing bonus, great benefits, and a salary that seemed surreal to Thad, who'd needed six promotions at his previous employer to get to thirty-two thousand dollars.

When he received the job offer from Coca-Cola, Thad had just begun his term in Cape Town in a whirl of new experiences. Soon that grand, MBA-driven vision of his future seemed all wrong, and something very different, much more speculative—a dream he'd set aside several years earlier—seemed precisely what he needed to pursue instead. Thad breathed deeply, then told his father he wanted to work in baseball, in the front office of a major league ball club.

If a face could register irony as well as displeasure, Thad would have seen more than acute disappointment wash over his father's countenance, for this irony bordered on the mythic. It was Thad's father who had taught him how to play ball and passed on his own passion for the game. Nothing defined Thad's childhood as much as baseball.

Thad's father had put a plastic Wiffle ball bat in his son's hands pre-T-ball, finding the time to instruct Thad even after an hour-and-a-half commute home to Alexandria, Virginia, from his accounting job in Baltimore.

On Sundays, April through September, the family piled in the car for the weekly pilgrimage to see the Baltimore Orioles play. Their season tickets, ten rows behind the first base dugout, offered Thad an intimate view of the players he idolized. As a grade-schooler he could hardly write a number without thinking of an Oriole: 1—Al Bumbry; 2—Billy Smith; 3—Billy Ripken; 4—Earl Weaver (the manager); 5—Brooks Robinson; 6—Paul Blair; 7—Mark Belanger. "I was a member of the Junior Orioles," he recalls. "Every Sunday, during the seventh inning, they'd pull five names out of a hat. If you were chosen, you'd get to meet the Orioles in the clubhouse afterward," Thad continued. "After many years, my name was finally called. I got to meet Mark Belanger and Al Bumbry—got to shake their hands, and I think they signed a ball for me. It was one of the best days of my young life."

Sunday after Sunday those ballpark sojourns, with their weekly drives to and from the stadium, the ritualistic same seats and same ballpark food, and the unpredictable on-the-field joys and disappointments, both anchored Thad's childhood and authored family lore. Baseball knit father and son together and helped define Thad's choice of college. On the drive home after those Sunday outings, Thad and his father would not only recap the game they'd just seen, but after pulling into the driveway, they'd often head to a local diamond and relive the games, Thad assuming the stances of all the Oriole hitters.

"I think part of the reason I excelled in creative writing was because I spent so much of my time converting this fantasy into reality by reliving what I saw," says Thad. He praises his father as a patient, never-overbearing coach, whose dedicated instruction gave his baseball career an early jump-start.

In high school, Thad excelled in math and creative writing. Baseball remained his passion. A good outfielder with a strong arm, he also pitched for his high school team his junior year and again his senior year, when he batted a sparkling .397. By then, he'd already decided to attend Haverford College, where he could continue to play ball and also pursue a top-notch liberal arts education.

The latter, he confesses, he pursued perhaps "a little too literally." He sampled courses like a kid choosing treats at a candy counter: oceanography, economics, Japanese, a course called Structure of Cities. "My friends joked that every semester I was declaring a new major," he says. By the end of Thad's sophomore year, he found himself one class into no fewer than sixteen possible majors, including the one he wished to declare. When he approached the head of the English department the second term of his sophomore year and she asked him to name all the English courses he'd taken, Thad's list began and ended with freshman English. To prove

Just because you're good at something in school doesn't mean it has to be the focus of your career.

his merit, he took an English course that summer at George Mason University near home; thereafter, he settled in as an English major.

As for life and a career after college, Thad entertained two near-term thoughts: teaching or following in the footsteps of his parents and older sister by continuing on for an advanced degree. Winter break of his senior year, he applied to take the GREs and interviewed with a couple of private day schools in the Atlanta area, looking to teach English and maybe coach baseball or basketball. But the private school atmosphere didn't resonate for him. Recalling his recreational baseball team experiences, Thad found the schools too homogeneous and elitist, and accordingly, he turned down invitations for second interviews. He decided to get a master's in English and a teaching certificate so he could teach and coach in public schools.

That was the plan, anyway, until an alumni-based externship program that same semester break set him on a different path. Thad spent most of the month of December working at Reebok International in Stoughton, Massachusetts, assigned to the company's Rockport walking shoe division. "I think it's healthy in life," advises Thad, "even if you've found one job that you think brings you fulfillment, to always be thinking of another job that may provide you with a greater degree of satisfaction." In light of his love of baseball and other sports, Thad had deemed it smart to explore what it might be like to work for a company involved with athletics.

As part of the externship program, Thad lived with a fellow classmate in the Boston area while he worked at Reebok helping launch a new line of walking shoes by interviewing customers in stores and buttonholing people he stopped on city sidewalks.

This three-week corporate stint intrigued Thad enough that when he came up dry exploring another career option—working for a major league baseball team—he decided to accept Reebok's offer of a more formal, summer internship at the company's Rockport Shoes division. Thad had written every team in the American and National Leagues, adding, of course, in his letter to the Baltimore Orioles, that he was a longtime fan. His thirty letters netted four responses. Only the Tigers, the Expos, the Orioles, and

> Take the opportunity to explore widely in college. You'll never get that much freedom again.

the Phillies even bothered to send him a rejection letter. "I kept and cherished each rejection letter," he says.

The internship paid a stipend of $1,250 a month. With some financial help from home, Thad made do. Finally, come winter, leading a rather lean lifestyle, he went to his boss and pushed for a full-time job. His salary only increased to eighteen thousand dollars, but now he received benefits and stock options. And he wasn't there for the money, anyway.

"Money has never been the driving career factor for me," Thad says. "I've been blessed with jobs that have been fulfilling and educational, and I've woken up most days dying to go to work because I've really enjoyed my jobs." At Rockport, Thad dug in as he had at Haverford, drinking in the corporate experience and thriving because of the communications skills he developed and honed in college. "I think my English major helped make me a more creative thinker," he says, noting, "When I worked for Rockport, my boss was a gifted man, but his brilliance was not complemented with as polished communication skills. I think now that might have been one of the reasons I was paired with him, to balance him out, adding diplomacy and communication skills. I created his PowerPoint and oral presentations."

Even so, Thad didn't get pigeonholed. His assignments bled into a number of different roles. "At every turn there was an entirely new educational experience, and I traveled extensively, twice a year to Las Vegas for shoe shows, to Dusseldorf for an international show, and to London to help direct a film for a commercial," he says. "I felt like I was surfing on a long wave that had yet to hit shore. There were such consistent opportunities to further my business education that for a long time I couldn't foresee any greater benefit from going to school than from staying put and keeping my eyes and ears open."

> "**I** think my English major helped make me a more creative thinker."

By 1997, as part of a design team building the company's first website, Thad was traveling twice a month to New York. He could hardly believe it; his three-month internship had stretched into three years. He realized it was probably time to move on. "I felt I owed it to myself and my family to get

When you're dying to go to work, you know you've found your true passion.

a master's degree," he says. "At the same time, I'm thinking, I've gotten six promotions and I'm still only making thirty thousand dollars. It might behoove me to bolster my resume with a master's degree."

However, based on his experiences of the past three years, instead of an advanced degree in English, Thad was thinking of an MBA, looking to bolster his blossoming Internet skills with a blue-chip business education and then find a job at a sports-related company. In the fall of 1997, he started classes at UCLA's Anderson School of Business.

Thad's business school classes proved challenging and educationally rewarding. But off-campus activities provided his biggest learning experiences and career lessons. First came the competition for an all-important summer internship, the experiential bridge between year one and year two of business school that for many MBAs results in a lucrative job offer. Thad interviewed on campus with Coca-Cola and was flown with three of his classmates to Atlanta for follow-up interviews. He was pretty sure he'd made the cut when his interviewer threw him a trivia question designed to test the depths of his professed love of baseball, which Thad had offered when asked what he was most passionate about. The trivia question was indeed a good one, but mere batting practice for as hard-core an Oriole fan as Thad. Asked to name the only four pitchers on a single major league team to record twenty wins or more in the same season, Thad rattled off the names as easily as seasons of the year: Palmer, McNally, Cuellar, and Dobson.

He got the internship. With only one suit in his closet, he borrowed three from a friend, wearing the suit jackets as little as possible, as he and his friend cast very different shadows. Thad is six foot three and weighs 185 pounds; his friend stands six five and weighs 220 pounds. Most days, Thad could drape the coat over the back of a chair early in the morning, and, in the heat of an Atlanta summer, not need to put it back on until heading home in the evening. His assignment, working on one of Coca-Cola's smaller brands, Barq's root beer, proved ideal.

"Other interns, on big brands like Sprite, spent their whole internship working on the two-liter bottle, whereas on Barq's, I got exposed to a lot more," he says. His big project examined the potential value of instituting a customer loyalty program. Thad's internship culminated in a fifty-slide,

> Internships are a great way to get your foot in the door.

hour-and-a-half-long PowerPoint presentation—and a verbal understanding that his work that summer had earned him a job after graduation.

As promised, that offer came in the fall, reaching Thad while on foreign study in Cape Town, South Africa. He had been so enamored of campus life at Haverford that he'd never wanted to leave for a term abroad. So he'd figured he'd do so while in business school. He was one of five UCLA students who shared a house a half mile from the ocean. The only trouble was, classes at the University of Cape Town ran Monday through Saturday and didn't leave a lot of time for the beach.

Thad did make time for a bit of traveling to better experience and take the measure of South Africa. He'd read about apartheid, but traveling with a classmate away from the city to one of the African townships, he came face-to-face with the legacy of that sorry chapter of the nation's history. "I learned that down there, the darker your color, the lower your class. As you move out of Cape Town—a lavish, rich city much like Southern California in climate and population—you come first to a township where the people are Indian. In the next township, you see mulattoes, then pure Africans." It was in the third township, volunteering to help a classmate teach English to schoolchildren, that Thad's career gyro was knocked haywire.

Thad came upon a three-square-mile settlement of dirt-floored, tin-roofed shanties with no plumbing or electricity. He was told that four hundred thousand people lived in the township and the average life expectancy for a male was forty years. When he and his classmate reached the "school," a bit of space carved out of a warehouse, the children they were to teach, kids ranging from five to fifteen years old, ran straight toward them. "I expected them to be fearful of white people, but they swarmed us. They all wanted to be loved and hugged. If there were fifty children there, I probably picked up forty of them," Thad says. "The ten I didn't pick up were the fifteen-year-olds."

Considering Thad's recent career news from Atlanta, the preponderance of signs for Coca-Cola in the township was almost eerie. "You only needed to drive two or three blocks in any direction and there'd be a sign for Coca-Cola," he says. "It was almost a status symbol to be drinking a Coke." Given the widespread poverty, that disconnect troubled Thad, adding to an emotional day that served like a wake-up call, or as he terms it, an epiphany. He started rethinking his intended career path that ran through Coca-Cola headquarters in Atlanta.

He found himself in a perfect place to do so. "Away from the norms and rigors of my life in the United States, I was almost in sensory under-load. I wasn't watching television. I had more time to think," Thad says, explaining that he started questioning the meaning of going to work for Coca-Cola and realized that, unlike the children he had hugged in the shantytown, he was blessed with the opportunity to act upon dreams larger than a bottle of soda and have a real shot at making them happen.

Was he passionate about a climb up the ladder at a consumer products company? No. He *was* passionate about baseball. What he really wanted to do when he finished graduate school, he now saw clearly, was exactly what he had sought to do years earlier when he blindly mailed all those letters to every major league baseball team. Thad wanted to work in the front office of a big league baseball team. He felt that desire in his very bones. He vowed to do his best to make that happen, even though it meant letting go of the bird—a very golden goose—he already held in his hand.

Breaking the news to Coca-Cola wouldn't be hard. Telling first his father and then his mother would be much, much harder, for Thad wasn't looking for advice to help make a decision. He had already made his decision—and he knew his father would consider it an imprudent choice and try to talk him out of it. For the first week of his father's visit, Thad avoided the issue. Then, on safari, as if goaded by the giraffe, Thad finally told his father his change in plans.

"I explained about the cathartic experiences I'd had and the net effect, that I'd decided to turn down Coca-Cola's generous offer and pursue a dream I had, which was to work in baseball," Thad says. "I saw his face— the look of consternation. His initial reaction was very curt, expressing disbelief. He said, 'I appreciate your feelings about your dream, but a job is a job, and this is an excellent career opportunity, and I don't think it's a good idea for you to turn this down.'

"He viewed work as just that, as work, not something you love. He said there's security associated with working for an organization such as Coca-

Cola and that I could make a lifetime career of it. 'You need to think beyond your whims of today,' he told me. We probably talked for two to three hours that night back at the cabin we were staying in."

Thad wanted to work in the front office of a big league baseball team. He felt that desire in his very bones.

Thad had anticipated his father's counterarguments almost word for word, and answered with a ready rebuttal. He told his father that he had two friends in baseball, Josh Byrnes, who'd been one captain ahead of Thad on the Haverford baseball team, and Paul DePodesta, whom Thad had known since childhood. The two had played youth sports together and high school baseball against each other. Byrnes had become director of scouting for the Cleveland Indians, and DePodesta was special assistant to John Hart, general manager of the Indians. So what he sought, while difficult, wasn't impossible.

"I explained that I wasn't passing up my dream job; I was passing up a tremendous opportunity, yes, but not one I was passionate about," says Thad. "And I asked him, 'Dad, are you passionate about your job?'"

"No," his father answered.

"Was your father ever passionate about his job?"

Again the answer came back no.

"It's a means to an end, for both of us. That's the way we were raised," his father answered.

At that point, a herd of approaching giraffe would have gone unnoticed, for finally father and son were beginning to see eye to eye. And how could Thad's father not understand his son's dream? For it descended from his own passion for baseball, which he'd so lovingly passed on to Thad.

Two days later Thad called his mother and told her. First came silence on the other end of the line. Then the expected question, "What does your father think of this?" Then the same counterarguments. And much sooner, acquiescence. "My mother is more of a heart person, whereas my father is more of a mind person," says Thad. "She caught on much more quickly to the excitement in my voice."

From there on, Thad's dream became the family's dream. "If you truly believe this is your passion," his parents told him, "this will not only be your dream, it will be our dream." With their support and their blessing, he returned to UCLA almost euphoric, determined to crack into baseball.

Needing names and contacts to leverage, Thad started with his two friends in baseball and the administrative offices of the Anderson School of Business. Learning that the general manager of the LA Lakers basketball team had attended the executive MBA program at Anderson, Thad reached out to him. He exchanged a couple letters, but nothing fruitful came of it. But sitting in the careers office researching MBAs in the greater Los Angeles area who worked in sports, Thad came across the name Fred Coons, a Wharton grad now in the office of business development for the LA Dodgers.

Thad contacted him early in January of his winter term, arranged for a meeting in Coons's office at Dodger Stadium, and made him an offer he couldn't easily refuse. Thad announced that he would work for free the next two terms, provided he could fold the work into an academic internship as part of his course work at Anderson. Winter term, Thad worked mostly on a detailed cost-benefit analysis of moving the team's Vero Beach minor league team to another city. Considering such factors as stadium size, local population, projected attendance, and parking and concession revenues, he evaluated such potential cities as Memphis, Louisville, and Daytona Beach. He had pledged eight to ten hours of work a week. Talk about overdelivering on a promise.

"I think thirty was the fewest hours I ever worked. I tried to spend every waking minute there," Thad says. And why not? He was reporting to work not at some steel-and-glass skyscraper or boxy corporate headquarters, but at Dodger Stadium, a field of his dreams, where the office walls bore pictures of Dodger legends Sandy Koufax, Don Drysdale, Ron Cey, and Dusty Baker. At first Thad worked at a small table in the corner of Coons's office, but his long hours soon necessitated a move elsewhere—which happened to be an empty desk out in a prominent hallway. There, he got to see everyone coming and going.

Spring term, easily wrangling a few classmates to help him, he took a page from his Coca-Cola internship and led a study of the potential bene-

To lead a fulfilled life requires tough choices. Sometimes it's better to turn down a sure thing in order to follow your passion.

fits of a fan loyalty program for Dodgers ticket buyers, something a few other ball clubs had just begun. With his academic year and his internship drawing to a close, Thad did everything he could think of to turn his unpaid, temporary position into any kind of ongoing job with the Dodgers. "I wrote no fewer than four or five job descriptions that would justify me sticking around," he says. "I did everything short of baking brownies and pleading."

But luck was not on his side—at least not yet. Thad later learned that it wasn't that he lacked ability, energy, or perseverance, only timing. The Fox Broadcasting Corporation had just bought the Dodgers, and a management shake-up loomed. The team's new owner was looking to subtract employees, not hire people. Thad graduated from business school without a job.

His classmates headed off to investment banking firms, consulting firms, and Fortune 500 corporations. Even unemployed, Thad had no second thoughts about his decision to turn down the Coca-Cola offer, and after his soul-nurturing taste of life inside baseball, a job with a view of a well-groomed diamond, he was more determined than ever to make good on his dream.

He redoubled his efforts to turn contacts into leads and increase his odds of networking to a job. He got back in touch with his friends in baseball, and he obtained a few new names through them. At the end of every conversation, before thanking a person for his time, Thad asked for the names of two others who might possibly be able to help him. He was still in California, living with a roommate, his money dwindling. Pride kept him from phoning home for help. "I figured I'd made my bed. I knew there might be trying times," he says. But when things got to the point where he was eating toast without butter for more than just breakfast, Thad took a stopgap job. He signed on with a company started by one of his grad school classmates, an online business plan–writing enterprise. Happily, his stay lasted no longer than one project.

First came a flicker of hope, then a glimmer, then a white-hot rush of joy. Thad's friend Josh Byrnes called with inside information on high-level front office doings. "He said that Dan O'Dowd, who had been assistant general manager of the Cleveland Indians while Josh was their director of scouting, was interviewing for the general manager's job at several teams and had talked to Josh about joining him as his assistant general manager. He said, 'Depending on where we end up, there might be a job available. Would you want us to consider you?'"

Thad didn't know what kind of job or what team. Nor did he care. He'd pretty much been figuring that by virtue of his business degree and experience with the Dodgers, he'd have to take an indirect route to his eventual goal of a coveted job on the operations side, arriving there by way of a job in the business office. "I figured I'd try to moonlight as best I could with the operations guys, and maybe after five or six years, be able to move laterally," he says. Byrnes was dangling a straight shot to operations, the brass ring without all those spins of the carousel.

Byrnes kept Thad apprised of how the wind was blowing. At one point it seemed that all signs pointed to a team in a Midwest city. O'Dowd would continue on and interview with the Colorado Rockies, Byrnes informed him, but that seemed a mere courtesy call. A few days later, Thad's phone rang.

"You said you were ready to move. Are you really ready?" Byrnes said. "He accepted an offer from the Rockies. We're going to Denver."

Thad met O'Dowd for the first time in October 1999, when he strode happily into Coors Field, the fifty-thousand-seat gem of a ballpark that had only four years earlier replaced Mile-High Stadium as the home of the Rockies. His first day on the job, his very first email was from his father. Two terse lines that went something like this: "Shirt size: large. Hat size: 7 and $1/4$. Jacket: better make it extra large because it will be going over the sweatshirt." This, Thad points out, from a die-hard Orioles fan—now the proudest Rockies rooter in Alexandria, Virginia.

Although he wasn't sure how, Thad wanted his business skills to add value on the operations side. Within the first six months, he had found a way—forecasting deferred ballplayer compensation packages and recommending investment vehicles to fund those packages.

Officially, his first year on the job as a baseball operations assistant making forty thousand dollars, he worked as an advance scout, meaning he stayed an opponent ahead of the team the Rockies were currently playing. Thad worked in a boardroom watching the games on his computer screen, clipping videos of opposing pitchers and charting pitches against opposing batters in search of the best way to get them out. Was it a slider down and away that caused the weak groundout to second? Who would chase the high fastball? His data filled the reference notebooks common nowadays in the dugouts.

"I was crunching the numbers every way I could," he says. The following year, also concentrating on the Rockies players, he found himself sitting with Clint Hurdle, then the team's hitting coach, going over the opposition batters. When he was finished, he brought up the subject of the then-slumping Rockies center fielder Tom Goodwin. Thad's intensive review of Goodwin's early season at bats pointed unmistakably to a hole in his swing. "He's overswinging on fastballs on the inner half of the plate," he told Hurdle. "If you look at twelve of his first fifteen strikeouts for the year, the pitch is in the exact same location." In other words, the front office rookie was instructing the former ballplayer and twenty-year veteran of the game—and being listened to. Hurdle wasted no time sitting Goodwin down with the videos and working with him to successfully correct the flaw in his swing. Thad felt like he'd hit one out of the park. Talk about living a dream.

Each year, his parents come out for a week's visit, timed for a long Rockies home stand, of course. Thad's father also spends another week with his son and his team during spring training. The circularity is not lost on Thad. His dad hosted him at Orioles games when he was boy; now he's hosting his father at Rockies games. "I think we've all shared in the fulfillment of my dream. And the satisfaction I've had in giving back to my parents has been worth more than anything I've been paid by this organization."

The workdays run long and run together relentlessly. Thad's first year with the Rockies, he managed exactly three days off. You won't hear him complaining. "If I work a ninety-hour week, typically twenty of those hours are spent watching baseball. We'll be sitting around discussing the team, but it's hard to define that as work."

Recently promoted to senior director of baseball operations, Thad now reports to general manager Dan O'Dowd. His friend Josh Byrnes is now assistant general manager of the Boston Red Sox. With the Rockies bent on running with a lean staff, Thad's duties range widely. His responsibilities include administering the intricate rules that oversee baseball transactions and roster movements; negotiating contracts and trades; managing the arbitration process; managing the payroll and clubhouse operations, and nonuniformed coaches and trainers; even visiting all the team's minor league affiliates and writing scouting reports on every player.

Thad would be hard-pressed to actually name all the reasons he loves his job, but here's one he'll never forget: Interleague play had brought the Rockies to the Bronx to play the Yankees, and Thad had welcomed the opportunity to go out on the field during pregame batting practice. Little did he know that his thrill at standing with a player's view of the most celebrated baseball park in the land, would soon be topped. Clint Hurdle, who'd moved on to become Rockies manager, looked his way and shouted, "Suit up. You're shagging."

Donning a uniform and spikes and borrowing a glove from a Rockies player, he settled in left center field between the team's pitching coach and a rookie center fielder named Choo Freeman. His first chance to snare a fly ball in Yankee Stadium rocketed off the bat of Rockies slugger Larry Walker, "a missile of a line drive hit right at me, one of those that knuckles en route," he would term it in an email sent to friends. The ball dipped, Thad jumped, and Walker's line drive bounced off the glove's thumb. A good-natured chorus rang out: "Error front office." A few swings later, Walker obliged by hitting another ball Thad's way. This one had more loft. Thad made the catch on the run, admitting to "shamelessly calling off Freeman, who actually was trying to get some pregame work done."

Hurdle's next command sent Thad to the batting cage, where Walker handed him the thirty-five-ounce bat of Preston Wilson, another Rockies slugger. Thad stepped in, right next to home plate, onto hallowed dirt, where so many of baseball's greats have stood: Ruth, Gehrig, Mantle, Cobb, Williams, and all the Oriole heroes of his childhood. Thad did not hit one out of the ballpark. But he did send a ball toward the left center field gap.

Looking to the future, Thad hopes he "can stay in Denver indefinitely. But I realize that may not be the reality." He speaks of politics playing a role in the upper realm of a baseball team's front office. "Right now I'm try-

> It's often difficult for parents to accept their children's career choices, especially when they're off the beaten path. But shared joy can come from achieving difficult goals.

ing to do the best job in the job I'm being asked to do and contribute the most I can to the organization. If I were to focus on becoming a general manager, I think I'd find the journey of getting there unfulfilling. I think a realistic goal is to be an assistant general manager someday. If something happens beyond that, I'll be tickled pink, but I'm not counting on that, nor am I measuring my success on that."

What about a World Series championship? "I joke with friends that I love coming to work every day, and for the last five years we've averaged just over seventy wins a year. Unfortunately, like every other team in baseball we play 162 games, which means we're losing an awful lot more than we're winning," says Thad, before adding, "I can only imagine the joy and excitement of coming to work every day when you're winning."

Thad's Smart Moves

- He risked his parents' disapproval when making a tough career choice—one he was certain of but which he knew would be initially unpopular with them.

- He has followed his heart, not his wallet, in making career decisions.

- He networked furiously, via friends and leads at the university career services office, to connect with the lead that got him started in his field of dreams.

- He invented his own internship as a grad student, volunteering to work for free, and then worked three times as many hours as promised.

Index

networks and understanding of the nonprofit world.

JONATHAN (page 123)—Worked for free in the district attorney's office in his hometown to build his reputation.

Competence Gaps

HARPREET (page 235)—Worked for a consulting firm to develop business skills and build mentoring relationships.

THERESA (page 141)—Solicited advice from alumni on how to start a nonprofit organization.

TODD (page 178)—Checked out every book he could find in the library on repairing stringed instruments.

WARREN (page 187)—Took classes on small business at a local community center.

Consulting

CARA (page 162)—Became a self-employed consultant for nonprofit arts organizations.

HARPREET (page 235)—Became employed by a nonprofit strategy consulting firm.

JUDITH (page 64)—Was drawn to technology and management consulting.

Cross-Cultural Understanding

CHRIS C. (page 212)—Began to understand the Arab point of view while serving in the Peace Corps in Morocco.

EMILY (page 225)—Founded an international art company to promote cultural exchange.

HARPREET (page 235)—Evaluated educational projects for UNICEF in Nepal.

JENNIFER (page 249)—Worked as an educational program evaluator and built a database of refugees while living in Kenya.

Education

CHRIS C. (page 212)—Spent a summer teaching in China and then two years in Morocco.

CHRIS N. (page 50)—While looking for jobs, served as a substitute public school teacher. Taught marine science at the Oceanographic Institute.

JENNIFER (page 249)—Always wanted to be a teacher. Realized that almost everything she had done, however varied, involved education.

RAY (page 287)—Taught math, which remains plan B for when his stunt career comes to an end.

WARREN (page 187)—Worked as a health educator before law school.

Entrepreneurship

ALISON (page 264)—Founded the Climb High Foundation, a nonprofit organization.

CARA (page 162)—Founded Marketing by Storm, which provides marketing and promotions for arts organizations in the Bay Area.

EMILY (page 225)—Co-owner of a stained glass company.

JUDITH (page 64)—Helped a fellow college student start Peace Frogs on campus.

RAY (page 287)—Started marching band camps.

THERESA (page 141)—Founded Harbinger Partners, a non-profit organization.

TODD (page 178)—Founded StringWorks, selling violins, violas, and cellos.

WARREN (page 187)—Founded Cake Love and Love Café.

Faculty and Administrator Relationships

CHRIS C. (page 212)—Was challenged in terms of his values and beliefs by weekly lunches with a college chaplain.

TODD (page 178)—Befriended by the university president, furthering Todd's musical and entrepreneurial talents and contacts.

KC (page 130)—South Africa

SHARON (page 87)—London

THAD (page 299)—South Africa

International Work

BETH (page 200)—Worked in a village in Benin, twelve miles from the nearest paved road, teaching basic business skills to local tradesmen.

CHRIS C. (page 212)—Taught English in China and Morocco, giving him valuable insight into the developing world.

EMILY (page 225)—Went to Taipei without concrete plan and found employment teaching English, modeling, and selling paintings and jewelry on consignment. Developed the idea of using art as a medium for cultural exchange.

HARPREET (page 235)—Explored a budding interest in international development by serving as manager of a broad educational reform project for the Aga Khan Development Network in Tajikistan.

JENNIFER (page 249)—Gained flexibility and confidence from her travel in Tanzania.

JUDITH (page 64)—Pursued an internship in India, where she was charged with executing a major corporate turnaround for a polymer company.

Internships and Apprenticeships

ALISON (page 264)—Was offered a summer internship at Mattel after creatively showcasing her communication skills to her future employer.

BRAD (page 40)—Worked as an intern over his Christmas break at Doctors Without Borders' L.A. office, where he learned the dynamics of the organization and built a reputation for hard work and enthusiasm.

CARA (page 162)—Interned at the promotions department of WBCN Radio, Boston, to get her foot in the door of a competitive industry.

JENNIFER (page 249)—Received a paid internship in Kenya with the United Nations High Commissioner for Refugees. Learned about disparities, needs, and corruption in resource allocation.

JUDITH (page 64)—Interned at the Bureau of Oceans and International Environmental and Scientific Affairs, sampling potential career interest in Foreign Service.

HARPREET (page 235)—Interned while in high school, which allowed her to try on a scientific career.

LIZ (page 277)—Learned that an internship she hated was equally as valuable as one she loved in defining her career direction.

SHARON (page 87)—Interned at Ralph Lauren and volunteered at the Nassau County Museum of Art.

THAD (page 299)—Did an MBA internship with Coca-Cola and an unpaid internship with the Office of Business Development for the Los Angeles Dodgers.

THERESA (page 141)—Interned at a law firm. Discovered law was ultimately not the right fit for her.

TODD (page 178)—Created his own jobs in college, gaining entrepreneurial skills along the way.

Journalism and Writing

DAVID (page 112)—Was a feature writer for a North Carolina weekly newspaper.

BETH (page 200)—Wrote for her college newspaper, notably covering a Walter Mondale campaign speech.

CHRIS C. (page 212)—Served as an op-ed editor for his student newspaper.

LIZ (page 277)—Coauthored *Murray's Guide to Cheese*.

SHARON (page 87)—Worked as a part-time freelance journalist.

HARPREET (page 235)—Continually assessed what skills she needed for future jobs and career moves.

JUDITH (page 64)—Kept her resume available so she was ready to take advantage of an unanticipated opportunity.

WARREN (page 187)—Conducted market research and took classes to prepare himself for a radical career change.

Public Speaking

ADELITA (page 98)—Excelled in debate in high school. Later applied her extemporaneous speaking skills in various government jobs and related public events.

ALISON (page 264)—Founded her own company promoting herself as a motivational speaker.

CHRIS N. (page 50)—Faced his fear of public speaking by signing up for a communications course.

DAVID (page 112)—Represented his foundation at an international conference, speaking on volunteerism in America. He was invited to speak at a conference on volunteering in Melbourne.

Risk Taking

ALISON (page 264)—Epitomizes strategic risk taking as she climbs mountains on every continent.

CARA (page 162)—Moved coast-to-coast, leaving behind family and business contacts; later, departed a prestigious, high-profile job and a steady paycheck to start her own business.

EMILY (page 225)—Went to Taiwan with no place to live and no job.

HARPREET (page 235)—Worked with at-risk youth for City Year between her sophomore and junior years, something outside her comfort zone. After graduation worked in Nepal and Tajikistan.

JENNIFER (page 249)—Learned to enjoy the challenges of the unfamiliar by traveling abroad.

LIZ (page 277)—Learned to trust her gut and take risks, a lesson learned through white-water canoeing.

Self-Discovery and Self-Assessment

BETH (page 200)—Sought quiet, distraction-free times to listen to her inner voice when making career decisions.

BRAD (page 40)—Asked himself how a job opportunity would fit into his life story.

CHRIS N. (page 50)—Viewed his career as a series of evolving adaptations.

DAVID (page 112)—Figured out what kind of work environment he needed.

EMILY (page 225)—Asked herself pointed personal questions to validate her career moves.

HARPREET (page 235)—Awarded herself a short sabbatical between jobs, allowing time to reflect on her previous experiences to better direct her next career move.

JUDITH (page 64)—Thought about her career by looking beyond her much-praised, obvious talent for science, realizing that she had other interests worth fulfilling.

KC (page 130)—Asked herself a comprehensive list of career questions.

LIZ (page 277)—Realized after taking two unsatisfactory Internet jobs that she needed a more introspective approach to finding the right career fit.

SHARON (page 87)—Asked herself whether she could see herself working eight-hour days marketing toothpaste or working to build shareholder value.

THERESA (page 14)—Keeps a journal of her thoughts and observations.

WARREN (page 187)—Gave himself some time after graduation to recover from career inertia and listened to his inner voice.

About the Authors

Sheila J. Curran is the Fannie Mitchell executive director of the Duke University Career Center, a position she has held since 2003. Prior to coming to Duke, Sheila was the director of Career Services at Brown University for seven years. Sheila holds a BA in Russian and Persian (honors) from Durham University in England; a graduate degree in education (distinction) from the University of London, England; and lifetime certification in human resources. Her earlier professional experience was in the human resources field at the University of Michigan, Gallaudet University, and Brown University. In 1996, Sheila switched careers from human resources to career services, and in doing so she discovered her true passion: helping liberal arts students and graduates attain their career dreams.

Suzanne Greenwald holds a Ph.D. in education policy from the University of Chicago, a master's degree in education from Harvard University, and a bachelor's degree in English and American literature from Brown University. She has conducted educational research at the comparative, international level at Oxford University as a research fellow, and at the level of higher education at Brown University as an institutional research analyst. Suzanne is an expert on school-to-work issues, work-related learning, and school-business partnerships, and she is coauthor of *Knowing, Learning, Doing: Enterprise Education and the Pedagogy of Experiential Learning.* She is currently employed at the Massachusetts Institute of Technology, serving as an educational advisor to the Cambridge-MIT Institute.

For more information, please visit **www.smartmovesforliberalartsgrads.com**